On the Genesis of
Thought and Language

ALEXEY KOSHELEV

ON THE GENESIS OF THOUGHT AND LANGUAGE

On the Emergence of Concepts and Propositions
The Nature and Structure of Human Categories
On the Impact of Culture on
Thought and Language

Translated by
Alexander Kravchenko
in collaboration with
Jillian Smith

Moscow & Boston
2020

Library of Congress Control Number: 2020930749

Copyright © 2020 LRC Publishing House
Copyright © 2020 A. D. Koshelev
Copyright © 2020 A. V. Kravchenko & A. D. Koshelev,
translation into English. Cover design by Sergey Zhigalkin.
On the cover Reversible Head with Basket of Fruit,
oil on panel by Giuseppe Arcimboldo.

All rights reserved

ISBN 978-1-64469-607-1
ISBN 978-1-64469-315-5 (electronic)

Typeset by LRC Publishing House
Russia, Moscow, Bolshaya Lubyanka, 13/16
http://www.lrc-press.ru/?lang=en

Published by Academic Studies Press in 2020
1577 Beacon Street,
Brookline, MA, USA
press@academicstudiespress.com
www.academicstudiespress.com

Contents

In lieu of a foreword 1
   1. Illustrative examples of the problems addressed in this book 1
      1.1. Categories and lexical meanings 1
      1.2. Objects and their parts 3
   2. Main topics discussed in this book 5
   3. Acknowledgements 7

Chapter 1
The evolutionary-synthetic approach and its concepts 9
   1.1. Cognitive units: the perceptual *vs.* functional dichotomy 9
   1.2. General development theory 12
      1.2.1. Development cycle 12
      1.2.2. Complete schema of development cycle 14
      1.2.3. Partial differentiation stage: the main and supplementary
            parts of objects 14
      1.2.4. Complete differentiation stage: role relationships 15
      1.2.5. Partial and complete integration stages 16
      1.2.6. "Flower" schema of a partitive system 18
   1.3. A basic-level concept and its development
      into a hierarchical system of parts 20
      1.3.1. Defining basic-level concepts 20
      1.3.2. Extended definition of a basic concept 20
      1.3.3. Artifactual and natural basic concepts 23
      1.3.4. Notional words and their basic meanings 26
      1.3.5. Concepts and their parts 26
      1.3.6. Development of concepts into systems of parts 29
      1.3.7. Flower schemas of partitive systems 31
      1.3.8. Differentiation of adjoining objects 32
      1.3.9. The partitive system of an object as a pathway of knowledge ... 34
   1.4. Structural unity of phenomenal objects 35
      1.4.1. Role system of situation participants 35
      1.4.2. Role system of object properties (adjectival system) 36

       1.4.3. Full lexical meaning 37
       1.4.4. Phenomena learning schemas 39
       1.4.5. Main factor in the development of mental representations 40
       1.4.6. Reference relation (Frege and Chomsky) 42
       1.4.7. The language of thought and its embodiment
              in different languages. 44
              1.4.7.1. Linguistic embodiment of the units of the language
                       of thought 44
              1.4.7.2. Linguistic expression of partitive relationships 46
1.5. The nature and structure of human categories. 47
       1.5.1. Definition of dual category 48
       1.5.2. "Age" structure of human categories. 55
       1.5.3. Basic meanings of the words *tree* and *banana* 58
       1.5.4. Distinction between semantic and pragmatic components
              in lexical meaning 60
       1.5.5. Model of a fruit tree. 62

Chapter 2
The genesis of human concepts and propositions. The initial stage of language. Aristotle and Chomsky on thought and language 64
2.1. Introduction 64
       2.1.1. The history of the problem. 64
       2.1.2. The proposed solution 66
2.2. Mental representations of agentive situations 68
       2.2.1. The notion of situation. 68
       2.2.2. Situation development 70
       2.2.3. The situation 'PERSON IS RUNNING' 71
       2.2.4. Identification of locomotive situations 72
       2.2.5. Specific situations 73
       2.2.6. Defining the term 'situation' 75
2.3. The development of basic situations into systems of protoconcepts ... 77
       2.3.1. Experimental data 77
       2.3.2. Decomposition of situations into Talmy's components. 79
       2.3.3. Definition of protoconcepts 80
       2.3.4. Definition of role relationships 81
       2.3.5. Integration of protoconcepts into protosituations 83
       2.3.6. The level of protoconcepts in the situation tree. 84
       2.3.7. Identification of situations of running 85
       2.3.8. Specific protoconcepts. 86
       2.3.9. Clarifying the identification process 89

Contents

- 2.3.10. Situations of observable actions 90
- 2.3.11. Hundreds of thousands of protoconcepts 91
- 2.3.12. Thousands of situations 93
- 2.4. The development of protoconcepts into systems of object and motor concepts 95
  - 2.4.1. Experimental data 95
  - 2.4.2. The formation of object concepts 96
  - 2.4.3. The formation of a motor concept (action) 97
  - 2.4.4. The formation of a predicative relationship 98
  - 2.4.5. The stage of conceptual integration 100
  - 2.4.6. The conceptual level of a development tree 102
  - 2.4.7. Specific concepts 104
  - 2.4.8. Clarifying the identification process 106
  - 2.4.9. The formation of conceptual situations of actions 107
  - 2.4.10. The outcome of the third cycle in the child's development 109
- 2.5. Matrices of concepts, propositions, and language 110
  - 2.5.1. Conceptual classification of the visible world. Conceptual matrix 111
  - 2.5.2. Propositional classification of the visible world. Propositional matrix 113
  - 2.5.3. The conceptual language of thought. Thought procedure 116
  - 2.5.4. The linguistic matrix as an initial stage of the child's language 117
  - 2.5.5. Distinguishing between general-cognitive and language-specific processes. Initial stages in language evolution 120
  - 2.5.6. Rapid growth of the child's lexicon 123
- 2.6. Aristotle and Chomsky on thought and language 124
  - 2.6.1. Aristotle's approach 124
  - 2.6.2. Chomsky's approach 126
  - 2.6.3. On the purpose of language 130
  - 2.6.4. Why are there languages, and so many of them? 135
- 2.7. Appendix. Does a child's language affect his formation of concepts? (supplement to subsection 2.3.6) 137
- 2.8. Conclusion 140
  - 2.8.1. On the indecomposability of concepts into elementary concepts 140
  - 2.8.2. Leaps in the child's cognitive development 143
  - 2.8.3. Spatial actions 144

Chapter 3
The effect of culture on language:
The case of the Amazonian tribe Pirahã 146
   3.1. Introduction 146
      3.1.1. On the Pirahã language: does culture affect language? 146
      3.1.2. Sapir and Baudouin de Courtenay on the effect of culture
           on language 147
   3.2. Models of activity development for individuals and ethnic groups ... 150
      3.2.1. The uniform progress of an ethnic group. 150
      3.2.2. The Pirahã tribe and pottery. 152
      3.2.3. Activities: crossing the Rubicon 154
      3.2.4. The minimal model of human activity development. 154
      3.2.5. The model of human activity development: basic concepts ... 156
      3.2.6. Case example: medical activity and its effects
           on the language and thought of an ethnogroup 158
      3.2.7. Case-study: stages in the development
           of Al-Sayyid Bedouin Sign Language, ABSL 163
      3.2.8. The final stage of human civilization. 165
      3.2.9. *Homo perfectus* 167
   3.3. Systematization of mental representations
        and conceptualization of linguistic meanings 172
      3.3.1. Two principles of development 173
      3.3.2. The child's conceptualization of color and other properties ... 176
      3.3.3. Does a child's language affect the process
           of differentiation?..................................... 178
      3.3.4. Words for color in Pirahã: the role of color in the life
           of modern industrial societies and the Pirahã Indians 178
      3.3.5. Lexical indicators of time 181
      3.3.6. Counting and count words.............................. 183
      3.3.7. Absence of the passive voice............................ 185
      3.3.8. On the universality of human concepts 188
      3.3.9. Concluding remarks................................... 190
   3.4. On the relative nature of 'exotic' linguistic properties 191
      3.4.1. Two principles of perception 191
      3.4.2. 'Exotic linguistic property' as a relative feature 196

References... 197

Name index.. 214

Subject index 219

Lexical index... 228

In lieu of a foreword

1. Illustrative examples of the problems addressed in this book

A well-known educator was once recalling an episode from his childhood when, for a long time, he had been trying without success to solve a complex math problem. An unexpected visitor—a friend of his father's and a famous mathematician—saw the boy's predicament and decided to help him. He did not try to solve the problem, however. Instead, he and the boy discussed in detail a specific simple case of the problem. After that, the educator recalls, he suddenly understood how to solve the problem generally.

I will try to follow the example of that mathematician. There are quite a few theoretical constructions in this book (see section 2). Some of them, such as the notion of category, the nature of lexical meaning, and the distinction between objects and their parts, can be illustrated by simple obvious examples. They are given below along with brief discussions. I believe that, for the reader, thinking over and solving these problems independently will be a quick introduction to the issues discussed in this book.

1.1. Categories and lexical meanings

The category "Games." In the Aristotelian tradition a category was defined as a class of objects in which each member had some objective characteristic feature that distinguished it from the members of other categories. More than fifty years ago, Ludwig Wittgenstein offered a critique of such an understanding of a category. He introduced the notion of "family resemblances" to define the category "Games" as he considered it to be non-classical, not having a unified description or clear boundaries. Analyzing the diversity of human games and their features, he wrote: "Don't say: "There must be something common, or they would not be called 'games'"—but look and see whether there is anything common to all" (Wittgenstein 1953: section 66). Furthermore, comparing different games, he demonstrated that they resemble one another in a variety of features, like relatives do in a large family.

In other words, he argued that games show "family resemblance" rather than possess a uniform characteristic feature. Wittgenstein's approach has played a crucial role in working out an alternative definition of category as a fuzzy class of objects that resemble some standard/reference, or prototypical, object from the class.

I do not share this position of Wittgenstein. I believe that the category "Games" does possess a uniform characteristic that distinguishes games from other activities. However, this is not an observable, or exogenous, characteristic like that Wittgenstein was looking for (there really isn't such a characteristic), but an endogenous, or functional, characteristic that is not accessible to external perception. We identify the members of one family not by their appearance or "family resemblance" (unrelated members can be more similar than relatives) but by endogenous (functional) characterization—the presence of kinship between them. As will be shown in the book, it is the endogenous (functional) characteristic that underlies the human concept of category. It is also important that this endogenous characteristic belongs to the basic meaning of the word. Because of this, the word *game* may be used correctly to refer to any game while it cannot be used correctly to refer to a non-game activity.

PROBLEM 1. Identify the characteristic feature of the category "Games" which strictly separates games from other, similar kinds of activity.

DISCUSSION. Evidence for the existence of such a feature is provided by the examples of incorrect uses of the word *game* to refer to some combat sports that appear at first sight to be bona fide games. Indeed, it is correct for some reason to use the word *game* to refer to football and tennis, but not to boxing and fencing; cf. the correct sentences (both in Russian and English) *Futbol / Tennis—èto igra, Football / Tennis is a game* and the incorrect or odd sentences *Boks / Fextovanie—èto igra, *Boxing / Fencing is a game.

Categories of actions "Person is walking" and "Person is running."

PROBLEM 2. Give explicit definitions of the identifying features for these categories.

DISCUSSION. In their typical manifestations walking and running are quite different, as can be seen in figure 1.

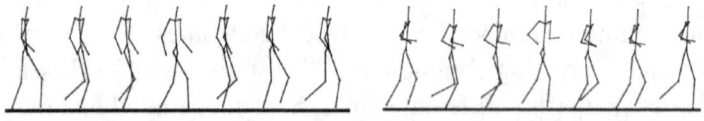

Fig. 1. Typical manifestations of walking and running

At the same time, these types of human motions may vary considerably. Roberta Golinkoff and colleagues emphasize the variety of types of running as follows: "running is running whether it is Carl Lewis circling a track or Grandma running to the telephone" (Golinkoff et al. 2002: 604).

Indeed, it is no easy task to identify the feature that distinguishes Grandma's running from fast walking. Yet native speakers do it easily and never confuse them, referring to them by the phrases in their main meanings: *Grandma is running* and *Grandma is walking*. It is hard to imagine someone moving on her feet in a manner that could be correctly referred to by both the phrases at once. Therefore, the main meanings of the Russian verbs *bežit* 'is running' and *idët* 'is walking' contain distinctive features.

Consider the well-known definitions of these verbs:

a. *Walk* 1. 'To move forward by putting one foot in front of the other' (Longman 2009: 1966);

b. *Run* 1. 'To move very quickly, by moving your legs more quickly than when you walk: He was running towards the door' (Ibid.: 1531);

c. *Čelovek X idët iz Y-a v Z* [lit., 'A man, X, is walking from Y to Z'] ≈ 'A person, X, moves over a surface from Y to Z, shifting their feet up and down and never completely losing contact with the surface crossed' (compare, by contrast, with *bežat'* 'run'—'periodically losing contact with the surface').

The seeming adequacy of these definitions reflects our familiarity with, and easy recognition of, various types of walking and running (see figure 1). Yet, obviously, the definitions (a–c) do not allow for a strict distinction between walking and running. It cannot be the feature "at a normal speed / fast" because one individual may walk faster than another individual can run. Neither can it be the feature "losing contact." Grandma may be running to the telephone without losing contact with the floor (a shuffling run). Therefore, in this case also native speakers rely on other, endogenous characteristics in referring to these types of motion.

1.2. Objects and their parts

Distinguishing objects and their parts. Discussing the problem of objects and their parts, David Marr, an AI researcher, raised some questions:

> Is a nose an object? Is a head one? Is it still one if it is attached to a body? What about a man on horseback? These questions show that the difficulties in trying

to formulate what should be recovered as a region from an image are so great as to amount almost to philosophical problems. There is really no answer to them—all these things can be an object if you want to think of them that way, or they can be part of a larger object (quoted by Pinker 1997: 258–259).

PROBLEM 3. Demonstrate that 'part of an object' is an objective notion that does not depend on the observer's view and formulate a description that defines a part of an object.

DISCUSSION. There are some indirect data indicating that the feature in question does actually exist. In Russian, there is a nominal genitive construction, YX-a 'Y of X', where Y is the name of a part of an object and X (in the genitive) is the name of the whole object: *nožka* (Y) *stula* (X-a) 'leg of the chair,' *kožura banana* 'skin of the banana'; this construction may be used correctly only if object Y (leg, skin) is part of object X (chair, banana). Therefore, the expressions *ručka dveri* 'knob of the door', *polotno dveri* 'board of the door' are correct; they mean that both the knob and the board are parts of the door. The expressions *glazok dveri 'peephole of the door', **počtovyj jašik dveri* 'mailbox of the door' are incorrect, hence neither the peephole nor the mailbox on the door are its parts. Similarly, it is correct to say *nos čeloveka* 'nose of the person', *golova čeloveka* 'head of the person' but the expression *lošad' vsadnika* 'horse of the rider' would be correct only in a different, derivative meaning 'the horse belongs to the rider' and not in the main meaning 'the horse is part of the rider'. Such examples allow us to assume that, observing objects X and Y, a native speaker of Russian is capable of "computing" in real time whether Y is part of X. Therefore, he knows whether a particular nominal genitive construction is correct or not. It would appear that this is true about native speakers of English as well. As is shown below in subsection 1.4.7, the nominal genitive has a corresponding construction in English in the form of the Y *of* X construction (here, as before, Y is the name of a part of the object and X the name of the whole object): *roof* (Y) *of the house* (X). For example, the expressions *knob of the door*, *board of the door* are correct, while the expressions **peephole of the door*, **mailbox of the door* are at least odd if not incorrect.

The structure of parts of objects. If we divide quite familiar objects into parts, as a rule one part is singled out among all the other parts as the most important one. For example, among the parts of a chair (the back, seat, and legs) the seat is the most important part because it is the seat that provides for the sitting posture of a person; among the parts of a lake it is water (in comparison with the shores and bottom), and among the parts of a banana it is its flesh (in comparison with the skin and fruit stem).

PROBLEM 4. What is the most important part of a cup?

CLUE. For this part, X, the expression *X of the cup* would be correct, similar to the expressions *sides of the cup* and *bottom of the cup*.

SOLUTIONS:

For Problems 1–2, see subsection 1.5.1; Problem 3—section 1.2 and subsection 1.3.5; Problem 4—subsections 1.3.6 and 1.3.7.

2. Main topics discussed in this book

This book is a translation of the supplemented text of my book *The Genesis of Thought and Language*, published in Russian in 2019 by LRC Publishing House in Moscow. In this edition, I discuss various aspects (cognitive, social, etc.) of the evolutionary-synthetic approach to the study of human concepts and their development and embodiment in language (Koshelev 2019).

It seems appropriate to list at the outset a few specific problems, solutions to which are proposed in this book:

1) How do human notions and the language of thought arise in a child? (sections 2.1–2.5);
2) Why is language acquired subsequent to thought and dependent upon it? (subsection 2.5.4);
3) Why are there any languages at all, and why are there so many? (subsection 2.6.4);
4) What is the primary function of language (this is not communication and not thought)? (subsection 2.6.3);
5) How are the basic meanings of words defined in the language of thought? (section 1.3, subsections 1.4.3 and 1.5.3);
6) How are the meanings of the subject and the predicate combined? (subsections 2.4.4 and 2.4.5);
7) How are semantic and pragmatic components of meaning differentiated? (subsection 1.5.4);
8) What is the essence of Frege's reference relation (Chomsky's problem)? (subsection 1.4.6);
9) What is the nature and structure of human categories? (section 1.5);

10) How does culture affect thought and language? (subsections 3.1.1, 3.1.2 and 3.3.9);
11) How does language contribute to the progress of society? (subsection 3.2.6);
12) What should be *Homo perfectus* so that it can solve the social problems of *Homo sapiens sapiens*? (subsection 3.2.9).

This book consists of three chapters.

Chapter One is an analytical review of the main ideas of this approach. The fundamental dichotomy "visual (exogenous) *vs.* functional (endogenous)" cognitive units is introduced; these units are used to give non-verbal definitions of mental representations of various objects, actions, and situations. In particular, definitions of such concepts as GLASS, CHAIR, BANANA, TREE, LAKE, RUN, and some others are given.

Chapter Two discusses how children form concepts, hierarchical relationships, and propositions (conceptual 'utterances'). Drawing on experimental data, I demonstrate that the initial units of the child's representation of the world are pre-conceptual cognitive units—mental representations of whole situations. In the course of two consecutive cycles in the child's cognitive development, these units transform into (a) primary notions—object and motor concepts, and (b) binary role relationships. Together these constitute the elementary language of thought that, in the process of thinking, is used to build conceptual structures—propositions. It is further demonstrated that immediately after the formation of thought the child begins to develop his native language in which object and motor concepts become initial meanings of nouns and verbs, while propositions become the meanings of the child's expressions. The chapter concludes with a discussion of the major components of this language, a contrastive analysis of the proposed approach, and Aristotle's and Chomsky's views on thought and language.

Chapter Three analyzes how a community's culture affects its language. It is demonstrated that the progress of a community, the main constituent of the civilizational component of its culture, enhances the development of the content component of language by extending the range of its lexical and grammatical meanings. In the context of this analysis, Daniel Everett's (2008) hypothesis that culture affects language structure is discussed. In the subsequent sections, models of the development of human and social activity are offered. These models comprise three components: **Activity** (main component), Thought, and Language (auxiliary components that ensure the successful realization of activities). The models are illustrated with examples of some concrete societies. The section is concluded by a discussion of the final stage in the progressive development of society and its members.

3. Acknowledgements

The ideas set forth in this book are the result of many years of research. Throughout these years I received support, advice, suggestions, and constructive criticisms from many wonderful people, including close friends and colleagues as well as anonymous reviewers. My sincere gratitude goes to all of them. I will only mention those who were directly involved in the discussions and provided helpful comments while the manuscript was being prepared, first of all Sergey Zhigalkin, Mikhail Kozlov, Alexander Kravchenko, Ekaterina Pechenkova, Tatjana Samarina, Ekaterina Yakovleva, and Jillian Smith.

My special thanks to Ludmila Zubkova for insightful discussions of many parts of the book and her valuable comments on some of the hypotheses put forward in it.

I also want to express my unwavering appreciation to the tireless editor of the book, Vera Stolyarova, and my excellent layout designer Sergey Belousov.

Alexey Koshelev,
6 January, 2020

Chapter 1

The evolutionary-synthetic approach and its concepts

The goal of this chapter is to give a compact overview of a number of basic concepts and provisions of an evolutionary-synthetic approach to the study of human mental representations (cognitive units of thinking) and illustrate them with concrete examples. This chapter covers perceptual *vs.* functional cognitive units (section 1.1); general development scheme (section 1.2); mental representations and their hierarchical structures (section 1.3); basic level concepts for artifact and natural objects (chair, tree, lake) (subsection 1.3.2); object, motor and developed concepts, etc. (subsections 1.3.6 and 1.4.2); basic lexical meanings and their semantic *vs.* pragmatic components (subsections 1.3.4, 1.4.3, 1.5.3 and 1.5.4), etc.

1.1. Cognitive units: the perceptual *vs.* functional dichotomy

A major issue in knowledge representation is identifying the elementary cognitive units that constitute our knowledge. Some research published several decades ago (Richardson 1969; Paivio 1971; Shepard, Metzler 1971; Pylyshin 1973; Kosslyn 1973, inter alia) stimulated a new round of discussions on how knowledge is represented in the mind (Kosslyn 1994; 2005; Barsalou 1999; Pylyshin 2003, inter alia). The bone of contention is the status of mental images and how they are represented. How are they stored in memory: in the form of propositions or as visual imagery such as holistic images? Are visual images stored in long-term memory or only in working memory? etc. There is no need to discuss these issues here as concrete parts of mental representations of the world will be described in chapter 2. It will be shown, in particular, that children initially form holistic representations of parts of reality that include visual images of these parts. Later, these representations are supplemented by their systemic correlates in the form of propositions.

Another important theme in the aforementioned discussion is the theory of dual coding developed by Paivio (1971; 1986; 2006). According to this theory, human knowledge is constituted by units of two types: verbal units that store linguistic information, and non-verbal visual units that store information about non-linguistic objects and events. At the same time, any information, even purely linguistic information, includes visual units along with verbal ones.

It must be noted that a similar principle of dual coding has long been used in explaining human concepts, particularly in dictionary definitions, when a verbal description of lexical meaning is accompanied by an image of the typical referent of the word being explained. For example, the definition of the word *banana* in Longman (2009: 114) is given as follows:

Banana—a long curved tropical fruit with a yellow skin, see picture.

A similar although more detailed definition is given by Iu. Apresian; there, the outward appearance of a banana is described verbally rather than with the help of an image:

Banan ('banana')—a southern fruit of an elongated and slightly curved form, usually a little longer than a human hand, with a thick smooth yellow skin and very tender and slightly mealy sweet flesh without seeds inside, which grows on a herbacious plant and is usually eaten raw (Aktivnyj Slovar' 2014, 1: 14).

One of the main features of my approach is that, along with visual units, I use purely **functional** units to represent human concepts (goal, purpose, motive, desire, hypothesis, inference, result, etc.) that have neither visual nor verbal components. They are in a strict opposition to visual (or, more broadly, perceptual) units because they are of a different nature. While mental images are **exogenous**—they are the effect of external stimuli on the human sensory apparatus—functions, by contrast, are **endogenous** because they are internal reactions of humans (human physiological and mental systems) to the images they perceive. I am, of course, speaking about typified units of both kinds stored in long-term memory.

In short, the following descriptions of human concepts will employ dual coding, where visual units will be paired **not** with **verbal** but with **functional units**. Let us clarify this with examples of definitions of basic concepts (basic lexical meanings).

1.1. Cognitive units: the perceptual *vs.* functional dichotomy

Concept BANANA (the meaning of the word *banana*) =

Visual prototype of a banana		Function of a banana
"An object of an elongated and slightly curved form, a little longer than a human hand, with a yellow skin and slightly mealy sweet flesh with a peculiar smell"	←	'Grows and ripens on a herbaceous plant; when ripe, used by humans as food that gives enjoyment by the taste of its flesh'

The definition on the left gives the perceptual features of a banana—they are perceptually accessible to an external observer—while on the right are perceptually inaccessible functional features (in single quotation marks). For example, the taste of a banana, its shape and size are all perceptual features, while enjoyment derived from its taste, as well as the knowledge of how it grows and ripens, are functional features. They cannot be directly perceived. They are the products of interpretation and logical inference. Thus, to enjoy the particular taste of a banana one has to eat it. Being an internal feature, a function is a **conceptualization** of an external image and its place among human goals and needs. When this function belongs to an image, an arrow (←) is used to indicate it (for more detail see subsection 1.3.2).

Concept PATH (the meaning of the word *path*) =

Visual prototype of a path		Function of a path
"Narrow strip of ground for walking"	←	'Of natural origin, used by people as a convenient way to travel from one location to another'

One can see a path and the people walking on it (image) but its natural origin and what it is for (why people walk on it) have to be known (function).

It must be emphasized that verbal definitions of the functional features of these concepts are not descriptions of their content. They are a mnemonic device used to refer to functional features which have an independent, non-verbal status. In the examples above they are (a) a means to an end: 'appease hunger', 'convenient way for pedestrians'; (b) a means of classification: 'natural object / artifact', 'food/not food'; (c) an organism's reaction, such as 'enjoy the taste', etc.

Image prototypes and functions are elementary atom-like cognitive units which, of themselves, do not have any meaning. As it is, a prototype does not contain any information about why it should be of interest (being useful or harmful) to an individual. By contrast, a function does possess such a feature, but it does not indicate to what prototype it belongs. Concepts—the "Image ← Function" pairs, united by a relationship of common locus (the function belongs to the image, as does its locus)—become elementary 'molecular' units which express **meaningful parts of reality**. Combined by various binary relationships (predicative, adjectival, etc.), these meaningful parts add up, not unlike in a 3D puzzle, into a universal human representation of the observed world.

In what follows, the dichotomy of visual *vs.* functional cognitive units will be discussed in detail and illustrated with examples. Taking a step ahead, however, I will note the dominating role of functional units in human representation of the observed world. Metaphorically speaking, the array of visual units of such a representation is like the observed matter in the Universe and the array of functional units is like dark matter, invisible in the electromagnetic spectrum but accounting, according to indirect data, for 85 % of all matter in the Universe.

1.2. General development theory

1.2.1. Development cycle. The decisive role in the study of the origin and structure of human concepts will be given to the general development theory as it is represented in the works of a number of outstanding researchers, such as J. Komensky, G. Hegel, H. Spencer, I. Sechenov, V. Solov'ëv, A. Bogdanov, H. Werner (the orthogenetic principle of development), K. Koffka, K. Lewin, and some others (cf. Werner 2004; Chuprikova 2007; Koshelev 2011; 2019: 31–33). According to this theory, development consists of a two-stage transformation of a whole homogeneous object into a system of its components. Initially, the object is divided into parts, separate 'particular' objects (the differentiation stage, marked as $\wedge$). Then these parts are combined into a system (the integration stage, marked as $\vee$).

1.2. General development theory

I will call this two-stage process a **development cycle**:

(1) Homogeneous whole
∧
Totality of independent parts (differentiation stage)
∨
System of independent parts (integration stage)

This cycle can be illustrated by the way in which a child develops a mental representation of an object, that is, a basic level concept (or basic concept, for short—see definition in subsection 1.3.2). Up to 18 months, a child's idea of an object is all its visible parts and features as a syncretic whole. Such a typified whole sets a global spatial image, or a **prototype** of the class of objects singled out by the basic concept. A second component of the concept is the general function syncretically aligned (←) with the prototype. For example, the basic concept CHAIR can be seen below:

(2) Concept CHAIR =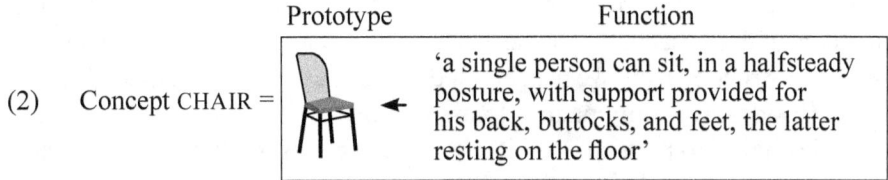

Here, the prototype is a typical spatial image of a chair and the function (shown in single quotation marks) is its typical purpose.

Thus up to the age of 18 months a child's mental representation of a chair is a holistic schema, (2), in which the prototype and the function form a syncretic whole. Later, at 24 months, this concept, as shown in the development schema (1), acquires a second level—a system of its parts or **partitive system** (3c), (4c) —and becomes a **developed concept**:

(3) Developed concept CHAIR =

    a. Whole (basic) concept   CHAIR
                                                       ∧
    b. Differentiation   BACK; SEAT; LEGS
                                                         ∨
    c. Integration (partitive system)   BACK—SEAT—LEGS

Or, in an abbreviated form (with the cycle marked as ◊):

(4) a. Whole concept   CHAIR
        Cycle of development   ◊
     c. Partitive system   BACK—SEAT—LEGS

Therefore, the development of a mental representation of a whole object consists, essentially, in the transformation of this representation into a system of parts.

At first sight the schema (3) seems to be quite clear. Upon a closer look, however, some questions arise to which the schema gives no answers. First of all, the algorithm for the assembly of parts at the integration stage is not clear. For example, if parts of the chair have been differentiated, becoming independent (3b), on the basis of what information are they then assembled into a system of parts (3c)? Should all the relationships between parts be taken into account during such an assembly and, if not, which of them exactly? For example, how should the connections of rear legs with the back of the chair be explained? In some chairs they connect with the seat and in others with the back. Of course, such particulars would be described in assembly instructions; but we need unified instructions on how to assemble any chair. Besides, it is only natural to assume that when children differentiate a whole chair into parts they do it with other objects, such as armchairs and stools, as well. What helps the child to avoid confusing different parts during assembly—for example joining a chair's armrests and the seat of a stool?

1.2.2. Complete schema of development cycle. As it has been shown by an analysis of some specific processes in children's development of mental representations (Koshelev 2019: 31–33, 203–210), the general schema (1) requires some clarification. Let us continue our reasoning for the concrete schema (3). First of all, two intermediate levels should be introduced: "partial differentiation" and "partial integration." In addition, the relationships between the differentiated object parts should be defined and explained.

1.2.3. Partial differentiation stage: the main and supplementary parts of objects. At the differentiation stage an intermediate level must be added to reflect **partial differentiation** of the whole representation of an object (marked as ⋏), that is, a state in which, on the one hand, the representation is not homogeneous anymore because its constitutive parts are already becoming prominent and, on the other hand, these parts are not yet conceived of as separate and continue to exist within a whole. For example, children are capable of comprehending the different roles of the seat, the back, and the legs of a chair while still perceiving them as its inseparable parts (cf. Koshelev 2019: 32).

As Koshelev (2019) has shown in his analysis of many various objects, their **differentiated parts are not equivalent**. One part carries most of the object's function; I will call it the **main part** (and highlight it in bold type). The other parts carry much smaller shares of the general function; they play the role of **auxiliaries in regard to the main part**. I will call them supplementary parts.

For example, the main part of a chair is the seat because it is the seat that allows an individual to take a sitting posture. The back and legs supplement the seat. They determine the character of the sitting posture: the legs of the chair allow an individual to sit at an elevation above the floor resting his feet on it, while the back of the chair provides support for his back. As a result, a new level (b) of partial differentiation appears in the schema (3); the concept remains whole at this level but it loses its homogeneity with the distinction of the main part and supplementary parts:

    a. Whole concept   CHAIR
                                         /\\
    b. Partial differentiation   BACK-**SEAT**-LEGS

It may be hypothesized that the partial differentiation stage in the case of a chair begins when the particular function of sitting, allowing for a human sitting posture, is singled out from the object's general function, and the seat is singled out from the prototype. Then the functions of supplementary parts are singled out (support for the back and legs of a sitting individual) along with their material carriers (the back and legs of the chair).

1.2.4. Complete differentiation stage: role relationships. In the course of further differentiation of level (b), as it is completely divided into parts, there **arise** independent **binary relationships** which fix the connections that existed between parts within the whole. Later, they will account for the correct combination of the differentiated parts into a partitive system. And as it turns out, it is enough to take into account only those relationships between parts which **connect the main part with supplementary parts** (for an explanation, see subsection 1.2.6). Let us call them **role relationships** and use single arrows to mark them. The relationship of alignment has already been mentioned above; other role relationships will be either numbered or given names. For parts of a concept, the role relationship is as follows:

Main part –N→ Supplementary part

The role relationship above shows how a supplementary part should be positioned in space in relation to the main part so that the function of the supplementary part can be added to the function of the main part. For example, the role relationship "–1→" (**SEAT** –1→ BACK) shows that the back (a) is behind the seat, above it, and tilted slightly backwards, and (b) due to such positioning its function is to provide support for the back of the sitting individual. As a result of complete differentiation level (c) features a set of parts, with the main part highlighted in bold type, and a set of role relationships connecting the main part with supplementary parts:

a. Whole concept   CHAIR
                                                     /\\

b. Partial differentiation   BACK- **SEAT**-LEGS
                                                       ∧

c. Complete differentiation   BACK; **SEAT**; LEGS; «←1–»; «–2→»

Other objects, such as an armchair, stool, couch, etc. are differentiated in a similar way.

Note. Not all of the remaining parts are supplementary parts, but only those which contribute directly to the general function of an object, adding their particular function to the function of the main part. For example, the spindles that connect the legs of a chair, being its physical parts, are not supplementary, or **functional** parts. Their function 'to strengthen the legs of a chair' does not contribute to the function of the seat—in contrast with the back and legs, it does not contribute directly to the sitting posture of a person.

In summary, at the stage of differentiation, when an object is divided into functional parts, firstly an intermediate level of **partial differentiation**, (b), is introduced and, secondly, two operations are performed: (1) the **main part is singled out** from among the differentiated parts and (2) in the course of such differentiation **binary role relationships** are formed connecting the main part with the supplementary parts. In other words, a role hierarchy is established among the functional parts: "**Main part** –N→ Supplementary part."

1.2.5. Partial and complete integration stages. After the stage of complete differentiation, integration begins. It is also a two-stage process. First, the main part is combined with each supplementary part (partial integration), forming

1.2. General development theory

dual systems: **SEAT** $-1\to$ BACK and **SEAT** $-2\to$ LEGS for a chair, plus **SEAT** $-3\to$ ARMRESTS for an armchair, etc. As a result, one more intermediate level, (d), appears in the schema (3); it reflects **partial integration** of object parts (marked as ⋎) and includes dual systems with their total functions:

   c. Complete differentiation   BACK; **SEAT**; LEGS; «←1–»; «–2→»
                                                                    ⋎
   d. Partial integration   **SEAT** $-1\to$ BACK; **SEAT** $-2\to$ LEGS

To complete the integration the child combines the dual systems with the same main part, in this case the seat. But seats were differentiated in different objects: a stool, chair, armchair. What systems that include a seat must be combined in order to get a chair? The general function of a chair is the most important reference point. Combining the dual systems with the same main part, the child aims to assemble the general function of a chair from the functions of these parts. Therefore he combines **SEAT** $-1\to$ BACK and **SEAT** $-2\to$ LEGS, thus arriving at the requisite partitive system:

   e. Complete integration   BACK $\leftarrow 1-$ **SEAT** $-2\to$ LEGS

The partitive system (e) is authentic with the holistic concept CHAIR as it has an identical function. The child does not combine it with **SEAT** $-3\to$ ARMRESTS because this would breach the system's authenticity with the chair.

In the end, we arrive at the following development cycle schema for the concept CHAIR:

(5)   a. Whole concept   CHAIR
                                                               ⋀
      b. Partial differentiation   BACK- **SEAT**-LEGS
                                                                 ∧
      c. Complete differentiation   BACK; **SEAT**; LEGS; «←1–»; «–2→»
                                                                  ⋎
      d. Partial integration   **SEAT** $-1\to$ BACK; **SEAT** $-2\to$ LEGS
                                                                ∨
      e. Complete integration   BACK $\leftarrow 1-$ **SEAT** $-2\to$ LEGS

Abridged, it may be represented as follows:

(5')   a. Whole (basic) concept   CHAIR
         Cycle of development   ◊
      b. Partitive system   BACK $\leftarrow 1-$ **SEAT** $-2\to$ LEGS

As before, the sign ◊ stands for a full development cycle.

18   Chapter 1. The evolutionary-synthetic approach and its concepts

The schema in (5) may also be represented by a tree-like schema of development, or **development tree**.

(6)   a.   CHAIR
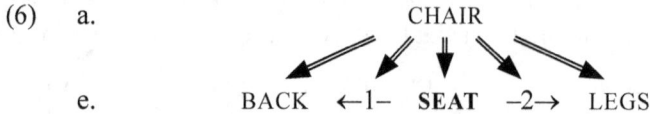
      e.   BACK ←1− SEAT −2→ LEGS

Its more explicit version is given in (32). The tree, (6), shows that the nodes of level (e) (chair parts) enter two hierarchical relationships: a partitive relationship "Whole ⇒ Part" and a role relationship "**Main part** –N→ Supplementary part." An object may have a varied number of parts, but the structure of its partitive system remains the same. For example, for a stool there is only one relationship, SEAT −2→ LEGS, while for an armchair a third relationship appears, SEAT −3→ ARMRESTS.

The analysis above clearly shows that partial differentiation—the appearance of level (5b)—begins when the main part (seat) and its physical image are gradually singled out from a homogeneous whole (5a). Only after this has been done may there begin the singling out of supplementary parts (their functions and material carriers).

Note. The partitive system (6e) is a special case of the role system (7e) as the result of development of any holistic representation:

(7)   Developed mental representation =

      a.   HOLISTIC MENTAL REPRESENTATION
                                  ◊
      e. Role system   (PART 1) ←1− (**MAIN PART**) −2→ (PART 2)

As may be seen, the role system (7e) is a set of parts of the whole grouped hierarchically around its main part—the top of the hierarchy. Since the main part carries a major share of the general function of the holistic representation it defines the type (functional characteristic) of the entire group. Thus, it may be claimed that the role system is isomorphic to the **syntactic constituent**—a group of words that has an apex defining the group type and other words dependent on the apex (see subsection 2.6.3). Therefore, the role system (7e) will sometimes be referred to as the **role constituent**.

1.2.6. "Flower" schema of a partitive system. Let us elaborate our hypothesis that during assembly of an object's parts into a partitive system it

1.2. General development theory

is just enough to take into account the connections between the main part and supplementary (functional) parts, that is, the role relationships. As differentiation of numerous spatial objects into parts has shown, the resulting partitive system has the structure of a flower as in (8a): the main part is at the center, like a pistil, and the supplementary parts surround it and are physically connected to it, like petals—compare with the schemas for a chair, (8b), and an armchair, (8c). The supplementary parts are spatially positioned relative to the main part such that their functions add up to the function of the main part (such a positioning is determined by the role relationships not shown in figure 1). Possible connections between supplementary parts do not affect the cumulative function of the partitive system and may be ignored.

(8)

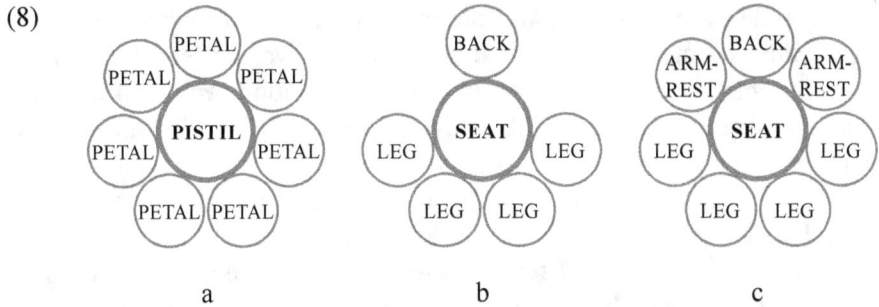

Fig. 1. The partitive systems of a flower, chair, and armchair as flower schemas (a), (b) and (c)

As it is, the flower schema of a chair, (8b), may serve as a universal instruction on how to assemble a chair delivered in a box from a furniture store: each supplementary part must be joined in the construction such that its function adds up to the function of the seat. The back may be physically connected both to the seat and the rear legs (depending on the specific assembly instructions), but in any case it must be positioned above the rear side of the seat with a slight backward tilt such that it can be leaned on by a sitting person. The same holds for the armchair schema (8c). Armrests are not always physically attached to the seat. Sometimes they are joined with the back and legs and sometimes (for armchairs made of metal) only with the back. The role relationship SEAT $-1\rightarrow$ ARMREST only shows the requisite **position of the armrest's function relative to the function of the seat**. Note also that, since a partitive system includes only an object's functional parts, the positionings of other parts (bracings of chair legs, etc.) are not defined by the flower schema.

1.3. A basic-level concept and its development into a hierarchical system of parts

One of the central themes of this book is how to analyze human representations of objects and actions and how to identify a system of cognitive units—components and relationships that constitute these representations. The initial requirement these cognitive units must meet is that they must be non-verbal, non-linguistic. In other words, I am making an attempt to form an initial language of thought, the units of which are used to build representations of visible objects and actions and are independent of language.

1.3.1. Defining basic-level concepts. Let us, first of all, focus on an analysis of simple concepts—mental representations that reflect spatial objects. In generally accepted terminology, these are basic-level concepts (or, simply, basic concepts). According to George Lakoff's definition, which sums up the direction of research taken by R. Brown, E. Rosch, B. Berlin, and others, a basic concept is formed by two interconnected features: overall outward appearance, or overall **shape**, and typical **motor interaction** with this shape, that is, interaction determined by the overall shape (Lakoff 1987: 36; Gallese, Lakoff 2005: 466). Citing Brown, Lakoff gives the following examples: a typical interaction with chairs is to sit on them, with flowers to smell them, with cats to pet them, with a ball to play with it in a certain way (Lakoff 1987: 31). In short, a basic concept is constituted as follows:

(9)   Basic concept = overall Shape + motor Interaction.

This definition gives a visual object-motor characteristic of a basic concept: both its constituents are perceptually accessible.

According to another similar view (Nelson 1973; Mervis 1987; Rakison 2000), basic concepts have a two-component structure:

(10)   Basic concept = Shape + Function.

Here, it is not interaction that is matched with the object's overall shape but the general function of shape—a feature inaccessible to direct perception.

1.3.2. Extended definition of a basic concept. I offer an interpretation of a basic concept that embraces both these definitions. It is based on the dichotomy of atom-like cognitive units introduced above: **visual** (or, broadly,

1.3. A basic-level concept and its development... 21

perceptually accessible) *vs.* **functional** (observer's intentions and interpretations). In more general terms, these are **exogenous** *vs.* **endogenous** units.

The shape or action of an object is a rather abstract feature which children develop relatively late. Therefore, instead of the term "shape" I will use the term "prototype," referring to the syncretic totality of all features of an object (shape, color, weight, etc.). Further, I will distinguish **object prototypes**—typical visual images of classes of objects similar in appearance, and **action prototypes**—typical dynamical images of classes of similar actions. For example, a prototype for the banana is a mental spatial image of a slightly curved ellipsoid, while a prototype for the action "eat a banana" a mental image of the action of a person who bites pieces off a banana, chews, and swallows them. It should be emphasized that both these prototypes are defined on a short time interval (a few seconds) of micro-t, on which the prototype of an object exists and the prototypical interaction with the object is recognized. In light of this clarification, the actions "peel a banana" and "eat a banana" are two strictly different independent actions (with respective independent prototypes and goals). However, the actions "bite off a piece of banana," "chew it," and "swallow it" are not independent actions; they are parts of the action "eat a banana" which, in their totality, allow for reaching an independent goal—"successively move pieces of banana to the stomach to satisfy the feeling of hunger."

Let us call a typical interpretation (mental or physiological response) of a prototypical object the **function** of this object. For example, the function of the prototype for a banana will be 'fruit of a banana tree; a portion of mealy sweetish food', and the function of the prototype for the action "eat a banana" 'particular gustatory enjoyment experienced in the process of the action "eat a banana" and subsequent satiation'.

Let us now introduce the notions of **object** concept and **motor** concept:

(11) **Object concept** = Prototypical object ← Function of object,

(12) **Motor concept** = Prototypical action ← Function of action.

To repeat, the arrow ← stands for the **relationship of spatial alignment** of its arguments, in this case, the prototype and function. The relationship shows that the function has a locus in the prototype. In other words, the function is carried by the prototype. As I believe the function to be the main argument in the pair, the arrow points to the prototype (from the main to the supplementary argument). In what follows, abbreviated names will sometimes be used: "concept" instead of "object/motor concept," and "function of object/action" instead of "function of prototypical object/action."

Here is an example:

(11a) Concept BANANA = Prototype 🍌 ← Function 'The fruit of a banana tree that grows on the tree and receives nourishment from it; a portion of mealy sweet food';

(12a) Concept EAT-BANANA = Prototypical action 👤 ← Function of action 'particular gustatory enjoyment and satiation'.

Thus, the concept BANANA is a **meaningful** Prototype, i.e. a typified mental image together with its function which is a uniquely human feature. The same is true for the concept EAT-BANANA.

The reasoning given above allows us to conclude that the components in Lakoff's definition in (1)—both the shape and the action—are an object concept and a motor concept, making up "Prototype ← Function" pairs of the types shown in (11a) and (12a) (for more detail see Koshelev 2019: chap. 3). This means that, explicitly, a basic concept is a unity of these pairs:

(13) Basic concept = object concept → motor concept =
(Prototypical object ← Function of object) → (Prototypical action ←
Function of action).

As before, the arrow (→) shows the relationship of spatial alignment of arguments and points from the main concept that exists on the interval of micro-t to the potential (and therefore supplementary) motor concept. In this way the object concept is an actual constituent—its prototype always exists on the interval of micro-t along with its function. By contrast, the motor concept is a potentiality—it is highly likely to appear on this interval but it may not. It may be absent while the object is directly perceived because at the moment of observation the object may be involved in various actions. However, an action defined by the motor concept is of a higher frequency and, therefore, more anticipated. It is interpreted as a motoric property of the object.

As noted above, a prototypical object is defined on the time interval micro-t not at a "point in time." This makes the unity defined in (13) ("object concept → motor concept") correct as both the components are defined on micro-t.

1.3. A basic-level concept and its development...

Here is an example of basic concept:

(14) Basic concept BANANA =

	Prototypical banana and interactions with it		Functions of a banana and interactions with it
concept BANANA ↓ concept EAT-BANANA		← ←	'Fruit of a banana tree; portion of food of a particular taste' 'experiences specific gustatory enjoyment and a slight satiation'

A concept is thus an elementary **informative** cognitive unit.[1] Its constituents, the prototype and the function, are abstract atom-like units that become independent only as the child develops cognitively. They exist in the child's initial mental representations only syncretically, in situations as whole globalities (see chapter 2).

1.3.3. Artifactual and natural basic concepts. Consider such artifactual concepts as CHAIR and (drinking) GLASS.

One of the merits of the definition of basic concept given in (13) is its strictly cognitive, non-verbal status: neither concept prototypes nor their functions (14)–(18) are described using the words of natural language. Bear in mind that the verbal definitions given above are not definitions of functions; they only indicate a person's **psychophysical states** caused by the corresponding prototypes. These states are determined by the subsystems of the human nervous system (such as limbic, vestibular, somatic, cerebellum, etc.) and are fixed by the neurobiological memory codes (for more detail see Koshelev 2019: chap. 3). Products of mental activity such as inferences, hypotheses, etc. also belong here. In other words, functions are the products (in a broad sense) of the physiological and thought systems of humans.

---

[1] I call a basic concept a **sensory** notion with a single visual (perceptual) constituent. There are, besides concepts, **functional** notions that lack a single constituent: "weed," "predator," "plant," "seek," "think," "work," etc.

24   Chapter 1. The evolutionary-synthetic approach and its concepts

(15)   Basic concept CHAIR = (Prototypical chair ← Function of chair) →
                                              (Prototype SIT ← Function SIT) =

	Prototypical chair and interactions with it		Functions of a chair and interactions with it
concept CHAIR ↓ concept SIT-ON-CHAIR		← ←	'Artifact designed for sitting on by a single person in a half-steady posture' 'while sitting a person feels support for his back, buttocks, and feet, taking a half-steady posture (maintaining balance to avoid falling sideways)'

(16)   Basic concept GLASS =

	Prototypical glass and interactions with it		Functions of a glass and interactions with it
concept GLASS ↓ concept DRINK-FROM-GLASS		← ←	'Container filled with a portion of liquid to be drunk by a single person' 'a person swallows the liquid by sips, experiencing its taste'

1.3. A basic-level concept and its development... 25

The natural concepts TREE and LAKE are defined similarly:

(17) Basic concept TREE =

Prototypical tree and interactions with it		Functions of a tree and interactions with it
(illustration of a tree and a person)	←	'Natural object, grows by itself and bears seeds (fruits), receiving nourishment from the ground';
Climb up the tree, pick its fruit, sit in its shade etc.	←	'a person interacts with the tree, experiencing a feeling of pleasure and receiving benefits'

(18) Basic concept LAKE =

Prototypical lake and interactions with it		Functions of a lake and interactions with it
(illustration of a lake and a person)	←	'Natural object, constantly keeps a large mass of still fresh water from spreading';
Swim, go fishing, perceive it as an object	←	'a person experiences a feeling of pleasure and benefits from interacting with the lake'

1.3.4. Notional words and their basic meanings. Basic concepts become central meanings of many notional words whose referents are unambiguously identified by their outward appearance. In particular, the concepts in (14)–(18) become the basic meanings of the words *banana, chair, glass, tree* and *lake*:

(14′) The meaning of *banana* = Concept BANANA (14);

(15′) *Chair* (meaning) = Concept CHAIR (15);

(16′) *Glass* (meaning) = Concept GLASS (16);

(17′) *Tree* (meaning) = Concept TREE (17);

(18′) *Lake* (meaning) = Concept LAKE (18).

The hierarchical structures (19)–(23) of these concepts, analyzed below, are the products of their transformation that simultaneously reflect the development of their stated lexical meanings.

> **Note 1.** It is only natural to ask to what extent the concept TREE in (17), that constitutes the meaning of the word *tree*, is universal for different communities. Our answer is that it is universal to the extent that the general function of this concept explaining how it "works" in these communities is one and the same. Imagine a hypothetical tribe in which the tree mythology interprets the tree as the place where the spirit of the tree dwells. The parts of the tree may be the same, but their functions would differ: the roots might be defined as 'fastenings that keep the tree from falling', the trunk as 'lateral protection of the inner space', and the branches as 'upper protection of the inner space'. Clearly, the concept TREE in such a case would differ, as the tree grows and bears seeds (fruits) not by itself (because of its connection to the ground) but by the power of the spirit that dwells in it.

1.3.5. Concepts and their parts. As children develop, their basic concepts also develop. In what follows I will be concerned only with the first, actual component: the object concept, i.e. the pair "Prototypical object & Function of object."

Notice that not all of the definitions of the functions of concepts given above are obvious. For example, why are just these functions selected for the prototypes of natural concepts TREE in (17) and LAKE in (18)? One could suggest different and quite acceptable interpretations. To justify the functions as they were formulated above I will lean on the following maxim derived from a number of concrete analyses: the **function of an object** (prototype) **equals the sum of the functions of its parts**. And since the division

1.3. A basic-level concept and its development...

of an object into parts is unambiguous, the function of an object as a whole may be determined if the functions of its parts are known.

Consider the structure of concept parts in (17)–(18). Some implicit knowledge tells us that a tree consists of three major parts: the roots, trunk, and branches (with leaves and seeds (fruits)). These parts have the same dual structure as the basic concept:

(17a) **ROOTS** = Prototype ← Function 'Receive nourishment from the ground';

(17b) **TRUNK** = Prototype ← Function 'Supports the branches and conveys nutrients from the roots';

(17c) **BRANCHES** = Prototype ← Function 'Support the seeds (fruits) and convey nourishment from the trunk'.

Adding the functions of these parts together yields the general function of a tree. Therefore, this function has been adequately formulated in (17). The same analysis can be applied to the concept LAKE:

(18a) **BOTTOM** = Prototype ← Function 'Prevents the water from draining';

(18b) **WATER** = Prototype ← Function 'A constantly maintained large mass of water that has properties useful for humans';

(18c) **SHORE** = Prototype ← Function 'Keeps the water from spreading'.

Adding up these functions likewise yields the general function of a lake.

But is the division of natural objects into parts really unambiguous? For example, might not a bird's nest in the tree be its part? Intuitively, the answer is no. And the explanation is not hard to find: a nest does not contribute to the general function of the tree; it does not participate in the tree's living. For similar reasons, an island in the middle of a lake is not part of the lake; it takes no part in maintaining the body of water. On the other hand, both the nest and the island are natural physical parts connected to the tree and the lake. This demonstrates the rule accepted in subsection 1.2.4 (see the note): the division of an object into parts involves only its **functional parts**, the parts whose functions contribute to the general function of the object. It is just such parts that will be analyzed further.

Note 2. There is a construction in Russian that provides linguistic evidence in support of the explanation given above. The nominal genitive construction *Y X*-GEN (*vetka dereva* 'the branch of the tree', *voda ozera* 'the water of the lake') is correct only if part Y (branch, water) of X (tree, lake) is a functional part of X (see Koshelev 2019: chap. 4, § 1). Therefore, the expressions above are correct, just as the expressions *berega ozera* 'the shores of the lake', *dno ozera* 'the bottom of the lake', *korni dereva* 'the roots of the tree', *stvol dereva* 'the trunk of the tree' are correct. But the expressions *ostrov ozera 'the isle of the lake', *gnezdo dereva 'the nest of the tree' are incorrect, which means that an isle and a nest are not functional parts of a lake and a tree, respectively. The following expressions are incorrect for the same reasons: **pristan'* 'pier' / *ryba 'fish' *ozera* 'of the lake', *skvorečnik 'birdhouse' / **mišen'* 'target' *dereva* 'of the tree' (of a target attached to a tree). That being said, it is reasonable to assume that a native speaker of Russian is capable of "computing" in real time whether a given part Y of object X is its functional part; therefore, he knows whether a particular nominal genitive construction is correct or not.

As was mentioned in subsection 1.2.3, the data provided by some concrete analyses of objects into parts allow us to formulate an important hypothesis: among the differentiated parts there is always a part whose contribution to the general function of the concept is the greatest. I call it the main part and highlight it in bold type. I call the other parts supplementary parts to the main part, which is typically at the center and surrounded by supplementary parts. Among the parts of the concept TREE the main part is **TRUNK** in (17b), and among the parts of the concept LAKE it is **WATER** in (18b).

Note 3. There is linguistic evidence showing how the main part of an object is distinguished: the referent of a name still remains its referent even without a supplementary part while the name becomes inapplicable if the main part of the referent is lacking. It is correct to say *derevo bez kornej / vetvej* 'a tree without roots / branches', or *ozero bez dna / beregov* 'a lake without a bottom / shores', but it is incorrect to say **derevo bez stvola* 'a tree without a trunk' or *ozero bez vody 'a lake without water', just as a dry riverbed cannot be called a river. It is true that this rule works only if the function of the main part is similar to the general function of the object. For example, the main part of a banana, its flesh, may be called a banana, while the main part of a chair, its seat, may not be called a chair. This seems to suggest that native speakers not only spontaneously divide concepts into parts (the second level of meaning, see subsection 1.3.6) but also "compute" the shares of the functions of the object parts.

1.3.6. Development of concepts into systems of parts. At first, the child's representations of perceived objects are in the form of holistic basic concepts of the type shown in (14)–(18). As the child develops, these concepts transform into systems of their parts. According to the general development theory (section 1.2), holistic concepts go through a two-stage development cycle. First (at the differentiation stage), concepts are divided into functional parts and binary relationships which are used to connect the now differentiated parts into a single whole. Later (at the integration stage), these parts and relationships combine into a system of parts (partitive system) of the concept. As a result, the basic concept (and with it, the meaning of the word) transforms into a hierarchical system with a tree-like structure, as shown in (5)–(5'). See examples below.

(19) Developed concept TREE (the meaning of the word *tree*) =

    a. Basic concept   TREE
        Full development cycle   ◊
    b. Partitive system   ROOTS ←1– TRUNK –2→ BRANCHES

The partitive system (19b) must be authentic to the concept (19a), that is, its aggregated function must be the same as its general function. This is ensured by the role relationships (see subsection 1.2.4), which show how **the function of a supplementary part must be positioned relative to the function of the main part** in order to be combined. The relationship "←1–" (ROOTS ←1– TRUNK) shows that the roots join to the trunk at the bottom and nourish it from the ground, while the relationship "←2–" (TRUNK –2→ BRANCHES) shows that the branches join to the trunk on the sides and convey nourishment from the trunk to the seeds (fruits) that grow on the branches. Because the supplementary parts constitute the remaining functional parts, they yield the general function of an object when correctly joined to the main part, making the partitive system **authentic** to it.

The following example is similar to (19):

(20) Developed concept LAKE (the meaning of the word *lake*) =

    a. Basic concept   LAKE
        Full development cycle   ◊
    b. Partitive system   SHORES ←3– WATER –4→ BOTTOM

While in earlier stages of concept development the meanings (17′) and (18′) of the child's words *tree* and *lake* included the concepts TREE and LAKE, these meanings now include the hierarchical structures (19) and (20). Thus the initial meanings of the child's words develop, transforming into hierarchical systems.

Let us analyze how the other objects, a glass, chair, and banana, are divided into functional parts, and describe their partitive systems.

The main part of the concept GLASS is its **INNER SPACE**. The supplementary parts, SIDES and BOTTOM, make it possible for the inner space to serve as a mobile storage for a portion of liquid that can be handled in different ways: one could drink it, splash it out, etc. Such a division into parts can be easily verified. It is quite correct to say *vnutrennee prostranstvo stakana* 'the inner space of the glass', or *dno stakana* 'the bottom of the glass', or *stenki stakana* 'the sides of the glass'. However, it is incorrect to say something like *voda stakana 'the water of the glass' (about water in a glass). Eventually, this is what we get:

(21) Developed concept GLASS (the meaning of the word *glass*) =

    a. Basic object   GLASS
         Full development cycle   ◊
    b. Partitive system   SIDES ←5– INNER-SPACE –6→ BOTTOM

The main part of the concept BANANA is its inner part, **FLESH**, and the supplementary parts are SKIN, which protects the flesh while it grows, and FRUIT STEM, through which the flesh receives nourishment from the branch. Thus we arrive at the following:

(22) Developed concept BANANA (the meaning of the word *banana*) =

    a. Basic object   BANANA
                                             ◊
    b. Partitive system   SKIN ←7– FLESH –8→ FRUIT STEM

Lastly, this is what we get for the chair:

(23) Developed concept CHAIR (the meaning of the word *chair*) =

    a. Basic object   CHAIR
                                           ◊
    b. Partitive system   BACK ←9– SEAT –10→ LEGS;

1.3. A basic-level concept and its development... 31

(compare with representations of chair in perceptual and amodal systems in Barsalou (1999: 578–579)).

As we can see, such different objects as a tree, lake, glass, banana, and chair all have the same partitive structure that consists of three elements.

Of course, the partitive systems of concepts do not always consist of three elements. In the case of a cup or an apple they have four elements. Consider, as an example, the seven-component system of a sipping cup with handles and a cap which ends with a cone-like tip (see figure 2). A child holds it with two hands by the handles and sips from the small holes in the tip of the cap. This cup contains its main part, the inner space, and six supplementary parts: the bottom, sides, cap, two handles, and tip.

(24)

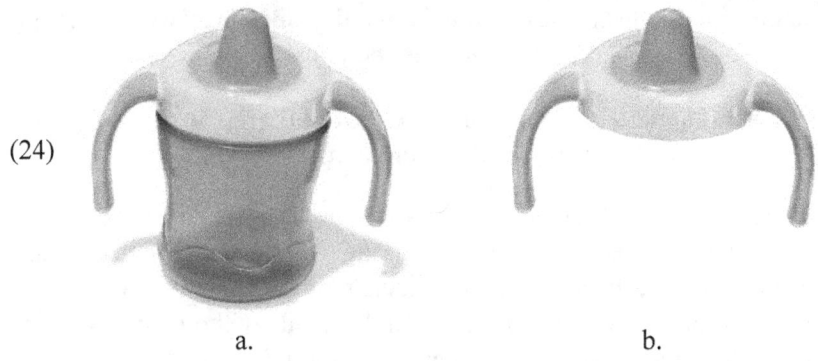

a. b.

Fig. 2. A sipping cup with handles and a cap

1.3.7. Flower schemas of partitive systems. As noted above, a partitive system has the structure of a flower. In figure 3 (p. 32), the flower schemas of parts of three objects are given: an armchair, a sipping cup, and a room; the latter includes the main particular function, inner space, and eight supplementary particular functions: the floor, four walls, the ceiling, the window, and the door. Numbered arrows show the role relationships between the **function** of the main part and the **functions** of the supplementary parts.

Let us emphasize again that role relationships show the positioning of the **functions** of supplementary parts relative to the **function** of the main part. In this context, a sipping cup with two handles and a cap is of special interest (see figure 2). The handles join to the cap (figure 2b), but their functions are added to the main function, the inner space, the positioning of which they help control. Similarly, the tip is positioned on the cap but its function is also

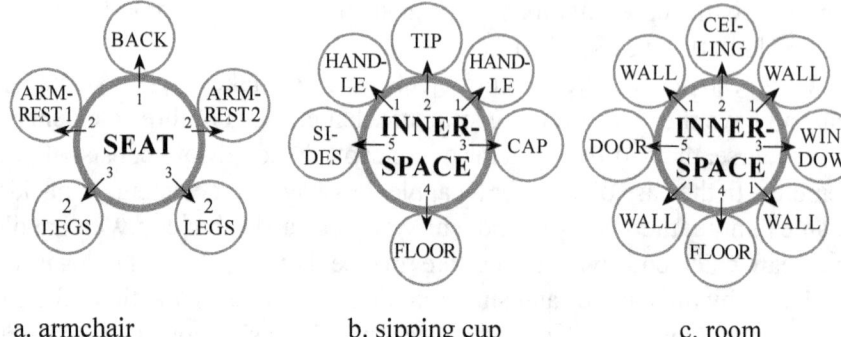

a. armchair   b. sipping cup   c. room

Fig. 3. Flower schemas for an armchair, sipping cup (see fig. 2), and a room. The labels SEAT, BACK, etc. designate the **functions** of the seat, back, etc., and the numbers inside the circles denote the **relationships (arrows)** connecting the main function with the additional functions

associated with the function of the inner space. Therefore, the partitive (role) system consists not of parts but of their functions.

1.3.8. Differentiation of adjoining objects. The above analysis allows us to claim that, when observing several adjoining objects, humans clearly distinguish separate objects and parts of objects in a group without confusing them. For example, a five-year old child understands without any explanation that the drawers in a desk are its parts and not independent objects, just as the desk cabinet door that hides them is not an independent object either. At the same time the child understands that a table lamp secured to the desk or a telephone sitting on it are independent objects and not parts of the desk. Therefore, without giving it much thought the child will use the expressions *jaŝik stola* 'the drawer of the desk', *dverca stola* 'the cabinet door of the desk', but not the incorrect expression **lampa stola* 'the lamp of the desk'. In this context, I disagree with David Marr's view, cited by Pinker (1997), that objects and their parts are not differentiated:

> As far as vision is concerned, it's not even clear what an object is. When David Marr considered how to design a computer vision system that finds objects, he was forced to ask:
> "Is a nose an object? Is a head one? Is it still one if it is attached to a body? What about a man on horseback? These questions show that the difficulties in trying to formulate what should be recovered as a region from an image are so great as to amount almost to philosophical problems. There is really

1.3. A basic-level concept and its development...

no answer to them—all these things can be an object if you want to think of them that way, or they can be part of a larger object" (Pinker 1997: 258–259).

To counter this view, let us recall some of the examples given earlier. Consider a wooden door with a metal handle, a peephole, and a mailbox attached to it on the outside. Knowing the function of the door, 'to shut and open an opening for entry and exit', and the function of the door handle, 'to hold it while opening or shutting the door', the observer interprets the door as part of the house and the handle as part of the door because the door with its particular function contributes to the general function of the house and the handle to the general function of the door. At the same time, the observer will interpret the peephole and the mailbox as independent objects that are not parts of the door as their functions are not connected with the function of the door.

Russian noun phrases provide linguistic evidence of these observations. The expression *ručka dveri* 'the handle of the door' is correct, while the expression *glazok dveri 'the peephole of the door' or **počtovyj jaščik dveri* 'the mailbox of the door' is not. It would be correct to say *dvernoj glazok* 'door-Adj-M peephole' or *dvernoj počtovyj jašik* 'door-Adj-M mailbox' (for more detail see Koshelev 2019: chap. 4, § 1). Similar considerations apply, on the one hand, to a man on horseback, as the man and the horse are independent objects possessing independent functions, and on the other hand, to parts of a human body such as the nose and the head, which have their particular functions; while such expressions as *golova čeloveka* 'the head of a human' or *nos čeloveka* 'the nose of a human' are correct, the expression **lošad' vsadnika* 'the horse of the rider' (in the sense 'the horse as a physical part of the rider') is not.[2]

The crucial difference between an object and its part is that **object is an independent notion**,[3] while its **part is not**. An object is independent insofar as its function is independent. The function is fully determined by the object's shape; therefore, it does not depend on the functions of other objects with

---

[2] I do not consider here the metaphorical meaning of this construction (derived from its basic meaning), 'the relation of possession of Y to X' (*lošad' žokeja* 'the horse of a jockey', *šapka brata* 'the hat of a brother') which does not imply physical contact at the moment of speech.

[3] To compare, in a once notable text on logic, first published in 1662, 'object' was the name of what was thought to exist on its own and be the subject of all that it was thought to be. In order to exist, an object did not require any subject (Arnauld, Nicole 1996: 30–31).

which the object is physically connected. The surroundings of an object may change, but its shape and, therefore, function will remain the same. For example, a chair, house, or tree may be transferred to a different location without any change in their functions. By contrast, the function of an object's part is not independent as it is determined partly by its own shape and partly by that of other parts—that is, their functions. If the immediate surroundings of part of an object change, the function of this part is lost. A door detached from the house cannot perform its function. Neither can the roots or branches of a tree: detached from the tree they lose their functions. That the function of an object's part is not fully determined by its shape may easily be seen: the shapes of the seat of a chair and the seat of a racing bicycle are quite different, just as the shape of a tall thin chair leg is different from the shape of a short thick sofa leg. Thus, while **basic concept** is an **independent notion** (separate mental representation), partitive concept, being part of the basic concept, is not an independent notion as it depends on other partitive concepts of the basic concept.

1.3.9. The partitive system of an object as a pathway of knowledge. Transformation of the holistic representation of an object into a system of its parts is a cognitive process whereby, first and foremost, the function of the object becomes known. Knowing parts of objects and their particular functions, I understand better how they "work" and how parts contribute to the functions of objects. For example, if a chair on which I am about to sit falls backwards, I can assume at once that its rear leg stopped "working" because it is the function of the leg, 'support the seat above the ground', that is not fulfilled. Yet this does not follow from a holistic representation of the chair. If a paper cup starts leaking, I can quickly figure out that its bottom ceased to perform its function. If a house plant is withering, our first assumption would be that it has not been watered or given nutrition and the root ceased to perform its function, etc.

The cognitive power of a partitive system is determined by the universality of its structure, which is characteristic of a great variety of objects, both artificial and natural, such as a chair, sofa, knife, spoon, pair of glasses, window, house, river, ravine, fruit, insect, bird, animal, etc. Among scientific objects, this structure is found in the interactional model of man (see chapter 3, subsection 3.2.4), the atom with its nucleus (main component) and electrons, the solar system with the Sun (main component) and the planets around it, etc. On the social level, two core social units correspond to this structure: the family (in its patriarchal interpretation, as consisting of the head of the family and other family members) and the collective (the head and the underlings).

1.4. Structural unity of phenomenal objects

In what follows, various examples will be given to demonstrate that the structure of a partitive system is manifested not only in how objects are divided into parts but in other types of division as well: objects into properties (an adjectival system), situations into participants, etc. In other words, the general role structure (7) of a partitive system is an invariant for the phenomenal (perceptually experienced) objects in the world.[4] From now on, partitive and other divisions of objects into components will be referred to by the general term **role systems** (see Note in subsection 1.2.5).

1.4.1. Role system of situation participants. At approximately 12 months children begin to form object and motor concepts—independent mental representations of objects and actions which participate in situations perceived as agentive. Prior to this, at 9–11 months, the child's elementary mental representations are holistic situations (see chapter 2). Later, in accordance with the development schema (5), the child begins to break holistic situations down into (a) participants: the main participant (motor concept reflecting the Agent's action) and supplementary participants (the Agent and other objects), and (b) role relationships that connect the main participant (Agent's action) with supplementary objects-participants.

For example, the mental representation of a holistic situation BANANA HANGING ON BRANCH is broken down into the main participant (the concept HANGING or FRUIT-SITTING) and supplementary participants (the concepts BANANA and BRANCH). In addition, two role relationships appear: predicative ("+→") and objective ("–On→"). At the stage of partial integration they help to form two dual systems of participants, **HANGING** +→ BANANA and **HANGING** –On→ BRANCH. Similarly to the assembly of parts into a partitive system, these systems form a role system of situation participants (25b) authentic to the initial holistic situation:

(25) Developed situation   BANANA HANG ON BRANCH =

     a. Holistic situation   BANANA-HANGING-ON-BRANCH

     b. System of participants   BANANA ←+ **HANGING** →On BRANCH

---

[4] Here and elsewhere the term "phenomenon" is used as member of the dichotomy "phenomenon *vs.* function," rather than "phenomenon *vs.* noumenon."

1.4.2. Role system of object properties (adjectival system). In our further discussion the term 'basic concept' will be used to refer only to its actual constituent, the object concept, with the motor concept omitted (full definition was given in (13)):

(26)   Basic concept ≈ Object concept = Prototypical object ← Function of object.

Children begin to divide objects into parts at roughly 24 months. However, they begin to single out separate properties of objects, such as size, weight, color, shape, etc. much earlier, at around 18 months. I will use the term 'shape' to refer to the spatial domain occupied by the object rather than to the object's surface. This will allow us to view an object as a totality of all its properties, one of which, the shape, will be considered the main property of the object (highlighted in bold type), and the other properties supplementary to it as they do not occupy independent spatial domains and have their loci in the domain of the shape. Thus, a role relationship of alignment between the shape and other properties of the object may be established (→) which shows that a supplementary property is aligned with the shape (main property), that is, it has a locus and is manifested in the spatial domain of the shape.

For example, for the properties of the concept GLASS, this relationship can be represented as follows: **GLASS-SHAPE** → LIGHT (the glass shape is not heavy), **GLASS-SHAPE** → GLASS (the shape is made of glass), **GLASS-SHAPE** → MEDIUM (size), etc. These dual systems are similar to the dual systems of chair parts (**SEAT** –1→ BACK and **SEAT** –2→ LEGS). Added up similarly, following the general pattern, these dual systems form a role (adjectival) system GLASS (26b) authentic to the holistic concept GLASS as a syncretic unity of properties.

(27)   Developed (adjectivally) concept GLASS =

   a. Basic concept

   b. Adjectival system

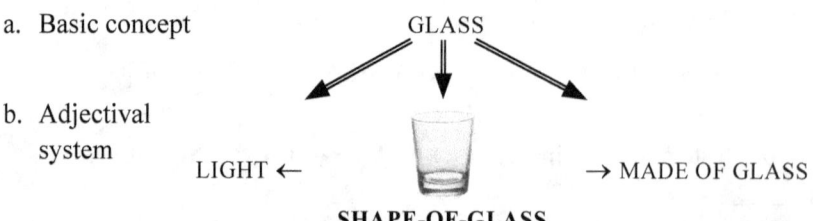

1.4. Structural unity of phenomenal objects

Consider another example, the adjectival system of a banana with a more ramified role structure. If, out of its many visible properties, we single out four supplementary properties—YELLOW, LIGHT, SOFT, and SWEET—we get the following:

(28) Developed (adjectivally) concept BANANA =

    a. Basic concept   BANANA

                                       ◊

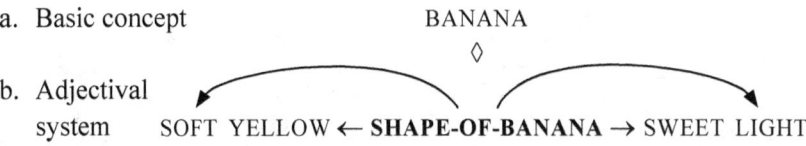

    b. Adjectival
        system   SOFT YELLOW ← **SHAPE-OF-BANANA** → SWEET LIGHT

As may clearly be seen, the partitive systems (19b–23b), the system of situation participants (25b), and the adjectival systems (27b–28b) are isomorphic. In other words, they all have a unified role structure: the main component is hierarchically connected with the supplementary components—cf. the general role system in (7e).

1.4.3. Full lexical meaning. Once stored in the child's memory, basic concepts quickly become the main lexical meanings of the words learned by the child. As the child develops, basic concepts also develop and transform into two-level tree-like hierarchies (see subsection 1.3.6).

Let us take a closer look at the lexical meaning of the word *banana*. Consider the concept (28) explained in (29), where the prototypes and functions of the elements are shown. The concept BANANA is shown on the level (29a) and its adjectival system (28b) on the level (29b) (double arrows show the differentiation of properties). Its main property may be represented as follows:

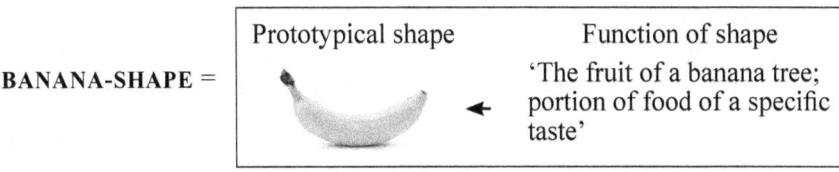

The function of banana shape, being its main property, inherits the main part of the function of the whole banana. Therefore, (28) may be made more explicit (see (29) below).

(29) Developed (adjectivally) concept BANANA =

a.

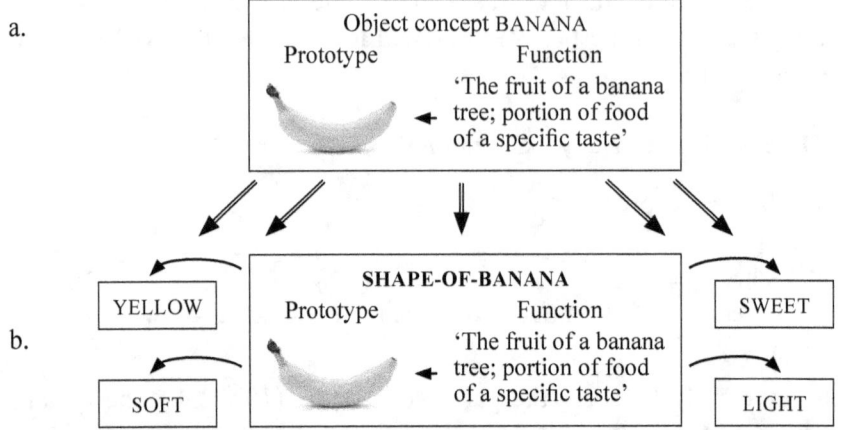

b.

Thus, the basic meaning of the word *banana* becomes more explicit as well:

(29′) *Banana* (basic meaning) = Developed (adjectivally) concept (29).

At the age of 24 months, the shapes of objects and actions stored in the child's memory begin to be divided into parts, and then they transform into partitive systems (see an analysis of this process in the case of the concept CHAIR in 1.2), cf. also Condillac 2001: 156. As a result, the child's two-level concepts become three-level, with the addition of the level of partitive systems. For example, the two-level concept BANANA (29) becomes the three-level (30) as shown on p. 39. On level (c) the prototypes for fruit stem, flesh, and skin are omitted; only their functions are given.

If the concept (30) is substituted for the basic concept BANANA in the tree (25) of the situation BANANA-HANGING-ON-BRANCH, the full structure of this situation will be easy to see.

Thus, at the stage when children's representations of objects and actions are divided into parts, we get the following three-level meaning:

(30′) *Banana* (basic meaning) = Developed (adjectivally and partitively) concept (30).

As far as cognitive development goes, this meaning may be considered the full meaning of the word as it does not develop any further in the native speaker's consciousness. It will be specified and discussed in more detail in subsection 1.5.2.

1.4. Structural unity of phenomenal objects

(30) Developed (adjectivally and partitively) concept BANANA =

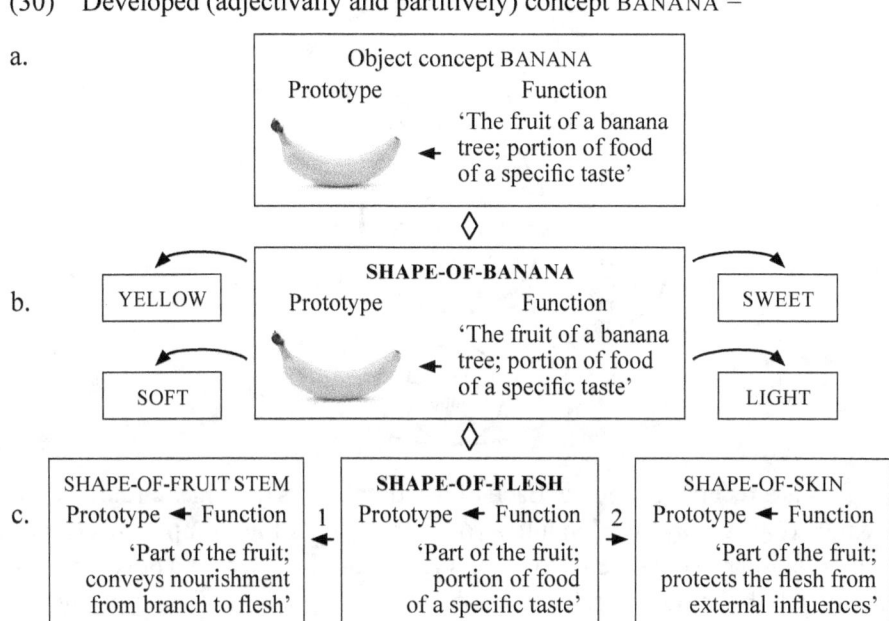

1.4.4. Phenomena learning schemas. The concept in (30) allows us to easily see how the child learns about bananas; it is a three-step process that depends on the child's cognitive development and accumulated experience. As the basic concept BANANA (level (30a)) appears in the child's memory, the child already understands that (a) there are objects of particular appearance (prototypical bananas) which are fruits growing on trees and which contain a portion of sweetish food, and (b) by eating this portion of food (which is done according to the prototypical interaction "eat a banana," see (14)) one can experience specific enjoyment and satiation (the function of the interaction). As the level of properties (30b) appears the child begins to understand that the properties of a banana and their roles are separate phenomena. Lastly, when the level (30c) appears, the child acquires knowledge of the parts of which a banana is composed and their functions.

The development tree for a mental representation of a spatial object may be generally diagrammed as "circles in a circle" (Gelernter 2016).

In this diagram the outer circle stands for a whole spatial object (situation, object, part of an object) and the totality of inner circles for the **role constituent** of its components (situation participants, parts of objects, parts of parts of objects):

(31)

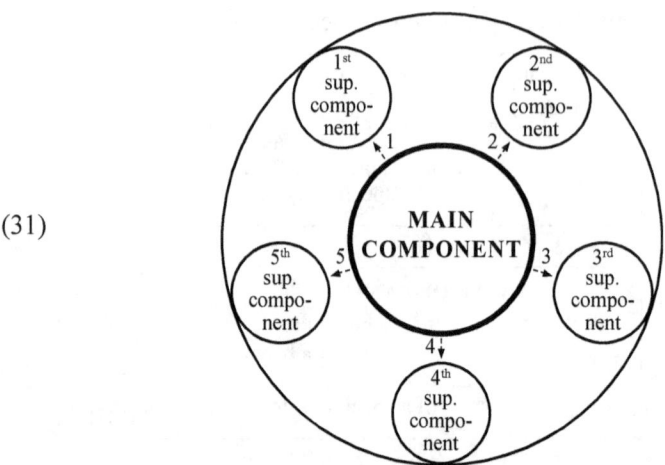

This is a recursive schema. Each of its components (an inner circle), being a whole object, may develop into a role constituent of its components (inner circles) similar to the schema in (31). As an example, consider a development tree in which the outer circle stands for a whole situation of the type shown in (25a) and the inner circles for its participants (25b). Being whole objects themselves, these participants develop into systems of their parts. Thus, each inner circle may develop into a schema like that shown in (31).

The schema (31) reflects cognition of a spatial object. It shows that quite diverse phenomena are conceived of as having the same role structure. That is to say, the world, as it is perceived by humans, is "cut out" according to the hierarchical schema, as in (31) (for more details, cf. Koshelev 2017: 411–414).

> **Note.** If this hypothesis is true, scheme (31) imposes structural restrictions on the variability of living organisms and, possibly, human languages, see the Note in subsections 1.2.5 and subsections 2.5.4, 2.6.2. For a discussion of these issues, see Chomsky 2010; Berwick, Chomsky 2016: 57–61.

1.4.5. Main factor in the development of mental representations.

The aim of our further discussion is to illustrate the following thesis: the development of mental representations is conditioned by the development (differentiation) of certain human inner functions (understood in the broadest possible sense).

The following two examples may serve as illustrations. Let us go back to the division of the holistic concept CHAIR into parts, as shown in (5). What factors trigger such a division? It seems that the main factor is the differentiation of its function into (a) particular functions: 'support for the

1.4. Structural unity of phenomenal objects 41

buttocks', 'support for the back', and 'the height of legs that allows a sitting person to rest their feet on the floor', and (b) role relationships that connect these functions. As a result, a system of particular functions is formed:

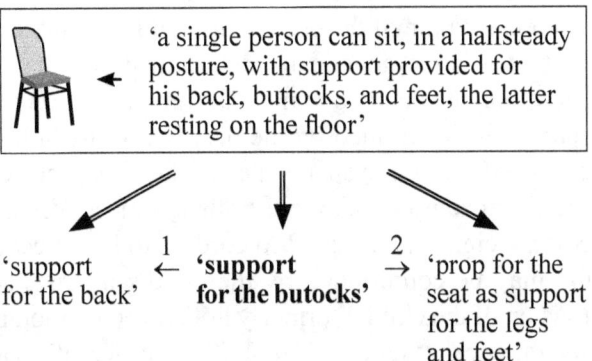

This system is at once projected onto the prototypical chair, singling out its physical parts as the carriers of these functions: first the seat, then the back and legs (they are not always obvious). Therefore, these parts obtain the conceptual structure "Prototype ← Function," and a partitive system is formed, (32b), as an explicit version of the system in (23b) in subsection 1.3.6:

(32) Developed concept CHAIR =

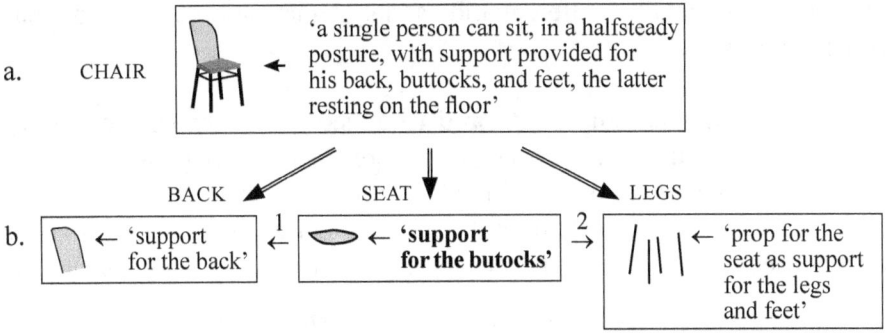

Naturally the question arises, Why is the general function of the concept CHAIR divided into particular functions? Looking for an answer, we should remember that the function of a chair is the psychophysical state of the person sitting on it. At an early age children perceive their bodies holistically, not systemically. Later, this representation is broken down into parts—the back, buttocks, legs, etc.—and transforms into a system of parts. The general function of the chair is also divided according to this system: the child's back singles out the back of the chair with its function of supporting the human back, the buttocks single out the seat, and the position of legs and feet single out the legs of the chair that provide for this position. If, finally, we ask why a holistic representation of the body transforms into a systemic one, the answer will be that it is the genetically determined physical development of children. Therefore, the development of the representation of a chair—its division into parts—is determined by the division of the holistic representation of the posture (psychophysical state) of the sitting person into parts.

Consider another example. Why are holistic objects divided into their properties—color, weight, shape, etc.? According to Ivan Sechenov (1952), such a division may be conditioned by the child's internal development, namely, the division of the child's formerly holistic perception into a system of separate physiological reactions. This leads to differentiation of the perceived properties of objects, cf.: "any and all sensorily accessible features or properties of objects are products of separate physiological reactions of perception, and the number of the former is strictly determined by the number of the latter" (Sechenov 1952: 354; for more detail, see chap. 3). In the same vein, Bower (1974) hypothesized that babies are born with a primitive unity of sensory modalities.

In summary, it may be hypothesized that the detailed systematization of the external (phenomenal) world characteristic of humans is prompted by the likewise detailed differentiation and systematization of their internal (functional) world.

1.4.6. Reference relation (Frege and Chomsky). N. Chomsky constantly emphasizes that human representations of perceived objects, unlike representations characteristic of other animals, do not have a clear connection with their referents since objects do not exist by themselves outside of human consciousness. They are closely connected with the mental sphere of man, cf.:

> In general, there appears to be no *reference* relation in human language and thought in the technical sense of Frege, Peirce, Tarski, Quine, and contemporary "externalist" philosophy of language and mind. Referring is an action, and the internal symbols that are used to refer do not pick out mind-indepedent objects. On investigation, it turns out that what we understand to be a house, a river, a person, a tree, water and so on, is not a physical construct of some kind. Rather, these are creations of what seventeenth-century investigators called

our "cognoscitive powers," which provide us with reach means to interpret and refer to the outside world from certain perspectives. [...] These properties of lexical items seem to be unique to human language and thought, and have to be accounted for somehow in the study of their evolution. How, no one has any idea (Chomsky 2010: 57–58; original emphasis; see also Berwick, Chomsky 2016: 85).

The reasoning given above seems to be one possible version of such an explanation. In this context, let us again look at level (b) of the developed concept CHAIR in (32). Actually, on this level the chair is represented by its functions as a structure: 'support for the buttocks' (main function), 'support for the back', and 'provides stable support for the buttocks and legs and feet' (supplementary functions); these are connected by role relationships. The latter determine the locus of supplementary functions in regard to the main function such that they are all realized simultaneously, adding up to form the general function. The prototypes for the back, seat, and legs shown on level (b) are not necessarily preserved. The parts of a real chair may be of any size and shape that provide for their functions. For example, it could be made up of force fields. Moreover, if we ask ourselves where these functions come from, the answer will be obvious: they are the three crucial supports that provide for the sitting person's certain psychophysical state. In other words, it is a neurobiological memory code that stores typified data from the different subsystems (limbic, vestibular, somatic, etc.) of the nervous system of a person sitting in a chair. Clearly, this state is completely separate from the chair being used.

Thus, the word *chair* is the name of a physical object designed to provide for the aforesaid state of a person. Understandably, to a cat or chimpanzee it will be a very different object. The same could be said about the concepts TREE, LAKE, etc.

It would only be fair to acknowledge that anthropoids also have concepts that contain functional components absent in the perceived physical objects. However, these functions are, firstly, much more implicit, as they merge syncretically with the physical components of these objects. Secondly, they are different from the functions identified by humans. Take the banana as an example—an object unquestionably comprehensible to anthropoids. It may be assumed that, to them, it has a syncretic function 'edible (satiating), of a pleasant taste'. More than that, they even know that the fruits hanging on banana trees become edible at a particular time of the year. However, their interpretation of how bananas appear on banana trees and why they become edible (should there be such an interpretation) would seem to be qualitatively different from the human interpretation—'the **fruits** of the tree which receive nourishment from the tree via its branches and, because of that, grow and ripen' (see the model for a fruit tree in subsection 1.5.5).

1.4.7. The language of thought and its embodiment in different languages. The structures of the properties of objects of the type shown in (27), and parts of objects shown in (19)–(23), as well as situation participants in (25b), are basic representations formed by the child. If instead of the holistic concept BANANA its developed version is inserted in the system of situation participants (25b) we may get a concrete idea about the structure of this situation, when its participants become developed (adjectivally and partitively) concepts. After 24 months many of the child's representations of situations acquire such a three-level tree structure, which also includes the developed structure of actions (see Koshelev 2017: 399–401) and which will not be taken into account for the time being.

Such three-level situation structures are formed, as children develop, before and independent of their acquisition of the mother tongue (see Koshelev 2019: section 2.7, chap. 2). Therefore, it may be assumed that, as a totality, they represent the universal language of thought. Its "lexicon" (a multitude of elements) is constituted by the conceptual nodes of situation structures. These fall into four classes: object and motor concepts (1st level), adjectival concepts (2nd level), and partitive concepts (3rd level). The syntax of the language of thought is defined by a set of relationships which fall into two classes: role relationships connecting the concepts on each level and two interlevel relationships, adjectival, "Object $\Rightarrow$ its Property" (BANANA $\Rightarrow$ YELLOW), and partitive, "Part of object $\Leftarrow$ Object" (FLESH $\Leftarrow$ BANANA). These connect the nodes of adjoining levels in the tree structures (on the language of thought, see also Koshelev 2019: subsection 2.5.3, chap. 2)

1.4.7.1. Linguistic embodiment of the units of the language of thought. One of the most important functions of language (its sentences) is the explicit description of arbitrary propositions—assessments of agentive situations, that is to say, any predicative strings of concepts from the three-level structure of a situation (on the functions of language, see subsection 2.6.2, chapter 2). As an illustration, let us consider the sentence *The boy is eating the flesh of a yellow banana.* It designates the following proposition:

1.4. Structural unity of phenomenal objects   45

BOY ←+ **IS EATING** → FLESH ⇐ BANANA ⇒ YELLOW

where the action **IS EATING** is the main situation participant (highlighted in bold type), BOY is the Agent performing the action, BANANA the Patient, YELLOW its property, "←+" the predicative relationship, "→" the object relationship, and "⇐" and "⇒" the relationships "Part ⇐ Object" and "Object ⇒ its Property," respectively. Clearly, for this proposition to be adequately designated, language must have, ideally, (a) names for the above-given concepts (object concepts BOY, BANANA, motor concept IS EATING, adjectival concept YELLOW, and partitive concept FLESH), and (b) syntactic relationships—correlates of the relationships which connect these concepts.

So, the units of the language of thought must be represented, in one form or another, in every language. Let us ask the hypothetical question, which units of the language of thought have a universal linguistic status, i.e. are certainly (or must be) expressed in all languages, and which units are linguistically expressed only under certain conditions?

It may be claimed that every language must have, firstly, separate names for object and motor concepts, and, secondly, means of expressing the relationship of predicativity that connects the action (motor concept as the main situation participant) and the Agent performing this action. This allows for the possibility of constructing a sentence—a linguistic unit expressing a proposition (see subsections 2.4.4–2.4.6 and 2.5.4, chapter 2). Thereby, two classes of words are formed in the lexicon of a language, nouns and verbs, and, respectively, two part-of-speech meanings. Moreover, other role relationships must also be linguistically expressed—the relations that connect the action with other situation participants; these relationships may be conditionally called case relationships. Otherwise the speaker will not be able to provide an explicit linguistic description of the participants in a situation.[5] In some languages case relationships are expressed morphologically, that is, by the case forms of nouns, and in some languages by prepositions and other language tools.

---

[5] It should be noted that children form case relationships at an early age. For example, children speaking Russian as their mother tongue form such relationships in their second year, which accounts for the acquisition of all six cases by 24 months (see Koshelev 2017: 94–96; Lepskaia 2013: 65–66; Voeikova 2015: 143–144; Tseitlin 2009: 168, 169, 175). Children speaking Turkish already acquire some case relationships at 15 months (Slobin 2004: 3).

As for the linguistic embodiment of other units of the language of thought, such as the class of adjectives as names of object properties or the two remaining relationships, adjectival and partitive, they are not as obvious. For example, a given language might lack the names for the visual properties of objects as a separate class of adjectives such as *thick, red, round, wooden*. In such a case their naming function can be taken on by nouns (see, for example, Grashchenkov 2018: 17–19). Then linguistic representation of the adjectival relationship "Object (basic concept) ⇒ its Property (adjectival concept)" may not be guaranteed. If, however, a given language does have adjectives, this relationship will also be represented.

Further, in a given language there might, in principle, be no names for parts of objects (handle, bottom, cover, etc.). For example, they could be substituted by nouns that name a part together with the object containing it; consider *plodonožka* 'fruit stem' in Russian, *doorknob*, *branch* ('part of a tree that grows from its trunk'), *hilt* ('part of a blade weapon that consists of a guard and a grip'), *blade* ('the cutting part of a blade weapon') in English. In such a case, the partitive relationship "Part ⇐ Object" may be absent in this language. If, however, a language does have names for parts of objects, the aforesaid relationship will be represented in this language.

1.4.7.2. Linguistic expression of partitive relationships. Both Russian and English are known to have names for parts of objects: *ručka, dno, kryška—handle, bottom, cover*, etc. Therefore, in keeping with what has been said above, these languages have the feature of partitive relationship "Functional part (partitive concept) ⇐ Object (basic concept)." It must be emphasized that its first argument is not just any part but precisely the functional part, because the partitive system of an object concept comprises only its functional parts, see (6e), (19b)–(23b), (25b), (32b). The task at hand is to identify the language tools for expressing this relationship in Russian and English.

As has been noted above (see subsection 1.3.8), in Russian the partitive relationship is expressed by the nominal Genitive construction *Y X-a* 'Y of X' (*kožura banana* 'banana skin', *dno stakana* 'the bottom of the glass'). If the part Y named by the word *Y*, is not a typical functional part of the object X, the nominal Genitive construction becomes incorrect (see Koshelev 2006; 2017: 327–338). Some experimental data allow us to believe that a similar partitive relationship in English is expressed by a construction with the preposition *of*, where the preposition has, among other things, the function of the Genitive: *Y of X*. Here, as before, *Y* is the name of the functional part Y of an object and *X* is the name of the whole object X: *roof* (*Y*) *of the house* (*X*).

The English construction *Y of X* is used in this meaning much less frequently than the Russian construction *Y X-a*. Nevertheless, in a number of examples one can see that the construction *Y of X* also becomes odd or incorrect if the word *Y* names a part of an object that is not among the typical functional parts of this object, cf. the correctness of the expressions: *door of the house* ('dver' doma'), *handle of the door* ('ručka dveri'), *middle of the road* ('seredina dorogi'), *trunk of the tree* ('stvol dereva'), *shore of the lake* ('bereg ozera') and oddness or incorrectness of the expressions: **garage of the house* (*'garaž doma'), **peephole of the door* (*'glazok dveri'), **mailbox of the door* (*'počtovyj jaŝik dveri'), *pit of the road (*'yama dorogi'), *nest of the tree (*'gnezdo dereva'), **island of the lake* (*'ostrov ozera').

1.5. The nature and structure of human categories

It is natural to think that the classes of objects singled out by basic concepts are the simplest, or basic, categories. Currently, two types of categories, or two approaches to their definition, are distinguished. According to the classical approach all members of a category possess a specific set of necessary and sufficient features that make them identical to one another and strictly separate them from the members of other categories. The alternative prototype approach stemmed from Wittgenstein's (1953: 66–71) ideas and his analyses of the word *game* and the notion of "family resemblances," the latter becoming a cornerstone for this approach (see Lakoff 1987: 16), Austin's (1961) discussion of the ambiguous semantics of the word *healthy*, and experimental and theoretical research done by Rosch (1973; 1978), Lakoff, and others. According to the prototype approach, members of a category may resemble one another by various features (like members of a family) while these features are grouped around a certain prototype which all members of the category resemble to a greater or smaller degree (for details, see Pinker 2013: chap. 7).

Over the past 50 years these approaches and their application have caused a lot of discussions among linguists, cognitive psychologists, and philosophers, see for example (Wierzbicka 1996: 157–160; Ramscar, Hahn 1998). While some scholars adhere to one or the other approach (classical or prototype), others are looking for a compromise in the use of both the approaches, cf.:

A third, compromise position would say that human concepts correspond to both classical and family resemblance categories. Classical categories are the "core" of the concept, used for reasoning. Family resemblance categories are "identification procedures" or "stereotypes," used for identification of category exemplars on the basis of available perceptual information, or for rapid approximate reasoning (Pinker 2013: 184).

1.5.1. Definition of dual category. On the whole, we share this position of compromise. At the same time, our analysis of basic concepts given above allows us to offer a more detailed interpretation of human categories. According to the dual structure "Prototype ← Function," of the basic concept in (26) a category is **simultaneously** defined by two characteristics of essentially different nature: internal (functional feature) and external (visual mental image). Therefore, human categories are dual: they include two partially coinciding and closely interconnected object categories.

The first (classical) category is defined by the functional feature that is perceptually inaccessible. An object belongs to it if and only if it possesses a functional feature. The second (prototypical) category is derivative from the first. It is defined by the visual or, broadly, perceptual prototype—a **typical mental image of the members of the first category**. An object belongs to it if and only if it resembles the prototype in which the typical perceptually accessible features are crystalized. Thereby, the prototype sets a fuzzy category of "family resemblances." This category does not possess any independent significance. It arises only because it is important for humans to be able to reason rapidly about the functional (informative) features of the objects perceived. If a perceived object resembles the prototype it is highly likely (though not necessary) that it has a corresponding functional feature. To ascertain whether this is the case, we "compute" the object's functional feature based on our knowledge and some indirect data.

As an illustration, consider two categories in Russian, "Stul'ja" 'Chairs' and "Kresla" 'Armchairs', which are defined by the basic concepts STUL 'CHAIR' and KRESLO 'ARMCHAIR', that is, the main meanings of the words *stul* 'chair' and *kreslo* 'armchair'. It must be noted that the Russian concepts STUL and KRESLO differ from the similar English concepts CHAIR and ARMCHAIR (see below for an explanation).

Let us take a closer look at the category "Stul'ja" 'Chairs', defined by the concept STUL 'CHAIR'. I will take its abridged definition given in (26) as compared to the full definition in (15).

1.5. The nature and structure of human categories

(33) Concept STUL 'CHAIR' = Prototype ← Function =

Prototype	Function
![chair] ←	'An artifact designed for sitting on by a single person in a half-steady (semi-relaxed) posture (while sitting on it a person cannot fall backward, though he can fall sideways) comfortable for sitting at a desk and working with one's hands'

The classical category "Stul'ja" 'Chairs' is defined precisely by the function. Objects of unusual shape belong to this category along with the typical objects if they have this function (see figure 4).

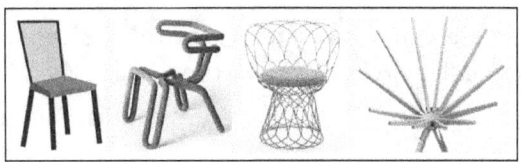

Fig. 4. Prototypical chair (left) and atypical (designer) chairs (right)

Let us bear in mind that basic concepts become basic meanings of words (see subsection 1.3.4):

Stul 'chair' (basic meaning) = Basic concept STUL 'CHAIR' (33).

Thus, a classical category defines the set of all the direct references of a word. The unusual shape of designer chairs in figure 4 does not prevent them from being referred to by the word *chair* in its categorical, non-metaphorical meaning.

We should not, however, forget about the provisionally omitted motor concept. If the shape of an object changes so that the motor concept changes, the latter does not belong to the classical category anymore even if its function remains the same. For example, a razor blade, safety razor, and electric razor belong to different categories even though they have the same function.

The prototypical category "Stul'ja" 'Chairs' is defined by a prototypical chair (figure 4, left). The category includes objects similar to the prototype (in shape and size). At the same time, but not always, most of the members of this category belong to the classical category. Thus, the category does not include the chairs shown in figure 4 to the right of the prototype. On the other hand, a chair made of paper mache will belong to the prototypical category "Stul'ja" 'Chairs' but not the classical (functional) category because it does not meet the functional requirement. It may be referred to by the word *chair* only in its metaphorical meaning showing that (a) the object referred to resembles the prototype and (b) the object does not possess the function of a chair.

Let us now consider the concept KRESLO 'ARMCHAIR'. It is similar, but not identical, to the concept STUL 'CHAIR'. The main distinction between chairs and armchairs is usually identified by the prototypical definition 'Armchair—chair with armrests'; compare the well-known definitions of the words stul 'chair' and kreslo 'armchair':

(34) a. *stul* ('chair') 1. A kind of furniture used for sitting on that has a back (for one person) (Ushakov, IV: col. 571).
  b. *kreslo* ('armchair') 1. A kind of chair with supports for elbows (Ibid., I: col. 1510).
  c. *chair* 1. A piece of furniture for one person to sit on, which has a back, seat and four legs: *a kitchen chair* (Longman 2009: 262).
  d. *armchair* 1. A comfortable chair with sides that you can rest your arms on (Ibid.: 77).

These definitions, however, are not adequate for the simple reason that they describe the difference between **prototypical** chairs and armchairs, while it is the difference in **function** that should be described. These different functions are as follows. Sitting in an armchair, a person can be fully relaxed and even doze off, yet his mobility is limited as it takes some effort to get up, turn around, etc. Sitting on a chair, a person is not so relaxed; he must balance the body not to fall sideways, but on the other hand he is more mobile.

These functional differences lead to the following definition:

(35) Concept KRESLO 'ARMCHAIR' =

Prototype		Function
	←	'Artifact designed for sitting on by a single person in a steady (relaxed) posture (the person cannot fall off it even when dozing) comfortable for resting'

Kreslo 'armchair' (basic meaning) = Basic concept KRESLO 'ARMCHAIR' (35).

Remember that function is a non-verbal cognitive unit that represents the typical psychophysical state of a person sitting on a chair (see end of subsection 1.3.2).

1.5. The nature and structure of human categories

It can easily be demonstrated that the differences between a chair and an armchair are determined by the differences in their functions, not their prototypes. Counter to definitions given in (34a–d), in Russian the objects with armrests (a–c) shown in figure 5 are called *stul* 'chair' and not *kreslo* 'armchair'. Contrarily, the objects without armrests (d–f), figure 5, are called *kreslo* 'armchair' in Russian and not *ctul* 'chairs'. The former have the function of a chair, and the latter the function of an armchair.

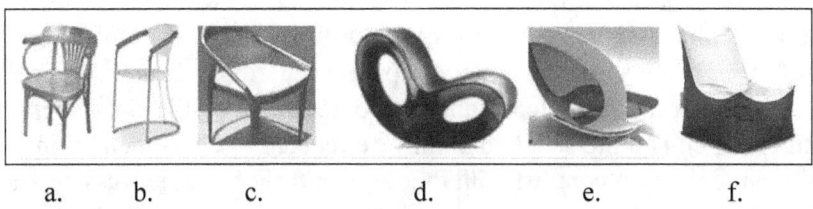

a.　　b.　　c.　　　d.　　　　e.　　　　f.

Fig. 5. The visual feature "presence / absence of armrests" is not a distinctive feature for the categories "Stul'ja" 'Chairs' and "Kresla" 'Armchairs'; compare the three chairs with armrests on the left and the three armchairs without armrests on the right

It is appropriate to ask, If the definitions in (34a–d) are so imprecise, why do we and lexicographers see them as intuitively quite adequate? The answer, briefly, is as follows. The prototypical component of the meaning (basic concept) in a native speaker's long-term memory is inseparably connected with the functional component which, being an identifying marker, it manifests. Therefore, when the prototype or its verbal description is perceived, the connected function is spontaneously and subconsciously foregrounded in the speaker's memory, actualizing the full meaning (the concept). Because of this the speaker gets the impression that the prototype represents the whole meaning. Only a pointed referential analysis allows us to discover the insufficiency of prototypical definitions of basic concepts (for more detail see Koshelev 2019: 47–50).

In definitions (33) and (35), the classical categories STUL 'CHAIR' and KRESLO 'ARMCHAIR' are defined by functions, and the prototypical categories by prototypes.

The situation with the English *armchair* and *chair*, which are similar to the Russian *kreslo* and *stul*, is somewhat different. The main meaning of the compound word *armchair* includes the main meaning of the word *chair*; therefore, these words do not define separate categories of their referents. "Armchairs" is a subclass of the category "Chairs"; members of this subclass have armrests. In this case, the definition of the word *armchair*, (34d), can be made more precise. In order to do so the function of an armchair—which is the sum of the functions of the armrests and chair—must be added to the image of an armchair (image of a chair + image of armrests).

As an illustration, consider the object (d) in figure 5. On first sight, to call it an *armchair* would be incorrect as it does not have armrests. The expression *comfortable chair* would be more appropriate. However, if we take a closer look at the edges of this object, they may well be seen as armrests of a sort; then, the name *armchair* becomes correct. Note that, in Russian, it is incorrect to call this object *komfortabel'nyj stul* 'comfortable chair', while the word *kreslo* 'armchair' would be quite acceptable regardless of whether we see any armrests or not. This acceptability is determined by the sitting person's posture, which is quite steady and may be relaxed—see 'Function' in (35). At the same time, in contrast with the English *armchair*, the Russian *kreslo* does not necessarily have to have the function 'support for the elbows'.

In chapter 2, subsection 2.8.1, the following thesis is formulated: definitions of main lexical meanings—their interpretations by means of a set of more simple lexical meanings—are imprecise. The precise definition of the word *armchair* given above—which is a modification of the definition in (34d)—is an exception to the rule, because it is tautological to an extent: the word *armchair* is interpreted with the help of the word *chair* contained in it.

Similarly, the functional features help to strictly define and differentiate the kindred categories of actions defined by the concepts MAN-RUNNING and MAN-WALKING. It should be noted that the kinematic images (versions) of running humans may differ very strongly and it is no easy task to define and differentiate them in a strict manner. For example, as will be demonstrated below, the well-known analytical definition of the basic meanings of the verbs *walk* and *run* notably fails to do it:

(36) Čelovek X idët iz Y-a v Z [lit., 'A man, X, is walking from Y to Z'] ≈ 'A person, X, moves over a surface from Y to Z, shifting one's feet up and down and never completely losing contact with the surface crossed' (compare, by contrast, with bežat' ['run']—'periodically losing contact with the surface') (Apresian 1974/1995: 108).

A native speaker, however, can always identify them easily and unambiguously. On the one hand, it does not matter to him "whether it is Carl Lewis circling a track or Grandma running to the telephone" (Golinkoff et al. 2002: 604). Both kinematic images are identified as running, regardless of how different they are. Yet a native speaker doesn't have a problem

1.5. The nature and structure of human categories

distinguishing between a "Grandma's" run and a fast walk, although in either case her feet don't lose contact with the floor, and her run doesn't have any "flying" phases, which are typical features for distinguishing a walk from a run. In addition, there is not much difference in speed between her fast walk and her slow run.

Just as in the case of the categories "Stul'ja" 'Chairs' and "Kresla" 'Armchairs', the strict distinction between a run and a walk lies in the domain of functional, rather than prototypical (visually perceptible), properties. Specifically, during a run a person periodically **loses the support** of the ground (while the touch contact with the ground may continue as in the case of "Grandma's run"). During a walk, however, the **support is kept** throughout. Because of this, a person's movement is much more stable when walking than when running (which is also a functional property). Let us formulate the final definitions (for detail see Koshelev 2019: chap. 3, § 4):

(37) Basic concept MAN-RUNNING =

Prototype		Function
"A person is moving fast over the ground shifting his feet up and down"	←	'A person, pursuing his spatial goal to **quickly** get to a certain location, alternately rests his feet on the ground and pushes off **forcefully** from the ground, **momentarily losing the support of the ground after each push**'

The man is running (basic meaning) = Basic concept MAN-RUNNING (37).

(38) Basic concept MAN-WALKING =

Prototype		Function
"A person is moving, not fast, over the ground shifting his feet up and down"	←	'A person, pursuing his spatial goal to get, **not quickly,** to a certain location, alternately rests his feet on the ground and pushes off **forcefully** from the ground, **not at any moment losing the support of the ground**'

The man is walking (basic meaning) = Basic concept MAN-WALKING (38).

The functions in definitions (37) and (38) set the classical categories of walking and running. When the sentences *The man is running* and *The man is walking* refer directly to perceived movements, the native speaker actually asserts that they are realizations of the corresponding functional features. The predicativity of these sentences consists in their subjectivity: functional features are the product of computations made by the native speaker based on the perceived images of movements and some other, indirect data. Along with the classical categories there are also prototypical categories of these movements set by their prototypes. Because of their indistinct boundaries, these categories partially overlap. For example, an old lady might say to her friend who is walking faster, "Why are you running so?" (metaphorical reference).

As mentioned at the beginning of section 1.5, Wittgenstein introduced the notion of "family resemblances" to define the category "Games" as he considered it to be non-classical, not having a unified description or clear boundaries. Analyzing the diversity of human games and their features, he wrote: "Don't say: "There must be something common, or they would not be called 'games'"—but look and see whether there is anything common to all" (Wittgenstein 1953).

Koshelev (2015: 146–168) gives a functional definition of the category "Games" which sets it as a classical category with clear boundaries. In particular, using this definition I explain why football and tennis belong to this category while boxing and fencing do not. Comparing Russian and English, I observe that both football and tennis may be referred to by the noun *game* (Rus. *igra*) and the verb *play* (Rus. *igrat'*), but boxing and fencing may not: the sentences *Football / Tennis is a game*; *Futbol / Tennis—èto igra*; *They are playing football / tennis*; *Oni igrajut v futbol / tennis* are correct, and the sentences **Boxing / Fencing is a game*; **Boks / Fextovanie—èto igra*; **They are playing fencing / boxing*; **Oni igrajut v boks / fextovanie* are incorrect, though we can say *Boxing / Fencing is a sport*; *Boks / Fextovanie—èto sport*.

Let us explain briefly the function of a game using a contrastive analysis of tennis and boxing. Let us take tennis first. Before the match begins the competitors usually warm up, test the court coating, practice strokes, etc. but these actions are not a game even though they are indistinguishable from it in appearance. There are even rules that must be observed: each competitor aims to parry the opponent's shot and send the ball back. The tennis players' actions become a game only when they express a **conventionally motivated** confrontation. In tennis, in contrast to real confrontation, the parties have nothing to "fight for" as there isn't any limited resource to be

1.5. The nature and structure of human categories   55

taken possession of. Therefore, this resource **is defined arbitrarily, in the conventional domain of the game**. In this domain the players, following the rules of the game, take "scoring a point" to be the main value (which is not a value at all in their everyday life). As every new point is played it is "won" by one or the other player, and the winner is the player who scores a certain number of points. Guided by this **proclaimed** value the tennis players fully immerse themselves in this arising conventional domain; they live in it, **fully distracted from real life**. This is the reason why warming up before the match is not the game itself; it has a sense in real life—to prepare for the match, get used to the court, etc.

Unlike tennis, boxing is very close to single combat, that is, a fight. The value of the opponents' actions, their effectiveness, is obvious and does not require any convention. That is why in boxing there is no conventional domain strictly separate from real life; therefore, there is no game. That is why the sentence *They are playing box* is incorrect.

The same is true about fencing, wrestling, track and field (running, jumping, hammer or javelin throwing), power lifting, etc. Fighting in sports is very much like real fighting in everyday life. In track and field, for example, running towards the finish line is an obvious variation of a real running race. Therefore, the conventional domains of tournaments in wrestling, racing, power lifting, etc. are situationally inseparable from rivalry in real life. In football, by contrast, an aspiration to score a goal has a strictly conventional value. From the point of view of everyday life, the actions of footballers appear to make no sense. Because of this, the conventional domain of the game here may be easily separated from everyday rivalry situations.

1.5.2. "Age" structure of human categories. Let us consider the objective definition (according to the formula in (26)) of the basic concept TREE given in (17):

(39) Basic concept TREE =

Prototypical tree		Function of tree
[image of tree and person]	←	'Natural object, grows by itself and bears seeds (fruits), receiving nourishment from the ground'

This concept characterizes a tree in its maturity, which is reflected in the prototype and the function of the tree, the latter being at its fullest. However, along with our knowledge of a tree in its prime, when the tree reaches the "zenith" of its life cycle, there is also, in our memory, knowledge about a tree's full life cycle, that is, about the entire sequence of age periods a tree goes through from start to finish (from sprout to moldering remains) (for more detail see Koshelev 2015: 188–192). The life cycle of a tree is shown in figure 6.

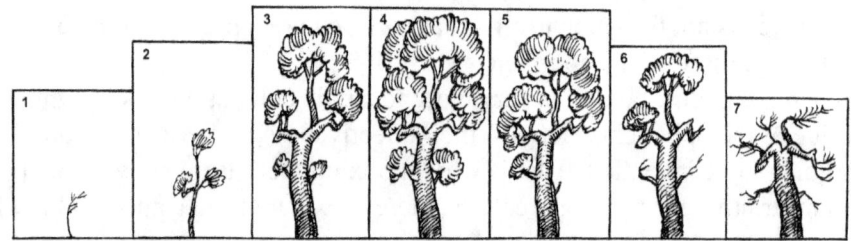

Fig. 6. The life cycle of a tree—a sequence of age concepts (the "Prototype ← Function" pairs that remain constant during the corresponding time intervals); these age concepts grasp the typical appearance and real function of a tree at a particular age

Each frame shows the prototype for a tree at a particular age: first a sprout, then a seedling (little young tree), then a more mature tree, then a tree in its prime, then an old tree and, finally, a withering or moldering tree. Each prototype expresses the characteristic appearance of a tree at a particular stage in its life, and its function expresses the degree of the full function of the tree in its prime—'grow, bloom, and bear seeds (fruits) taking nourishment from the ground' (in figure 6, the functions are not shown). The central stage, (4), reflected by the concept (39), is characterized by the visual and functional features at their fullest. The first and the last frames are considerably smaller than the others because a sprout or a dying tree do not have many of the tree's functions; they are close to the borderline of the classical category "Trees." Yet, at each of these stages the tree may be referred to by the word *tree* in its basic meaning.

The basic concept (39) is defined on a short time interval of a few seconds (micro-*t*) sufficient for recognizing a tree and its prime time. But an age period of a tree may last many years. Let us agree to call the concept of the type shown in (39) a **concept of age**, or **'age' concept** of a tree; it sets the prototypical appearance and function of a tree in a given age period (young, mature, old, etc.) and is defined on a long period of time (between one and a few score years) that corresponds to the given period in the life of the tree.

1.5. The nature and structure of human categories

The question arises, How is the life cycle of a tree represented in human memory? It is natural to assume that, at the beginning, the child does not yet have an idea of this cycle. Obviously, at first the child's memory stores a mixture of age concepts of united by the general prototype of a tree ("has roots and a solid trunk") and the general function ('grows by itself'), as shown in (40a). The child does not yet comprehend them as characteristics of the various periods in the life of a tree.

(40)

a.

b.

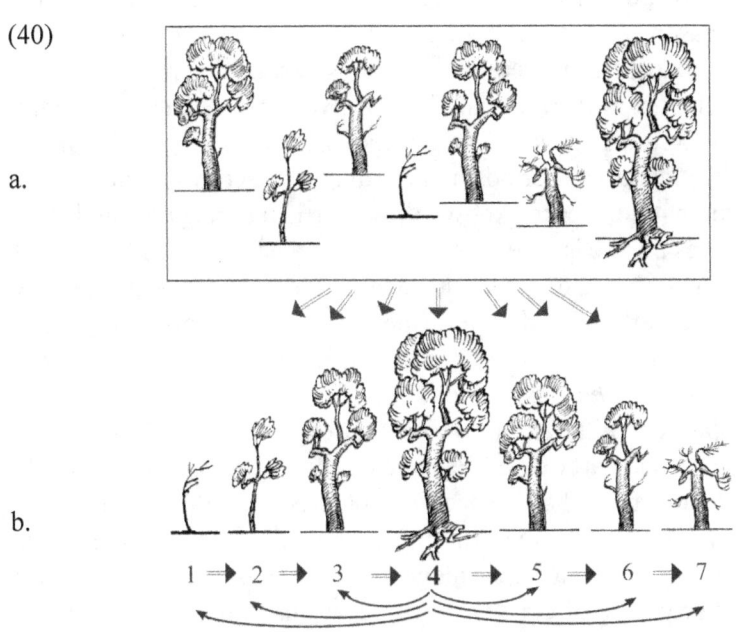

Fig. 7. The child's initial idea, (40a), of the life of a tree—a mixture of concepts reflecting the various periods in the life of a tree. This mixture forms the life cycle TREE, (40b), as a hierarchical system of its age concepts, with the main concept (4) having the full function of a tree and supplementary concepts which have either not reached the full extent of the function, (1)–(3), or partially lost it, (5)–(7). The role relationships (single arrows) connect the main concept (4) with the supplementary concepts. The relationship "Earlier ⇒ Later" sets the sequence of age concepts

It may be hypothesized that as the child's cognitive development continues this mixture is differentiated, according to the development schema in (5), into a sequence of age concepts set by the relationship "Earlier ⇒ Later" shown in (40b). Additionally, the concept (4) in this sequence, having the full function of a tree, becomes the main concept and the other concepts supplementary.

Simultaneously, role relationships (single arrows) are formed that show (a) the share of the function of a supplementary concept in the function of the main concept and (b) its remoteness in time from the main concept (before or after it). Next, at the integration stage, a hierarchical **system of age concepts** of a tree arises, (40b), which we call the **life cycle** TREE. In this cycle the main concept acts as a point of reference for the supplementary concepts.

Moreover, each age concept itself is a similar system of season concepts with the main season concept, reflecting the fruit bearing period and supplementary season concepts. The seasonal system has annual periodicity.

Life cycles characterize every category of live objects. They divide the category into age groups and serve native speakers perceiving a live object a basis for identifying its age period and including it in a corresponding class. It is because the native speaker knows these particular concepts and their specific prototypes that he is able, upon seeing for the first time a live object from a known category—a dog, tree, banana, flower—to almost unerringly use adjectives and participles that describe the age period of the observed object: *an old / young dog, a young / mature tree, a ripe / green (not ripe) banana, a blooming / withering flower.*

The situation is a bit different for the categories of artifacts. Their life cycle has only the second part of the life cycle of a living being. Being freshly made and new, an artifact has a specific prototype and all the properties in their entirety. Then, with time, the prototype changes and the entirety of properties is lost. Therefore, a category of artifacts breaks down into a similar "age" sequence of classes. Because of this, a native speaker can easily apply age characteristics to members of the already known categories (chair, car, suit, house): *a new / ancient chair, a used / old car, a new / worn out suit, a time-worn / decrepit house.*[6]

It may be hypothesized that life cycle is a universal characteristic of a category that does not depend on the speaker's language or ethnic identity.

1.5.3. Basic meanings of the words *tree* and *banana*. As we have repeatedly stressed, basic concepts constitute the basic meanings of words named by these concepts. It is natural to ask, What is the name of a life cycle? It may easily be demonstrated that it has the same name as its main concept. For

---

[6] For a detailed analysis of the meanings of, and conditions for, the use for the adjectives *old, young, new* see Koshelev (2015: 187–197), where the concrete life cycles of certain live and artifact objects are also analyzed.

1.5. The nature and structure of human categories

example, the name of the life cycle TREE will be the word *tree*, which names the basic concept (39). Indeed, the word *tree* in its basic meaning is used equally well to refer to a very young tree and to an old, dying tree. Of course, this word is most often used to name a mature tree in its heyday—the main concept of the life cycle. But in any case, a specific characteristic is often added to the name of the concept to make it more definite: *a young / old tree*.

The resulting basic meaning is as follows:

(41)   *Tree* (basic meaning) = life cycle TREE (40b).

What has been said is also true about the word *banana*. The life cycle BANANA is shown in figure 8.

(42)

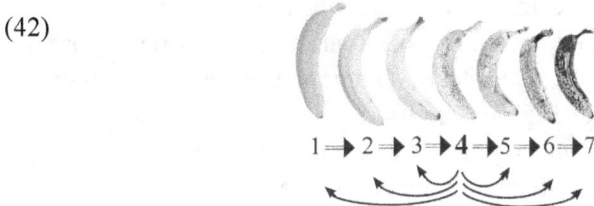

Fig. 8. The life cycle BANANA (42)—a hierarchical system of age concepts, with the main concept (4) of dark-yellow color with brown specks which has the full function of a ripe banana, and supplementary concepts which either have not reached full ripeness—(1) green, (2) light-green, (3) yellow—or are overripe in various degrees: (5) dark-yellow with brown specks, (6) yellow-brown, and (7) black-brown. The role relationships (single arrows) connect the main concept (4) with the supplementary concepts. The relationship "Earlier ⇒ Later" sets the sequence of age concepts

The developed concept BANANA in (30) has the features SWEET and YELLOW characteristic of the banana (4) in figure 8. But a banana may be green and sour if it is unripe, or black-brown and bitter if decayed. Thereby its function changes partially: such a banana does not have the full value of a 'portion of food'. However, both the green and the decayed banana may be correctly referred to by the word *banana* in its basic meaning; cf.: *unripe banana, green banana, bad banana*. This is possible because the direct referents of the word *banana* are bananas of any degree of ripeness—except, perhaps, some extreme conditions (not shown in figure 8) such as the initial stage of a banana ovary and the final stage of a fully decayed banana that has lost its shape.

The resulting basic meaning is as follows:

(43) *Banana* (basic meaning) = life cycle BANANA (42).

The direct referents of the expression *a ripe banana* are members of the classical category "Bananas" defined by the developed concept BANANA (30), or, which is the same thing, by the main concept (4), while the referents of the expression *an overripe banana* are members of the category defined by the supplementary concept (6) as shown in (42).

Let us now return to the issue of variability of the properties of the classical category "Bananas." This variability involves, first of all, the prototypical properties. As has been shown above, they may change up to a certain degree within the boundaries of the category. For example, there is a variety of small bananas, half the size of a human palm, and a variety of red bananas; or take the square watermelon that has not lost its name *watermelon*. Different varieties of apples show very high variability in size, taste, and color within the classical category. Let us emphasize again that we are discussing ripe bananas. The typical sour taste and green color of an unripe banana do not cast doubt on its inclusion in the classical category "Bananas."

Let us summarize. The classical category "Bananas" is defined by a mixture of perceptual and functional properties set by the developed concept (30). However, at the center of this complex are functional features: belonging to the fruits that grow on a banana tree, a specific gustatory and olfactory sensation and a characteristic motor feeling caused by the interaction with a banana. Indeed, should we stumble upon a typical ripe banana that tasted like an apple, we could call it a *banana* only metaphorically. Or, should we learn that the banana, with its typical smell and taste, is the product of organic synthesis, that is, something artificial, it would not belong to the classical category "Bananas." Finally, if there appeared bananas much larger in size than a human palm they might make up a separate category because the manner in which people interact with them might change considerably (they could not be conveniently held in a hand, etc.)—compare with the razor example.

1.5.4. Distinction between semantic and pragmatic components in lexical meaning. There is considerable controversy around the problem of strict distinction between the semantic (linguistic) and pragmatic (encyclopedic) components found in dictionary definitions. Thus, Langacker (1987), distinguishing the concrete specifications of a banana (color, taste, smell) and its abstract specifications (the knowledge that bananas are eaten as food and

1.5. The nature and structure of human categories

grow in bunches on trees in the tropics), raises the question: which of these specifications are linguistic (or semantic) and which extralinguistic (pragmatic)? He gives the following answer:

> The distinction between semantics and pragmatics (or between linguistic and extralinguistic knowledge) is largely artifactual, and the only viable conception of linguistic semantics is one that avoids such false dichotomies and is consequently **encyclopedic** in nature (Langacker 1987: 154; original emphasis).

The meanings of the words *tree* and *banana* formulated above—the life cycles TREE (40b) and BANANA (42)—allow for an alternative answer. Consider this issue in relation to any basic concept. Let us distinguish between the two types of its features, endogenous, or semantic, which characterize the concept itself regardless of its context, and exogenous, pragmatic features determined by the context. In subsection 1.3.8 it was demonstrated that a basic concept is a separate notion (mental representation) independent of its environment. Therefore, the semantic features of a basic concept are its constituents, prototype and function, as well as their properties and parts, that is, all the features which arose from the constituents in the course of cognitive development and which appear on the two subsequent hierarchical levels. In addition, the life cycle of a concept, not connected with the context in any way, is semantic (endogenous). For example, the following are semantic characteristics of a chair: its shape, function, color, weight, material, roughness/smoothness, etc.; its parts—the legs, seat, and back, and its "age"—new, used, or old. All other characteristics of a chair should be considered pragmatic, contextual. Examples of pragmatic characteristics could be the specific manufacturer, price, purpose (garden or kitchen chair), whether it is part of a furniture set or not, who it belongs to, whether it is strong and comfortable or, to the contrary, flimsy and uncomfortable, whether it is beautiful or ugly, etc.

With this in view, the perceptual specifications of a banana from Langacker's list—the color, taste, and smell, and the functional specifications—to grow, be used as food, and have a peculiar taste (the kind of taste is defined already by a perceptual specification), are semantic. Other specifications, namely, where and how bananas grow ("they grow in bunches on trees," "they come from tropical areas"), are pragmatic features. The classical category "Bananas" would not change if some variety of bananas grew in the north rather than tropical areas and as separate fruits rather than in bunches.

A similar analysis may be applied to the specifications in the definition of the word *banana* offered by Iurii Apresian (see section 1.1). In the expression *a southern fruit* it is not only the word *southern* that names a pragmatic feature but the word *fruit* as well. The subclass of fruit belongs to an ethno-specific rather than universal (common to all humankind) model. Not all ethnic groups single out this subclass in the class of fruit. The expressions *of an elongated and slightly curved form, with a thick smooth yellow skin, very tender and slightly mealy sweet flesh, without seeds inside, grows on a herbacious plant* and *is eaten raw* all name the semantic features.

In conclusion, it must be noted that neither Langacker nor Apresian describe the hierarchical structure of the features of a banana and its parts represented in the developed concept BANANA (30) and its life cycle (42).

1.5.5. Model of a fruit tree. The meanings of the words *tree* in (41) and *banana* in (43) express the **model of a fruit tree**—part of the universal perceptual model of the world. Briefly, this model could be described as follows. A fruit tree is a living object with a hierarchical partitive structure: a solid trunk that grows from the roots in the ground and is above it (the main part), the roots that grow in the ground, and the branches that grow from the trunk above the ground (supplementary parts). The tree keeps growing by itself (using its inner resources), using the roots to absorb nourishment from the ground, pass it on to the trunk and from there to the branches. It goes through a full life cycle, from birth and maturation to ageing and dying. In its mature stage (the medial period in the life cycle) it periodically (seasonally) bears fruits that grow and ripen on its branches that supply nourishment. Fruits also have a hierarchical partitive structure: a specific body of flesh (the main part), the skin which covers it, and the fruit stem which connects the fruit with the branch on which the fruit grows (supplementary parts). The skin protects the flesh of the fruit from external influences and the fruit stem transfers nourishment from the branch. Many varieties of fruit have a stone or seeds inside their flesh. Fruits also go through their life cycles, from an ovary to ripeness and over-ripeness. When ripe, fruits take a specific (easily recognizable) form: their flesh becomes edible and has a specific color, taste, and smell. When over-ripe, fruits lose, partially or fully, their taste qualities and edibility. Their appearance and smell also change. Ripe or over-ripe fruits usually fall from the branches to the ground. Under suitable conditions a new tree of the same species begins to grow from the seed or stone (should the fruit contain it). It goes, in turn, through its own full life cycle. The concept LIVING, which defines the category of living objects, was defined by Koshelev

1.5. The nature and structure of human categories

(2015: 211–220), who also offered a definition of the concept GROWING which characterizes the growth of live objects.

The line of reasoning given above allows us to suppose that the described model of a fruit tree is universal, composed of semantic features, and non-pragmatic in any of its parts. It is inherent in the mental representations of all humans familiar with fruit trees and their fruits regardless of their education, ethnicity, or language.

A series of facts and their discussions given in chapters 2 and 3 allows us to hypothesize that, as children develop, their model of a fruit tree also develops by stages, each stage consisting of two steps: the first step—the initial formation of general notions (a tree, fruit, life cycle, etc.)—is determined mostly genetically, while the second step—the formation of concrete versions of these general notions (banana tree and bananas, apple tree and apples, life cycles APPLE TREE and APPLE)—depends on the child's everyday experience accumulated as a result of encounters with fruit trees and their fruits (see subsection 2.8.2). Therefore, the life cycle BANANA-TREE as a concrete version of the life cycle TREE (40b) and the life cycle BANANA (42) as a concrete version of the life cycle FRUIT become part of the child's memory.

Chapter 2

The genesis of human concepts and propositions.
The initial stage of language.
Aristotle and Chomsky on thought and language

This chapter discusses how children form concepts, hierarchical relationships, and propositions (conceptual "utterances"). Drawing on experimental data, I demonstrate that the primary units of the child's representation of the world are pre-conceptual cognitive units—mental representations of whole situations. In the course of two consecutive cycles in the child's cognitive development, these units transform into (a) primary notions—object and motor concepts, and (b) binary role relationships. Together, these constitute the elementary language of thought that, in the process of thinking, is used to build conceptual structures—propositions.

It is further demonstrated that immediately after the formation of thought the child begins to develop his native language, in which object and motor concepts become initial meanings of nouns and verbs while propositions become the meanings of the child's utterances. The chapter concludes with a discussion of the major components of this language, a contrastive analysis of the proposed approach, and Aristotle's and Chomsky's views on thought and language.

2.1. Introduction

2.1.1. The history of the problem. In an analysis of the basis of human thinking, three issues come to the fore: the formation of (a) concepts, (b) the relationships between them, and (c) propositions. Let us consider the first issue. If we leave aside the ideas of the great thinkers of the 18th century (Descartes, Pascal, Leibniz), which go back to Aristotle, that it is possible to express all human concepts with the help of a small set of elementary concepts that are clear in themselves (see Wierzbicka 1996: 9–16) and turn to modern semantics, we may read the following:

2.1. Introduction

I first read about the formal description of meaning more than half a century ago, in 1961. The description proposed was as formal as that of the structure of wordforms or sentences. The writers were Alexander Zholkovskii, Nina Leont'eva, and Iurii Martem'janov: Zholkovskii et al. 1961 (Mel'čuk 2016: 142) [...] Together with A. Zholkovskii, Iu. Apresian, A. Bogusławski and A. Wierzbicka, I believe that the meaning of a word can and must be described in terms of simpler meanings—that is, decomposed. The decomposition of a meaning into simpler meanings is similar to the decomposition of living matter into cells, of any matter (including cells) into molecules, of molecules into atoms, of atoms into composite particles, and of composite particles into elementary particles (Ibid.: 88).

Pinker (2007: chap. 3) offers a detailed analysis of the issue from a somewhat different perspective: how do 50,000 concepts—the meanings of the words a person uses—appear in his memory? Fodor (1981: 284) believes that (1) practically all concrete meanings of words are atom-like and cannot be decomposed into more elementary concepts, and (2) all of them, including object concepts like "trombone," "carburetor," and "doorknob," are innate concepts in the sense that the potential for acquiring such a number of concepts is genetically determined and only their concrete composition depends on human experience (for a similar view, see Chomsky 1988: 32; 1991: 29; 2000: 65–66).[1]

It should be noted that the idea of innateness, or early emergence of initial concepts in infants, was widely discussed in the early 1970s—see an analytic review in Wierzbicka (1996: 16–24). Taking Chomsky's view mentioned above, Wierzbicka contrasts it with her own approach based on the ideas of 18th century thinkers: the possibility to reduce all linguistic meanings to a small set of innate (and therefore universal) semantic primes which are clear to all native speakers of a particular language and do not require explanation. She believes that it is not culture-specific concepts such as 'bureaucrat', 'table', 'boomerang', etc. that are innate, but only those which are found in all languages, such as 'person', 'thing', 'do', etc. All other concepts are acquired by means of language as a cultural tool (Ibid.: 19).

---

[1] In a recent book, Everett (2017) observes: "There is just no source of conceptual content inborn in all humans. Concepts are never inborn, they are learned" (p. 118), and adds: "It is, of course, possible that there are concepts inborn in humans. But this is a problematic idea" (p. 129).

Pinker (2007) holds a similar view. He believes that many concepts are compositional and argues, in particular, that "verbs are composed from a smaller number of conceptual particles" (Ibid.: 102).[2] By contrast, Lakoff (1987) insists that concepts are not decomposable into more elementary ideas: "Thought has *gestalt properties* and is thus not atomistic; concepts have an overall structure that goes beyond merely putting together conceptual 'building' blocks by general rules" (p. xiv; original emphasis).

Another problem of human thought bears on the formation of conceptual relationships and "utterances," or propositions. If, again, we leave aside Aristotle's ideas and their later interpretations—such as a critical evaluation in a textbook on logic, for example (Arnauld, Nicole 1996)—and turn to modern conceptions, we consider one of the most consistent views on human thought to be that Chomsky's. He also claims that the problems of thought mentioned above are crucial in the way of explaining language evolution (in his terminology, it is the formation of "word-like atoms" and how they are glued into "hierarchical structures"):

> To account for the emergence of the language faculty [...] we have to face two basic tasks. One task is to account for the "atoms of computation," the lexical items—commonly in the range of 30,000–50,000. The second is to discover the computational properties of the language faculty (Berwick, Chomsky 2016: 66).

According to Chomsky, hierarchical structures that characterize human language (internal or I-language) are generated by the two-argument iterative operation Merge, whose input are word-like atoms or previously constructed expressions (Ibid.: 70). At the same time, Chomsky thinks that it is absolutely not clear how word-like atoms are formed, cf.:

> By all accounts the origin of mind-dependent word-like elements remains a big mystery—for everyone, us included. In a recent book on language evolution, Bickerton (2014) shrugs his shoulders as well (Berwick, Chomsky 2016: 149).

2.1.2. The proposed solution. In what follows, a more or less alternative view is offered, namely, that concepts—basic meanings of notional words—are acquired by infants not at once but by stages, as pre-conceptual mental representations develop. In fact, a more general problem will be

---

[2] A different approach to lexical decomposition is offered by Pustejovsky (1991: 2013). Yet another view may be found in Evans (2014: chap. 6).

considered: the following steps in the genesis of human thought: (a) the formation of concepts, (b) the formation of relationships between concepts, and (c) the formation of propositions (predicative expressions) from concepts and relationships.

While analyzing these stages, I will describe the way in which children develop some concepts, hierarchical relationships, and propositions. In particular, it will be demonstrated that initially (at 9–11 months) it is the child's whole mental representations of agentive situations that serve as primary cognitive units for the representation of the sensory world. Because separate participants in such situations are not yet singled out, the situations themselves are pre-conceptual syncretic (merged) units. However, it is from these units that, beginning at 14 months, the child develops primary concepts in the course of two consecutive developmental cycles—separate situation participants which play different roles: **Action**, Agent, Patient, Goal (movement destination), etc. **Action** becomes the main participant and the other participants become supplementary to it. Simultaneously, hierarchical role relationships are formed: "**Action** –N– Supplementary participant N" which implicitly connects the action with its participants in a holistic situation. As a result, in total agreement with the development schema (5c) in subsection 1.2.5, whole situations are divided into separate participants and hierarchical role relationships. Then, at the stage of partial integration (5d), separate participants are combined into dual hierarchical structures as follows:

(**Action**) –1– (Agent);
(**Action**) –2– (Patient);
(**Action**) –3– (Goal), etc.

At the stage of complete integration (5e), these structures are combined, depending on the action (main participant), into propositions of the following type:

(Agent) –1– (**Action**) –2– (Patient).

Thus, there are two stages in the formation of propositions from concepts: dual hierarchical structures (dual concepts) emerge which are then combined in a proposition with the schema of a role system (7c) given in subsection 1.2.5. This is the schematic genesis of thought in children. In what follows, actions will be referred to as motor concepts, and other situation participants as concrete concepts.

2.2. Mental representations of agentive situations

The subject of our further analysis will be the child's representations of simple agentive situations and their development in ontogeny. As important components of the child's representation of the world,[3] these representations develop along with the child's cognitive development and transform into three-level tree-like structures with the whole situation as an apex, the system of object and motor protoconcepts as its second level, and the system of concepts as its third level. Thus, a mental representation of a whole situation is formed as a proposition composed of concepts, initial human notions.

2.2.1. The notion of situation. At 9–11 months, infants perceive and interpret the world by means of a set of whole situations with which they are quite familiar (and which, to them, have become typical situations). These are the primary units for comprehending the perceived world. Infants do not yet distinguish separate objects and actions as separate participants in a situation.[4] The visual images[5] of objects and actions are interpreted by infants only within a whole image of a situation, cf.:

> Rita F., 11 months, had a distinct conditioned reflex for the sight of a dish of porridge. The appearance of this stimulant in a normal situation, when the dish with porridge was set on the table at which the infant was sitting, caused movement towards the dish and the opening of the mouth. However, the use of this stimulant in a different setting, such as a playpen or a window seat, caused only a brief orientational reaction, while the food reaction was lacking

---

[3] This is indirectly attested by the child's first (two-word) expressions: "at about 18 months, children's verbal two-component expressions are formed based on fixing the action and the object of this action [...] *Xoču kisu* ('Want kitty'), *Kušat' supik* ('Eat soup-DIM') (Lepskaia 2013: 62). And later, by the age of 24 months, the structure "noun + verb" remains dominant (Clark 2009: 158–159).

[4] Compare with Vendler's (1967b) view of events as ontologically primary components of reality.

[5] I use the terms 'visual image / prototype' and 'spatial image' with reference to visual and spatial mental imagery. As has been shown by A. Baddeley (1996), S. M. Kosslyn (1973; 1994; 2005), J. Richardson (1980), R. N. Shepard, J. Metzler (1971), and other researchers, these are quite independent visual representations used in solving various tasks. Following other researchers, I interpret visual images as percepts, the products of direct visual perception.

2.2. Mental representations of agentive situations

altogether. The same infant displayed a clearly defensive reaction to the hat put on her head before going out for a walk, and always screamed and tried to throw it off. Such a reaction was always observed while the infant was being dressed. Yet if the infant saw the hat in a different setting, it caused only an orientational reaction (Kol'tsova 1980: 36; translation A. Kravchenko).

A similar case is described by Bloom (1973): a girl uses the word *car* only when she is looking from the window at cars down on the street; when on the street and seeing cars before her, she does not call them 'cars'.

Such children's holistic situations (or, in Lepskaia's (2013: 41) terms, "non-discriminated integral unities") will be represented as syncretic pairs "Prototype (mental image) ← Function" identified in 3-dimensional space on a short (from 10 to 15 seconds) time interval, micro-t. Here, the function (in a broad sense) is the child's psychophysical state as a totality of feelings, sensations, etc. caused by the current situation and the child's actions in this situation. The prototype is a typical mental image of a situation—a totality of external stimuli (first of all, visual) that cause this psychophysical state. The arrow ← shows that the function is spatially aligned with the prototype.[6] Consider an example:

(1) Situation CHILD EATING PORRIDGE (takes place on the time interval micro-t) =

Prototype	←	Function
"The child is sitting on a chair at the table with a plate of porridge before him; scooping a portion of porridge with a spoon, he transfers it into his mouth (this part is not shown in the picture)"		'The child experiences a fused complex of feelings and sensations: (a) of the moving hand with the spoon transferring a portion of porridge from the plate into the mouth; (b) of the taste of porridge; (c) of the action of swallowing; (d) of the welcome feeling of satiated hunger while swallowing one portion of porridge after another, etc.'

---

[6] The term 'event' is often used along with the term 'situation'. Since 'event' does not have a strict definition as a term, the term 'situation' is used (for its definition, see subsection 2.2.6).

It is only natural to ask, How do children construe situations of the type shown in (1)? I consider such situations to be an outcome of the cognitive development of the child's previous state (see subsection 2.4.10).

2.2.2. Situation development. As the child develops, situations of this type stored in the child's memory also develop. Strictly schematically, the development of a situation (mental representation) consists in gradual differentiation of its integral function into particular functions: the function of a hand with a spoon—'the feeling of porridge being placed in the mouth', the function of porridge—'the feeling of tasting porridge', the function of the plate—'used to put porridge on, which will be further transferred to the mouth (the sight of porridge on a plate causes anticipation of hunger satiation)', etc. These functions are singled out because of the differentiation of the child's initially syncretic nervous system into subsystems: limbic, vestibular, somatic, cerebellum, etc., which begin to separately fix current motives and goals, body posture, movements of the hand with a spoon, etc. caused by the child's participation in the situation. Therefore, the child's initially fused sensations are also differentiated into tactile, gustatory, motor sensations and so forth.[7] As a result, a neurobiological code of situation (1) is formed in the child's memory—an assembly of separate typical sensations in different modalities which emerge in the course of the child's participation in the situation.[8] The separate particular functions prompt differentiation of their visually perceived performers: the prototypes of hand movement, porridge, plate, etc. Thus, concepts emerge as pairs, "Prototypical movement of a hand with a spoon ← The function of a hand with a spoon," "Prototypical porridge ← The function of porridge," etc.

The leading role in the development of a mental representation is played by the differentiation of its integrated function into particular functions; this leads to a differentiation of its prototype into the prototypes of separate situation participants. Then, separate situation participants are integrated into a system of participants that becomes a developed mental representation of the situation, (1).

---

[7] For example, Bower (1974: chap. 5) speaks of the primitive unity of sensory modalities in children which are differentiated as the child develops.

[8] In his pioneering research of memory mechanisms, Tsien (2008) and his colleagues (Tsien et al. 2013) connect low-level (neurobiological memory codes) and higher-level (conceptual structures) representations of the same phenomena (human actions, states, etc.); see also Koshelev (2019: 164–177).

2.2. Mental representations of agentive situations

2.2.3. The situation 'PERSON IS RUNNING'. Let us take a closer look at these processes using a simple example—a situation of locomotion (2). This situation merges the function and the visual prototype as a syncretic image composed of three participants: the running person, the ground on which the person runs, and the spatial goal of the person's movement.

(2) Situation 'PERSON IS RUNNING' (takes place on micro-t) =

Prototype ←	Function
"A person a) is moving fast, b) shifting his feet up and down, making contact with the ground (dark strip), c) toward a spatial goal (vertical half-ellipse) located ahead"	'A person a') in order to move fast, b') pushes off forcefully with his feet from the ground, c') wishing to reach his spatial goal quickly'

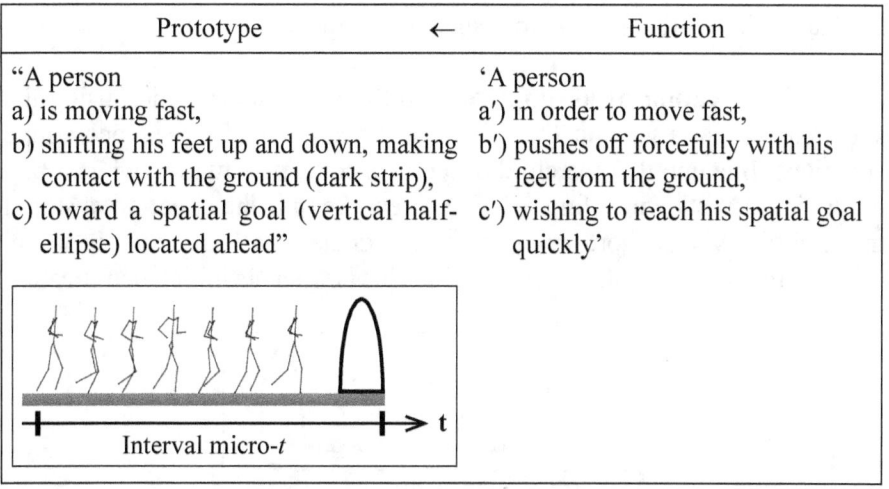

Closer to the neurobiological memory code, a more detailed description of the function may be depicted as follows:

'A person experiences sensations caused by
(a') the fast movement of his body (signals from the proprioceptive system and the vestibular apparatus),
(b') the forceful pushes of his feet from the ground (proprioceptive signals),
(c') approaching the fulfillment of his desire to quickly reach the goal (half ellipse) (signals from the limbic system reflecting the motive of the action)'.

Here, the visual properties (a)–(c) define the prototypical situation while the functional properties (a')–(c') allow for their interpretation as a description by means of an assembly of typical sensations that accompany the activity of running. This is an internal description inaccessible to observation. The use of the words of natural language in the descriptions of the functions in (1) and (2) only serves to designate the components of the memory neuro-code. Of course, in the case of young children what may be designated as 'desire' is just a syncretic affectation-motivational component that prompts the child's movement or interaction with an object.[9] It is only later, in concepts, that it becomes a separate functional component.

The situation (2) is stored in the child's long-term semantic memory (cf. Baddelley 1996: chap. 8; Tulving 1993; Givón 1998: 3). As has already been noted, at first (up to 12 months) functional properties are stored as syncretic properties and the components (a)–(c) of the prototype are, therefore, also undifferentiated; later, the function and then the prototype begin to be gradually differentiated into more specific components.

2.2.4. Identification of locomotive situations. Let us consider, using the situation in (2) as a schema, the child's identification of observed locomotive situations. Imagine that the child observes a concrete situation when a boy is running, (*) shown in figure 1. For a few seconds the situation is stored in the child's visual short-term memory, Baddeley 2001, and then in visual working memory, Chunharas et al. 2019. This is when its initial identification

(2)

(*)

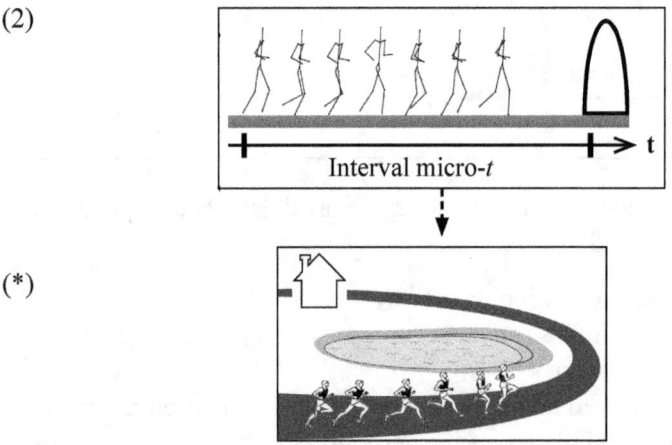

Fig. 1. Basic situation (2) used for initial identification of the concrete situation of running (*) observed by the child. Thereby the child understands that the function of situation (2)—'the runner's desire to reach his spatial goal quickly'—is realized in the observed situation

---

[9] As was emphasized by Vygotsky (1986: 262), "[e]verything has some affect so arousing that for the child, it acquires a character of a 'compulsory' affect [...]. As Lewin graphically expresses it, a ladder lures the child to climb, a door, to be opened or closed, a bell, to be rung [...]. In a word, for the child in this situation, each thing [...] has an affective valence which provokes him correspondingly to action, that is, leads him."

2.2. Mental representations of agentive situations 73

takes place: it is correlated with the prototypes of various basic locomotive situations stored in the child's long-term memory. Suppose the prototypical situation (2) turns out to be the closest to the image of the observed situation. Then this image is identified as a concrete manifestation of a prototypical situation "A person is moving fast toward the house, shifting his feet up and down, making contact with the ground." In this case, the image is assigned the function of the situation (2): "A person pushes off forcefully with his feet from the ground, wishing to reach the spatial goal quickly."

At the same time, separate parts of the image—the boy, the road, and the house—are not singled out; outside the image, they are not interpreted as separate parts.

2.2.5. Specific situations. The situation in (2) will be called a **basic situation**, and the names of basic situations will be given in capital letters. Just like a basic concept, a basic situation defines a dual category of various situations of a human run. On the one hand, the function of the situation (2) defines a classical category, 'PERSON IS RUNNING' (= A PERSON IS RUNNING ON THE GROUND TOWARDS A SPATIAL GOAL). On the other hand, its prototype defines the prototypical category of such situations (on dual categories, see subsection 1.5.1 in chapter 1).

In the course of multiple identifications of concrete situations of running of the type (2)–(*), the basic situation (2) begins to be differentiated into more concrete, **specific situations** "A MAN IS RUNNING ON THE ROAD," "A BOY IS RUNNING ON THE PATH," and the like, which are in a generic relationship with (2) (marked as ▷). Thus, we get a supplemented representation of the situation (2):

(3) a. Situation A PERSON IS RUNNING
$$\triangledown$$
  a'. (A MAN IS RUNNING ON THE ROAD,
A BOY IS RUNNING ON THE PATH,
A WOMAN IS RUNNING ACROSS THE FIELD…)

To emphasize: the prototypes of specific situations differ not only by the prototypical runners (men, women, etc.) but also by the prototypical kinds of running (see Footnote in subsection 2.3.8).

The structure in (3) is a complete mental representation of the basic situation of a human run. It is formed in two stages: (1) the formation of the actual basic situation—level (a), and (2) its subsequent development into specific situations—sublevel (a'). In the end, these specific situations become elementary units in the child's interpretation of the world.

As level (a') emerges, recognition of the image in (2)–(*) becomes a two-stage process. First, from the set of his basic locomotive situations, the child selects the situation (3a) A PERSON IS RUNNING, whose prototype is the closest to the image. Then, from the set of its specific situations (3a'), he selects the one closest to the image. In this case, it is A BOY IS RUNNING ON THE ROAD. As a result, only this specific situation is left on level (a') in (3'):

(3')   a.   Situation A PERSON IS RUNNING
                                            ▽
       a'.   A BOY IS RUNNING ON THE ROAD

The situation (3') becomes a mental representation of the image of a running boy. It allows the child to have a more concrete but still integrated notion (3'a') of the perceived image (compare it with (2)) that takes into account the specifics of the main participant and the surface on which he runs:

(3'a')

(*)

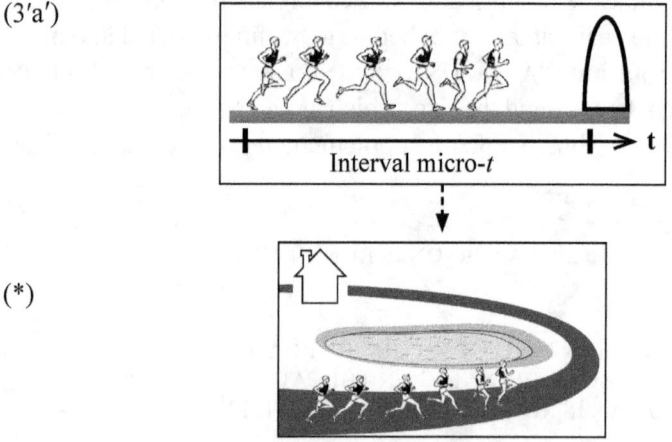

Fig. 2. A specific situation, (3'a') A BOY IS RUNNING ON THE ROAD, used in identifying the perceived situation of running

As can be seen, specific situations do not belong to concepts. They are too complex to become the meanings of notional words.

2.2.6. Defining the term 'situation'. Let us look at the term 'event' first, setting aside its common definitions, such as "a basic unit in organizing experience, memory, and meaning" (see Pruden et al. 2008: 163–164), and taking Zacks and Tversky's (2001: 3) definition used by Pruden et al. (2008: 164): "Here we consider the following archetype for an event: a segment of time at a given location that is conceived by an observer to have a beginning and an end. We will call the process by which observers identify these beginnings and endings, and their relations, event structure perception." Some researchers have pointed to the difficulty in its application. Thus, Hanson and Hirst (1989: 136) argue that these beginnings and endings are not always easy to identify: when a person reaches for a slice of toast and picks it up, the transition from the event "reaching" to the event "picking up" may be smooth, yet the lack of a strict borderline between the two does not mean that "reaching" and "picking up" are not discrete events. They also argue that these events may be incorporated in another, more general event such as "having breakfast." Similarly, the event "filling a car tank with gas" may be broken down into smaller units, such as "paying for the gas," "opening the gas tank," "picking up the gas hose," and "pulling the fuel pump lever."

Let us go back to the definition (1) of basic structure as the dual structure "Prototype ← Function," which develops on the time interval of several seconds, micro-t. First, this definition has a non-verbal status as both its components are non-verbal cognitive units. Second, it does not require an observable beginning or ending in the change of an object's locus. For example, there is neither a beginning nor ending in the basic situation (2) "a person is running." Third, the time interval in the definition, limited by several seconds, precludes complex situations such as "filling a car tank with gas."

Moreover, since the situation must be identified on this time interval its main characteristic, the Agent's action, must be integral and possess an independent function. Therefore, "reaching for a piece of toast," "opening a gas tank," "filling the tank with gas" are basic situations, while "picking up the gas hose" and "pulling the gas pump lever" are not because they are the related parts of the basic situation "filling the tank with gas." Similarly, "reaching (for a piece of toast)" and "picking up the toast" are parts of the basic situation "taking a piece of toast," which do not have independent functions (for a detailed analysis, see Koshelev (2019: 228–230)). To emphasize, the singling out of function in the definition of a basic situation is important because it is the independence of the function that defines a situation as whole.

On the other hand, the situation "purchasing gas" is not basic either, because this action is not perceptually salient and cannot be recognized as such in a few seconds. Neither is the situation "filling a car tank with gas" basic: it consists of a sequence of basic situations, "opening the gas tank," "filling the tank with gas," "paying for the gas," and "closing the tank," each with an independent prototypical action. Therefore, it cannot be non-arbitrarily identified on the time interval of a few seconds.

Fourth, and last, when speaking of an agentive action I mean only a directly identifiable or **sensory** action. To clarify the meaning of the term 'sensory action', let us consider two meanings of an action verb: uninterrupted (I call it **basic** or **sensory** meaning)—*Ivan pilit derevo / edet k perekrestku* 'Ivan is sawing a tree / going to a crossroads' (at the moment of speech, the observer sees this action—Ivan is sawing / going), and interrupted, or current meaning—*Ivan pilit staroe derevo / edet s raboty domoj* 'Ivan is sawing an old tree / going home after work' (at the moment of speech, the observer sees another action—Ivan has sat down to rest / has stopped at the newsstand to buy a paper). In the first case, the action is identified within the time interval of a few seconds, micro-t, while in the second case identification of the action requires a much longer period of time and additional knowledge (contextual and encyclopedic). Similarly, the sensory meaning of the verb *p'ët* 'drinks / is drinking' is that a person takes a series of sips and swallows, transferring the liquid from the mouth to the stomach. Thus, if the utterance *Ivan p'ët čaj* 'Ivan drinks / is drinking tea' is produced at the moment when Ivan is taking a sip or two, the verb is used in its sensory meaning. If, however, the utterance is produced at the moment when Ivan, in the process of having a cup of tea, stirs it with a spoon, or, having taking a few sips, continues talking with a friend, the verb is used in its current meaning, which is derivative from the sensory meaning. Similarly, if the utterance *Strelka dvižetsja* 'The hand is moving' refers to the moving second hand of a clock, the verb is used in its sensory meaning. If the utterance refers to the minute or hour hand, the meaning of the verb is not sensory because the movement of these hands cannot be identified on the micro-t time interval of a few seconds.

It should be noted that a basic situation may last much longer than the interval micro-t if it is not interrupted by another basic situation. For example, a basic situation "A person is walking" lasts as long as it is not interrupted for at least a few seconds. During these several seconds the observer may identify another basic situation—for example, the person may stop, jump over a puddle, or dash across the street. If, after that, he continues walking, it is already a new situation "A person is walking."

2.3. The development of basic situations into systems of protoconcepts

At around 12 months, the child enters the next stage of cognitive development. As shown in the development schema (5) in chapter 1 (subsection 1.2.5), the child's mental representations of basic situations are first differentiated into separate participants and role relationships, and then integrated into a systemic representation of a situation.

2.3.1. Experimental data. The above thesis is supported by some experimental data. It has been shown (Xu, Carey 1996; Xu 2002; 2007) that by the end of their first year infants begin to differentiate separate components which differ in shape in a locomotive situation. These are *sortal concepts:* they reflect the infant's initial classification of objects (see Note in subsection 2.3.3). Some research also shows that at the end of the first or the beginning of the second year children's mental representations of situations begin to feature preverbal components (Talmy 1985: 57, 61): 'Motion' (change of location), 'Figure' (the moving object or agent), 'Ground' (the reference-object), 'Path' (the course followed by the Figure object), and 'Manner' (the mode of motion), as well as 'Source' (the point of departure) and 'Goal' (destination). Over the past 30 years, a considerable amount of cognitive linguistic research has been done in this area, as well as on the issues of lexicalization and grammaticalization of the differentiated components and relationships between them (e.g., Choi, Bowerman 1991; Choi, Gopnik 1995; Tardif 1996; Choi et al. 1999; Casasola, Cohen 2002; Maguire et al. 2003; Mandler 2004; 2006; Pulverman et al. 2004; Lakusta et al. 2007; Golinkoff, Hirsh-Pasek 2008). The main conclusion resulting from much of this research (Pruden et al. 2008) and further elaborated in an analytical review by Göksun et al. (2017) seems to be that by the beginning of the second year children are capable of representing whole situations using a set of basal pre-linguistic components and constructions made of these components. This calls to mind Mandler's (1992; 2004) hypothesis that pre-linguistic children build simple image-schemas which consist of basal components of events—'primes' they develop at an early stage.[10]

---

[10] There is another, less categorical view (Slobin 1996; Wagner, Lakusta 2009) that deep semantic structures and semantic roles (Jackendoff 1990; Dowty 1991) affect

As we are mainly interested in how basal components of children's representations of events (basic situations) are formed, some relevant experimental research should be mentioned here. For the time being, we leave aside the issues of lexicalization and grammaticalization of these components.

Casasola et al. (2003) demonstrated that at 10 months infants notice the differences between Path and Manner in human locomotion (for example, a child crawling (Manner) before a bush (Path) *vs.* a child hopping (Manner) before a bush (Path)). These observations were made about children living in Mandarin Chinese and Hispanic-speaking environments (Pulverman et al. 2007; 2008).

In an experiment described by Lakusta et al. (2007), infants at 12 months of age watching the movements of a duckling perceived them as different if the difference was only in their sources or goals (see also Seston et al. 2009; Lakusta et al. 2017). Infants at 10 and 13 months differentiate between the invariant paths and manners, respectively. Thus, perceiving the same Path, for example "under (something)," represented by different manners (for example spinning, twisting, etc.), they notice when the Path in the test events changes but not when the Manner changes (Pruden et al. 2004).

Infants growing up in an English-speaking environment distinguish the figures (for example, a man or a woman) crossing a railroad and the Surface these figures cross (for example, a railroad and a tennis court) in dynamic events at 10 and 13 months, respectively. These infants also distinguish kinds of Surface which are differently coded in the Japanese verbs of terrestrial motion (for example, a railroad crossing a grassy field) (Göksun et al. 2008; 2009).

Along with Talmy's (1975; 1985) components, at a very early age infants begin to form spatial relationships. Already at 6 months infants in different linguistic environments understand the spatial relationships Containment-Support[11] (usually expressed by prepositions *in, inside* and *on*) and can distinguish situations with such relationships (see Baillargeon 2004; Hespos, Spelke 2004; Hespos, Baillargeon 2008; Hespos, Piccin 2009).

---

how children develop conceptual primes: "In this review, we discuss an approach to studying that begins with linguistic theory—specifically, semantic structures in language" (Wagner, Lakusta 2009: 177); see, however, Lakusta et al. (2017).

[11] The relationship Containment is found when one object is inside another object (a key in the keyhole, an apple in a vase, a book in a jacket). The relationship Support is found when an object is freely located on the surface of another object with which it is in physical contact (a cup sits on a table, a book lies on a shelf).

2.3. The development of basic situations into systems of protoconcepts

2.3.2. Decomposition of situations into Talmy's components. Using these and other data, it may be hypothesized that at the beginning of their second year children decompose basic locomotive situations into Talmy's components and role relationships.

When they appear, Talmy's components are merged pairs "object feature → processual feature" defined on the time interval micro-t, just as in the case of a basic situation. Therefore, they will be referred to by two words connected with a hyphen: a noun that names the object feature and a verb that names the processual feature. Specifically, the locomotive situation (2) 'PERSON IS RUNNING' is decomposed into the following participants: **PERSON-IS RUNNING** (main participant, highlighted in bold type), SURFACE-LIES, and GOAL-EXISTS (supplementary participants). The process feature (IS RUNNING) of the main participant defines the situation. It cannot be replaced by any other feature (STANDS, LIES) without the situation changing as well. By contrast, the processual features of supplementary participants are indeterminate and, therefore, can change while the basic situation remains the same. For the surface on which locomotion takes place, the typical feature is LIES—that is, the surface is unmoving and at ground level. But there may be a moving surface (a moving walkway, as in airports). The goal of locomotion can also be either unmoving or moving, therefore this process feature is expressed by a general verb.

Object-processual objects localized in space on the interval micro-t may be called **protoconcepts**. During the next stage of the child's cognitive development they break down into two basic-level concepts, object and motor.

Note. Cognitive psychologist Xu (2007) raises the following question: "Are basic-level categories and basic-level sortal concepts the same thing?" (p. 404). According to our analysis, **sortal concepts coincide with protoconcepts** because, firstly, they both appear at the end of the first—beginning of the second year and, secondly, they include a current motor constituent. With regard to sortal concepts, this was proved experimentally (Xu et al. 2004: 175–178). Infants at 12 months distinguished a cup and a bottle as differing in shape and in actions that could be performed with these objects but failed to distinguish a common cup and a sipping cup (see (24) in chapter 1). Apparently, the difference in the shape of these two cups was compensated for by the similarity of actions performed with them. As will be shown in section 2.4, basic-level concepts appear roughly at 14 months—later than sortal concepts.

2.3.3. Definition of protoconcepts. Let us define the protoconcepts in situation (2).

(4)   Protoconcept **PERSON-IS RUNNING** =

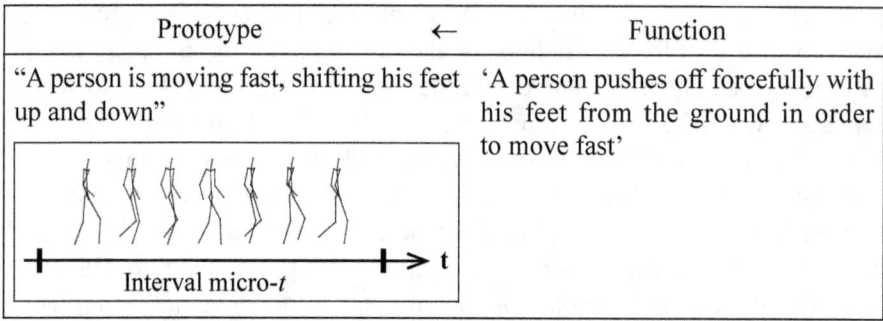

Prototype	←	Function
"A person is moving fast, shifting his feet up and down"		'A person pushes off forcefully with his feet from the ground in order to move fast'

To emphasize: the prototype only describes a running person and does not contain images (prototypes) of the surface on which movement takes place or the goal, cf. (2), figure 1. The main feature of a human run is often believed to be the periodic loss of contact with the surface (see the definition, (33), in chapter 1). However, even without this information it can be seen that a person is running by the inclined torso, arms bent at the elbows, etc. In other words, a typical run is recognized only by the kinematics of the body and body parts, without taking into account the ground surface (cf. Koshelev 2019: 164–177).

Surface is not included in the definition of the function either. One could object that movement by forceful pushes from the ground (running) cannot be separated from the surface, which is implied because the runner pushes off from it. But such an impression is the result of interpreting the expression *forceful pushes with one's feet* in its trivial linguistic meaning. However, here the expression is a term that refers to the runner's proprioception, the sensations caused by the pushes. These sensations are separate from the physical pushes, they do not include them. The hard surface in this case is the external cause of the sensations caused by the pushes.

The protoconcept SURFACE-LIES has a certain image (prototype). It is a flat straight strip that lies at ground level. Its purpose is "to be used for locomotion," therefore it must be hard for the moving object to push off from it with the feet (or wheels).

The resulting protoconcept is as follows:

2.3. The development of basic situations into systems of protoconcepts

(5)   Protoconcept SURFACE-LIES =

Prototype	←	Function
"A straight flat strip at the ground level" 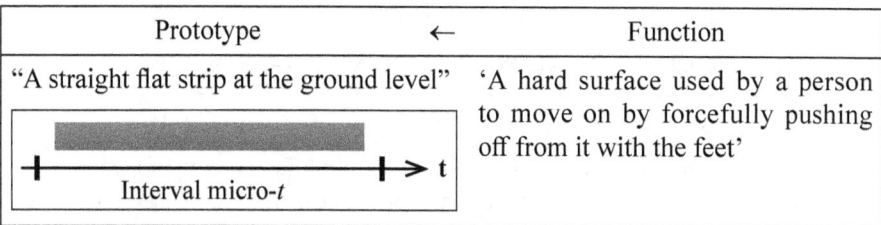 Interval micro-*t*		'A hard surface used by a person to move on by forcefully pushing off from it with the feet'

The protoconcept GOAL-EXISTS does not have a certain prototype because this function may be performed practically by any object or place (such protoconcepts (as well as concepts) are called **functional**). But its typical locus is known—it is ahead of the moving person in the direction of movement.

(6)   Protoconcept GOAL-EXISTS =

Prototype	←	Function
"An object ahead of the moving person in the direction of movement" 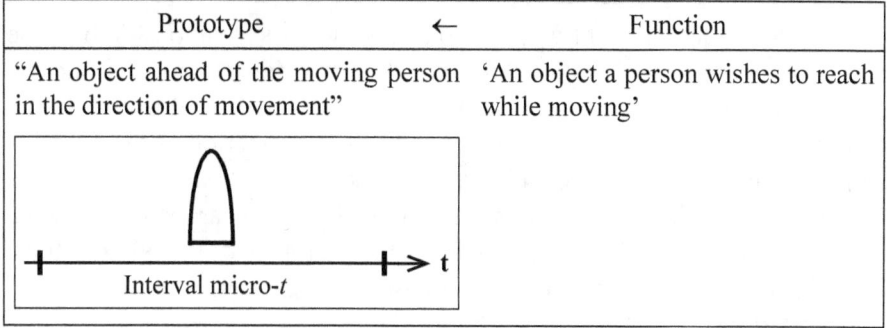 Interval micro-*t*		'An object a person wishes to reach while moving'

As can be seen, the main participant carries the major part of the general function of the situation, while the functions of other participants supplement it.

2.3.4. Definition of role relationships.

As the running situation (2) is differentiated into protoconcepts, two binary role relationships are formed which connect the main participant, protoconcept **PERSON-IS RUNNING**, with two supplementary protoconcepts (see the development cycle schema (5) in subsection 1.2.5). Each role relationship defines the locus of the supplementary participant relative to the main participant such that their functions are combined.

Let us consider the relationship –On→. It shows that SURFACE-LIES is directly under the main participant **PERSON-IS RUNNING**. The main participant is in physical contact with the surface (the prototype of the relationship) in order to be able, while moving, to use it as support and push off from it with the feet (the function of the relationship).

(7) Role relationship –On→ (**PERSON-IS RUNNING** –On→ SURFACE-LIES) =

Prototype	←	Function
"A person is moving fast, shifting his feet up and down and making contact with the surface"		'To move fast, a person forcefully pushes off from the surface with his feet'

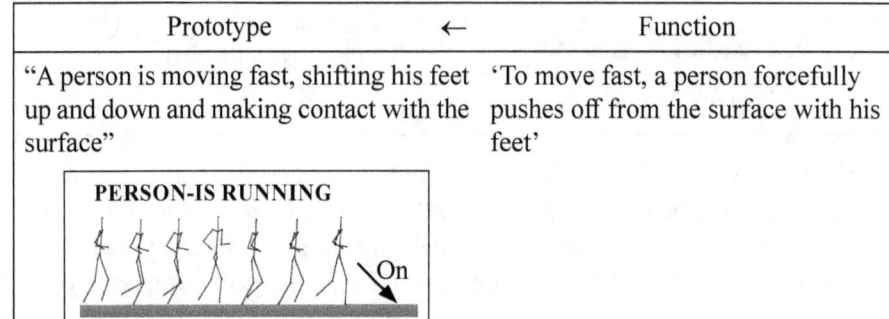

It is correct to connect two protoconcepts by a role relationship because both arguments of the relationship have the same (dual) structure and are defined on the same time interval, micro-t. The prototype of the relationship comprises the prototypes of the arguments and the function of the relationship, the particular functions of the arguments.

The relationship –To→ is defined similarly. Its second argument is ahead, in the direction of the Agent's movement (the prototype of the relationship); it is an object or point which the Agent wishes to reach quickly (the function of the relationship). Therefore:

(8) Role relationship –To→ (**PERSON-IS RUNNING** –To→ GOAL-EXISTS)[12] =

Prototype	←	Function
"A person, shifting his feet up and down, is moving fast toward a goal—an object ahead of him"		'A person forcefully pushes off with his feet from the ground in order to quickly reach the goal'

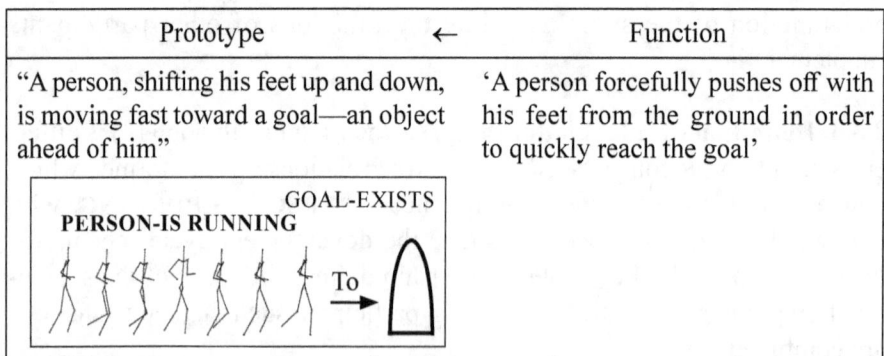

---

[12] To emphasize: the role relationships –To→ and –On→ are designated by prepositions for the sake of clarity. Actually, the prepositions *k* 'to' and *po* 'on-DIR' appear

2.3. The development of basic situations into systems of protoconcepts 83

As can be seen, role relationships are cognitive units with the same dual structure "Prototype ← Function" as their arguments.

2.3.5. Integration of protoconcepts into protosituations. Next, in accordance with the development cycle (5) in subsection 1.2.5, comes the stage of partial integration—the formation of dual systems of protoconcepts similar to the dual systems of chair parts such as SEAT –1→ BACK:

PERSON-IS RUNNING –On→ SURFACE-LIES,
PERSON-IS RUNNING –To→ GOAL-EXISTS.

At the subsequent stage of complete integration they are combined, according to the main protoconcept, into a system of protoconcepts. This system will be referred to as **protosituation**:

(9)   Protosituation PERSON-IS RUNNING = SURFACE-LIES ←On– **PERSON-IS RUNNING** –To→ GOAL-EXISTS

A protosituation is a proto-assertion, because the main protoconcept **PERSON-IS RUNNING** contains a grain of predicativity (for details, see subsection 2.4.4).

Let us expound on the protosituation in (9):

(10)   Protosituation PERSON-IS RUNNING =

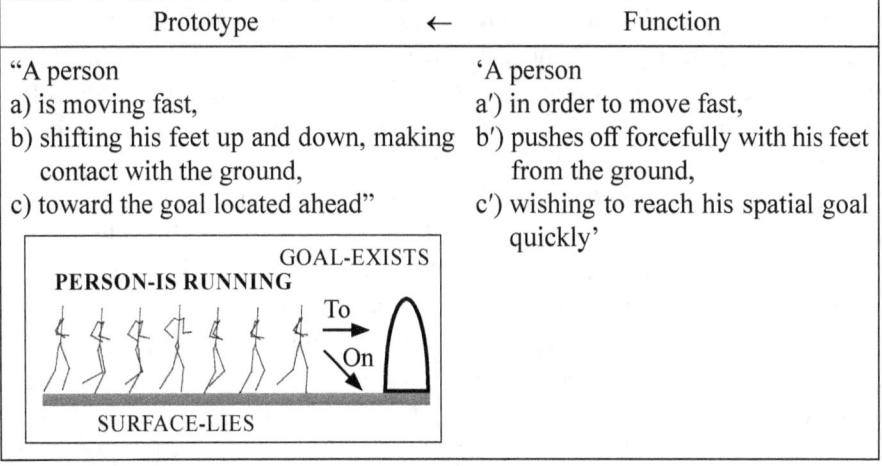

Prototype	←	Function
"A person a) is moving fast, b) shifting his feet up and down, making contact with the ground, c) toward the goal located ahead"		'A person a') in order to move fast, b') pushes off forcefully with his feet from the ground, c') wishing to reach his spatial goal quickly'

---

in the speech of Russian children close to 24 months, much later than prepositions for other relationships.

The prototype of a protosituation is a combination of prototypical participants and role relationships and the function a combination of their functions. As can be seen, the protosituation (10) is authentic with the basic situation (2) PERSON-IS RUNNING because their functions are identical. However, the function in (10) is more detailed as it consists of the separate functions (interpretations) of separate situation participants.

2.3.6. The level of protoconcepts in the situation tree. Let us go back to situation (3). The development cycle in question has formed the level of protosituation (b) in the tree:

(11) a. Situation A PERSON IS RUNNING

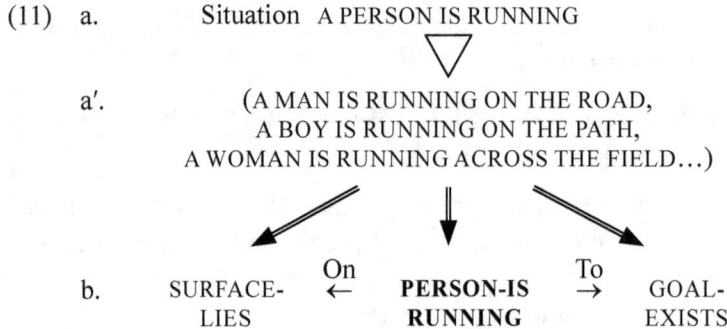

a'. (A MAN IS RUNNING ON THE ROAD,
A BOY IS RUNNING ON THE PATH,
A WOMAN IS RUNNING ACROSS THE FIELD...)

b. SURFACE- ←On— PERSON-IS —To→ GOAL-
LIES RUNNING EXISTS

Remember that double arrows stand for the relationship "Whole ⇒ Part (Component)," which appears as a result of the decomposition of situations (11a) into protoconcepts. To clarify, the protosituation, (11b), obviously emerges as a result of the child's differentiation between the specific situations, (11a'), which are concrete and clear, and the basic situation, (11a).

It may easily be seen that the protoconceptual component (11b) is isomorphic to the partitive component (6e) of the parts of a chair (see chapter 1). The following picture gives a much clearer idea of the tree in (11).

Notice that the protosituation (11b) is in fact a 3D dynamic puzzle, a composition of three protoconcepts and two role relationships defined on the time interval micro-t. It is reasonable to ask if the decomposition of a whole situation into protoconcepts is affected by the language the child begins to use at 12 months. As suggested by the data from a series of experiments (see section 2.7), the answer is most probably negative. And this attests to the universal character of the developed situation (11).

2.3. The development of basic situations into systems of protoconcepts   85

(11a)/(2)

(11b)

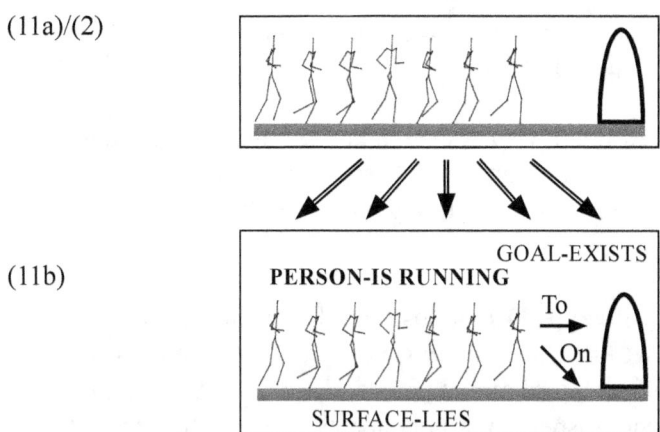

2.3.7. Identification of situations of running. Once formed, the protosituation, (11), is stored in the child's long-term memory and begins to be used instead of the whole situation (11a)/(2) in the subsequent identifications of observed locomotive situations, such as a picture of a running boy (*):

(11b)

(*)

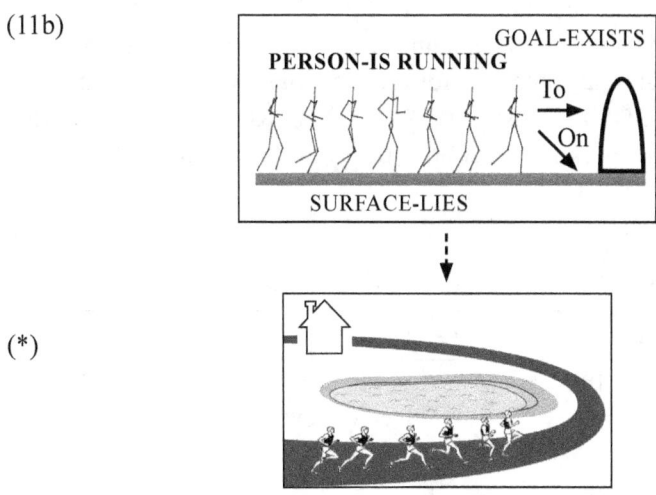

The protosituation (11b) structures this picture, changing it from a whole situation into a system of separate participants-protoconcepts connected by role relationships. The Agent **PERSON-IS RUNNING** projected on the running boy makes him the main participant and the focus of the situation. The black strip with which the boy's feet come into contact is interpreted as a protoconcept, SURFACE-LIES; thereby it acquires its own meaning—the function of the surface. Similarly, a house located in the direction of the boy's movement is interpreted by the protoconcept GOAL-EXISTS, acquiring the function of the goal.

This is an important point in the development of mental representations by a child: parts of a basic situation (spatial protoconcepts) receive their own interpretations for the first time, even though they are still not individual but contextually determined.

2.3.8. Specific protoconcepts. Decomposition of basic situations into basic protoconcepts SURFACE-EXISTS, **PERSON-IS RUNNING**, etc. is the first stage in the development of whole situations. Then comes the next stage, the formation of object, or specific protoconcepts—real participants of pro-tositutations—similar to the formation of specific situations, (11a'). This stage depends mainly on an external factor, namely, the child's experience accumulated in the course of multiple identifications of various situations with running humans such as (*).

It must be remembered that any object situation unfolds on the interval micro-t, i.e. it is a "live image" (short video clip). Therefore, its differentiated parts must also be 'live images'. The main participant **PERSON-IS RUNNING** ascribed to various running Agents yields a variety of specific protoconcepts: MAN-IS RUNNING, BOY-IS RUNNING, WOMAN-IS RUNNING,[13] etc., with the same transposed function: 'forcefully pushes off with the feet in order to move quickly'.

Here is an example:

(12)   Specific protoconcept A BOY-IS RUNNING =

Prototype ←	Function
"A boy is moving fast, shifting his feet up and down"	'A boy forcefully pushes off with his feet to move quickly'
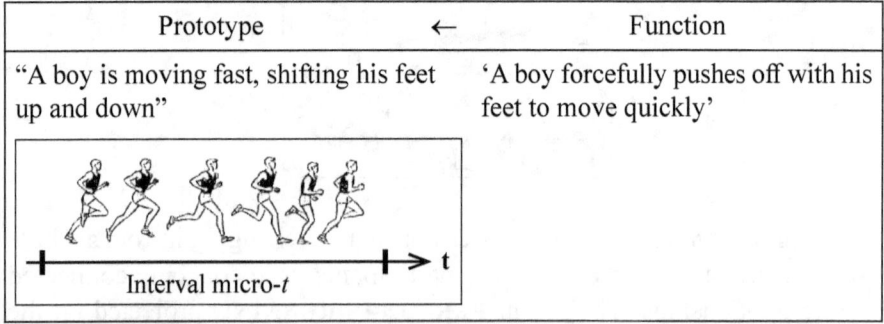	

---

[13] That human memory stores different prototypes of a man's run and a woman's run has been demonstrated by the experiments conducted at the biomotion lab at York

2.3. The development of basic situations into systems of protoconcepts

The specific protoconcepts ROAD-LIES, PATH-LIES, etc. of the basic protoconcept SURFACE-EXISTS are formed similarly.

Let us now look at the function of these images, starting with the protoconcept SURFACE-EXISTS. As a matter of fact, it does not always have the function of a surface in a locomotive situation. For example, the boy may be running towards the road (goal). Yet in the majority of cases SURFACE-EXISTS has just this function; therefore, this protoconcept and its specific protoconcepts ROAD-LIES, PATH-LIES have a fixed function—'hard surface for moving on'. Thereby they are all separated from the situation of running and acquire an independent, exosituational status determined by their function. Seeing one of them, we understand its function regardless of its current role in a given situation. For example, if the boy is running towards PATH-LIES we understand that, regardless of its current role (the goal of the movement), it serves as a surface for moving on. The reason of this independence is that all these protoconcepts have a single prototype—"a straight long strip at the ground surface (under the feet)." And the function-action is ascribed to this prototype (see (5)).

Here is an example:

(13) Specific protoconcept PATH-LIES =

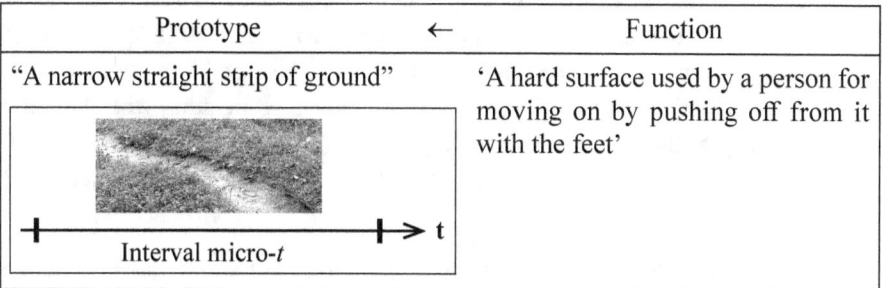

Prototype	←	Function
"A narrow straight strip of ground"		'A hard surface used by a person for moving on by pushing off from it with the feet'
Interval micro-t		

Let us now consider the protoconcept GOAL-EXISTS. Its function may be realized by very different protoconcepts: HOUSE-STANDS, LAKE-LIES, CAR-IS MOVING, RIVER-RUNS, etc. Yet its function does not have its 'own' protoconcepts as manifestations of this goal that have recognizable shapes. This function may be realized by participants with very different prototypes (shapes). In other words, the function of goal is performed by the participants which became basic protoconcepts in other situations.

University in Toronto, Ontario, directed by Prof. Dr. Nikolaus Troje (http://www.biomotionlab.ca).

On the second level (b′) of the development tree (11) (see (16b′)) each basic protoconcept forms a variety of specific protoconcepts:

(14) a. PERSON-IS RUNNING ▷ (MAN-IS RUNNING, BOY-IS RUNNING, WOMAN-IS RUNNING…);

b. SURFACE-EXISTS ▷ (ROAD-LIES, PATH-LIES…);

c. GOAL-EXISTS ▷ (HOUSE-STANDS, LAKE-LIES, CAR-IS MOVING…).

To emphasize, not only are BOY-IS RUNNING, BOY-IS SITTING, BOY-IS STANDING specific protoconcepts, but also BOY-IS RUNNING, WOMAN-IS RUNNING, MAN-IS RUNNING, etc.

> **Note.** Some indirect evidence that a child's mental representations have a level for protoconcepts is provided by children's use of some words to refer to both objects and actions. Clark (2009: 82) mentions the following observation made by Griffiths and Atkinson (1978). English-speaking children at 18–24 months used the word *door* not only in its main meaning but also in the action-meaning 'open' or 'let something out', for example with the meanings 'open the box', 'uncap a jar', 'take the clothes off the doll'. Other children of the same age used the word *open*. It may be assumed that in the first case the word *door* acquired its initial meaning in the form of a basic protoconcept, DOOR-IS OPENED, which later was not differentiated into components. Therefore, these children used the word *door* additionally to refer to the actions of opening, associating with them the processual meaning of the word. Eliseeva (2015: 105) describes the case of a girl, Lisa T., who used about half of her first 50 words to refer both to objects and to actions typically performed with these objects (cf. also Gvozděv (1949, 2: 4)).

Specific protoconcepts combine into specific protosituations. Because of their concrete character, they become composite 'live situations' in the full sense of the word, cf.:

(15) a. ROAD-LIES ←On– **BOY-IS RUNNING** –To→ HOUSE-STANDS,

b. PATH-LIES ←On– **WOMAN-IS RUNNING** –To→ BUS-STANDS,

c. HIGHWAY-LIES ←On– **BOY-IS RUNNING** –To→ CAR-IS MOVING.

Protosituations (15a–c) are examples of concrete proto-assertions.

The formation of specific protoconcepts completes the formation of the level of protoconcepts (b–b′) of the tree (11). The result is the following two-level development tree:

(16) a. Situation A PERSON IS RUNNING

a'. (A MAN IS RUNNING ON THE ROAD,
A BOY IS RUNNING ON THE PATH,
A WOMAN IS RUNNING ACROSS THE FIELD…)

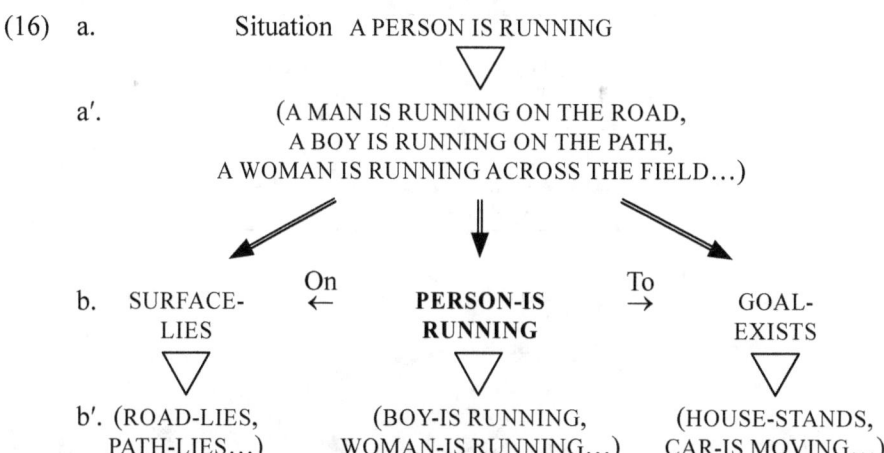

b. SURFACE-   On   PERSON-IS   To   GOAL-
    LIES   ←   RUNNING   →   EXISTS

b'. (ROAD-LIES,   (BOY-IS RUNNING,   (HOUSE-STANDS,
    PATH-LIES…)   WOMAN-IS RUNNING…)   CAR-IS MOVING…)

The sublevel (16b′) on this tree considerably expands the child's ability to represent situations with running humans. Using specific protoconcepts and role relationships, the child can now not only decompose familiar specific situations (11a′) but also build a large number of new situations observed for the first time or simply imagined.

2.3.9. Clarifying the identification process. Let us go back to the process (11b)–(*) of recognition of an image of a running boy. Upon identifying it, with the help of level (16b), as a basic protosituation PERSON IS RUNNING, the child moves to the level (16b′) and chooses there the most suitable specific protoconcepts. In the end, the following reduced tree is formed in the child's memory:

(17) a. Situation A PERSON IS RUNNING

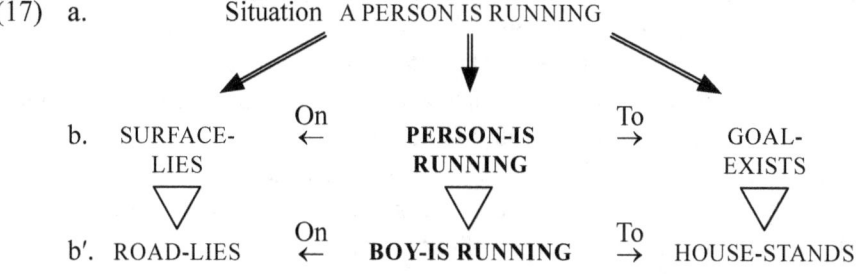

b. SURFACE-   On   PERSON-IS   To   GOAL-
    LIES   ←   RUNNING   →   EXISTS

b'. ROAD-LIES   On   BOY-IS RUNNING To   HOUSE-STANDS
                  ←   →

The specific protosituation (16b′) is also a new mental representation of the perceived image, which can be spatially visualized as follows:

(17b′)

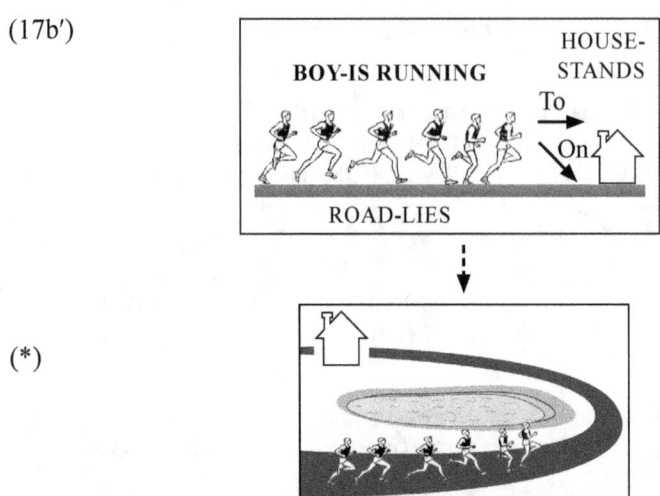

(*)

Fig. 3. Specific protosituation (17b′) used for concrete identification of the perceived situation of running (*)

The specific protosituation (16′b′) is more detailed compared to the specific situation (3′a′) shown in the tree (3). It takes into account the features of each participant.

Thus, specific protoconcepts become new, more detailed (as compared to specific situations) elementary units of the child's representations of situations.

2.3.10. Situations of observable actions. In the previous subsection we considered situations with a moving Agent. Similar developmental processes take place in the case of children's representations of situations with the actions of visible Agents: "A person is drinking / reading / dancing," etc. As some experiments have shown, infants display attention to concrete actions and single them out in a situation at a very early age (see analytical reviews in Pruden et al. 2008; Wagner, Lakusta 2009; Göksun et al. 2017).

In an indirect way this is attested by the fact that at 12 months infants begin to perform actions with objects for which these objects are intended. This fact is based on a vast array of experimental data. Cf.:

> At 11–12 months, first attempts to use objects according to their intended purpose are registered: drink from a cup, scoop up porridge with a spoon, comb hair with a comb, etc. (Kol'tsova 1973: 27, 33).

2.3. The development of basic situations into systems of protoconcepts

[…] Actions with objects gradually change from 'handling' to 'instrumental' […]. [A]t eight to nine months, the infant picks up a doll, a rattle, or a building block in a similar fashion and knocks them on the rim of the playpen or on the cradle guardrail; there is no clear differentiation between these objects. Two or three months later the infant already rocks the doll, stacks building blocks, rolls the ball, shakes the rattle, etc. (Kol'tsova 1973: 81, 83).

From the first six months of the second year, the dominant activities are actions with objects (manipulative up to 1 year, and instrumental from then on) (Isenina 1986: 43–44) [translation A. Kravchenko].

Infants can master instrumental actions with objects only on condition that, firstly, they single out object-motor protoconcepts from whole situations and, secondly, are capable of distinguishing, at least partially, between an object and object-directed action within protoconcepts. Therefore, infants are quick to recognize typical object-directed actions. True, such actions of infants may be called instrumental only conditionally. According to Vygotsky, infants already know about typical actions with objects but they don't comprehend their purpose, they only imitate the actions of adults. Discussing the actions of a two-year-old child who was nursing her doll and performing other actions—feeding, putting to bed, etc.—Vygotsky made the following observation: "But it is interesting that the child has no conception of the doll being her daughter, that she is the doll's nurse or mother" (Vygotsky 1986: 267).

Without going into much detail about the development of whole actional situations, I assert that the second level in the child's development tree is formed similarly: first, basic protoconcepts appear such as **PERSON-IS DOING-SOMETHING** (main participant), INSTRUMENT-ACTION, etc., and corresponding role relationships used to form basic protosituations (proto-assertions). Then, these basic protoconcepts also form a sublevel where their specific protoconcepts are accumulated. These are combined into specific proto-assertions such as the following:

PERSON-IS EATING-PORRIDGE –Off→ PLATE-STANDS,

PERSON-IS WAVING –Instr→ PENNANT-MOVES.

2.3.11. Hundreds of thousands of protoconcepts. Instant reaction to various observed changes is crucial to humans. Perhaps this is why human memory stores a multitude of specific protoconcepts which provide a detailed classification of significant human movements, gestures, facial expressions, and other typical actions; the art of acting is based on this. For example, there are many different 'hand waving' gestures: one can wave cheerfully, tiredly, hopelessly, demandingly, irritably, nervously, discontentedly, impatiently, indifferently, dismissively, generously, vaguely, in a farewell, in greeting; one can wave somebody off (meaning "don't bother me"), keep somebody at a distance (meaning "stay where you are"), invite someone to approach or to follow, wave someone to a seat, wave to someone to stand up, give a go-ahead, and so forth.

How does a child begin to differentiate and comprehend a score of meanings of the aforementioned gesture "wave of a hand?" They all emerge via differentiation of a multitude of whole situations with an Agent making this gesture. In the class of situations in which the state of affairs is hopeless for the Agent, this gesture (its particular shape) receives its particular function "express hopelessness"; in the class of situations where the Agent is irritated, this gesture, already of a slightly different shape, is interpreted as "expressing irritation," and so forth.

Thus, an array of specific protoconcepts HAND GESTURE-1, HAND GESTURE-2, etc. with a dual structure is accumulated in the development tree such as (16):

HAND GESTURE-N = Shape-N of the hand's motion $\leftarrow$ its Function-N.

If we are unable to clearly visualize a certain version of this gesture, such as the gesture "wave (to smb.) indifferently," for example, it is just because in our daily experience we haven't encountered a sufficient number of corresponding whole situations.

Of course, language does take part in the formation of these protoconcepts, determining or specifying the interpretation of an observed situation by the child as, for example, hopeless for the Agent, nervous, etc. But this participation is not primary; language is bypassed in the decomposition of situations into protoconcepts.

Another example is an array of specific protoconcepts of the basic protoconcept PERSON-IS DANCING-WALTZ: a man / woman / girl dancing, the dance of an old or disabled person, etc.; a waltz can be danced at a fast pace, in a constrained manner, hesitantly, awkwardly, professionally, tiredly, solemnly, carelessly, arrogantly, primly, etc. There are also various styles and kinds of waltz: the Viennese Waltz (rigorous, prim), the English Waltz and the Boston Waltz (slow), the Argentine Waltz (with the elements of tango), etc.

2.3. The development of basic situations into systems of protoconcepts 93

We also recognize without difficulty a plethora of various kinds of animal movements, in particular the fast, leisurely, or slow run of a dog, cat, leopard, monkey, ostrich, rooster, goose, etc., including the run of young animals, all of which may vary.

Specific protoconcepts often set separate sub-classes within the class of a word's referents. For example, the class of referents of the verb *tečët* 'flows / runs' includes over 10 such subclasses: the RIVER FLOWS SLOWLY / QUICKLY / RAPIDLY; WATER FROM TAP RUNS EVENLY / UNEVENLY / WITH GREAT FORCE / WITH LOW FORCE / BY FITS; oil, warm tar, and honey all flow in a different manner. All these protoconcepts are stored in our memory and are easily identified by an observer.

We distinguish the run of a child (a boy or a girl), an old man or woman, an athlete, a disabled person, a ballerina on the stage, a man with a heavy bag in his hand or a sack on his back or a cart he is pushing before him; we distinguish running on tiptoe, jogging, mincing or shuffling along, and so forth. We also recognize the run of near relations, friends, famous sprinters, etc. As may be seen, along with the basic motor concept IS RUNNING (PERSON-IS RUNNING), the perceptual model stores a great number of unnamed specific protoconcepts of running that form a detailed taxonomy of the class of referents for the given verb. The human walk has a no less rich taxonomy, which is more individual as the walk of a person is more recognizable than the run of the same person.

If we consider the number of basic protoconcepts stored in the memory of every individual, it may be assumed that it is larger than the number of basic concepts derived from them (the meanings of notional words) at least by an order of magnitude.

2.3.12. Thousands of situations. To top it all, protoconcepts themselves emerged as an outcome of the differentiation of many whole visual situations of locomotion and action. These are the initial human conceptions of the phenomenal world. It may be assumed that human long-term memory stores at least thousands of such situations.

During the next stage of the child's development basic protoconcepts are divided into basic concepts, which are combined to form basic situations. As was shown in subsection 1.3.8, a basic concept is an independent notion while its parts are not. A situation formed by concepts is also an independent cognitive unit because the function that defines it is separate, independent of the functions of other situations that may be somehow connected with it.

However, its independence is of a different kind; it is an elementary predicative unit, and when it is divided into concepts this predicative property is not inherited by any of the concepts.

One could ask, Why, unlike parts of an independent concept, are parts of an independent situation—its participants—independent? As it is, concepts acquire independence apart from the roles they play in different situations, cf. "to run on the roof" (the roof is used as a 'road' but remains a roof) and "to run to the road" (the road plays the role of goal but remains a road). And parts of concepts do not have such independent functions: the handle of a door, bag, or kettle all have different shapes and are not used in any other common role. The idea may be well illustrated by the portraits painted by G. Arcimboldo, a 16th century Italian artist; they consisted exclusively of fruits, vegetables, plants, and flowers. One such portrait is shown in figure 4. In the picture on the left, an assortment of fruits creates an image of a human head: the pear becomes a nose, the apples cheeks, the pomegranate a chin, and so forth. The reversed picture on the right ceases to be a human face and becomes a basket of fruit. In this picture, the pear ceases playing the role of a nose but remains a pear, and so on.

Fig. 4. G. Arcimboldo. Reversible Head with Basket of Fruit, 1590

Thus, situations and concepts are two types of elementary independent notions, predicative and non-predicative. Concepts are not decomposable into simpler concepts (independent notions) and situations are not decomposable into simpler propositions (compositions of concepts) (see subsections 2.5.1, 2.5.2, and 2.8.1).

2.4. The development of protoconcepts into systems of object...

In summary, basic situations—two-level trees of the type shown in (16) (as will be shown, they later become three-level trees)—are not directly connected with one another. They are independent unities of scores of situations. They become interconnected in more global models of reality such as the model of a fruit tree (see subsection 1.5.5).

2.4. The development of protoconcepts into systems of object and motor concepts

Very soon, in accordance with the development schema (5) (see subsection 1.2.5), protoconcepts begin to be partially differentiated into their object and motor components. For some protoconcepts this differentiation appears to be complete by the age of 14 months. This is the time when the child moves to the next level of situation representations, with more abstract and more fragmentary elementary units—object and motor concepts, or, to put it simply, objects and actions.

2.4.1. Experimental data. Some research provides evidence that at 14 months the object and the motor components of a protoconcept acquire an independent status; in other words, the child develops separate ideas of objects and actions:

> The singling out of separate objects from a "situation image" takes place [...] rather early—at the beginning of the child's second year (Kol'tsova 1980: 36; translation A. Kravchenko).
>
> At 12 to 18 months, functional actions with objects begin to take shape. Objects exist without and separately from the child as syncretic unities of their physical and functional properties. Operations on objects are determined by their features [...] The child begins to distinguish actions (Isenina 1986: 43–44, 101; translation A. Kravchenko).

This proposition is clearly evidenced in a clever experiment described by Waxman (2008: 110–113). Infants at 14 months were tested for their ability to form two categories, an object category "Larp," in which balloons of various shapes waved by the experimenter were called a *larp* (for example, *The man is waving a **larp***), and a motor category "Larping," when different actions with a balloon were described by the verb *larping* (as in *The man is **larping** a balloon*). Waxman's initial hypothesis was that "if infants have specific expectations for both verbs and nouns, then they should map words from these grammatical categories differently, mapping verbs specifically to event categories and nouns specifically to object categories" (p. 111). The test trials supported this hypothesis; therefore, at 14 months, infants already differentiate between objects and actions in their mental representations.

Differentiation of object and motor components of protoconcepts is the result of a stage in the cognitive development of infants which begins at around at 12 months. Differentiations which begin earlier are also completed by about this age. According to Pruden et al. (2008: 176–177, 179), beginning at 14 months infants learn to extract the invariant Manner of movement (walking, running, jumping) from scores of different movements of Agents, and the invariant Agent from scores of its various movements with different Manners.[14] As Song et al. (2006) demonstrated, it is also at this time that the invariant Agent is formed when movements of different manners are performed—for example, as when five different Agents moved by 'jumping' or 'marching'. It would appear that infants at 14 months can form an invariant category of goal (but not of source) that includes various goal-objects and spatial relationships (Lakusta, Carey 2008).

Some subsequent research (Göksun et al. 2017; Pruden et al. 2012; 2013) extends and elaborates on many of these findings—see also section 2.7, where the issue of how the child's language affects the formation of concepts is discussed in detail.

2.4.2. The formation of object concepts. In light of the above, it may be assumed that at 14 months the child enters a new developmental cycle. As a result, on the one hand basic protoconcepts of the type PERSON-IS RUNNING, SURFACE-LIES and the like are differentiated into basic concepts, object (PERSON, SURFACE, etc.) and motor (IS RUNNING, LIES, etc.), while on the other hand a role relationship appears which combines these concepts into dual conceptual systems. Let us begin our analysis of differentiation of protoconcepts with the main protoconcept PERSON-IS RUNNING. It is defined on a short time interval, micro-t, and in the process of differentiation is divided into two basic concepts also defined on this time interval: an object

---

[14] Clark (2009: 91–92) discusses the hypothetical order of priority in distinguishing and naming the roles of situations participants by children at the beginning of the second year: the doers, actions, and states of manipulated objects come first, and the objects related to a location, receiver, or possessor come next.

concept PERSON and a motor concept IS RUNNING (the names of basic concepts are also given in capitals). As will be demonstrated below, the motor concept becomes the main concept.

The separate concept PERSON will be represented as the protoconcept PERSON-EXISTS, **generalized according to the action**, which is not defined on this time interval. This means that at every moment on the interval micro-*t* the person exists—but how, and what is actually happening (whether the person is sitting, running, or eating), is not known. This protoconcept PERSON-EXISTS, abstracted from the action, will be called 'basic object concept PERSON' and its prototype will be shown as a motionless human figure on the interval micro-*t*:

(18) Object concept PERSON (PERSON-EXISTS) =

Prototype ←	Function
"A typical image of a human showing his structure and visual features" 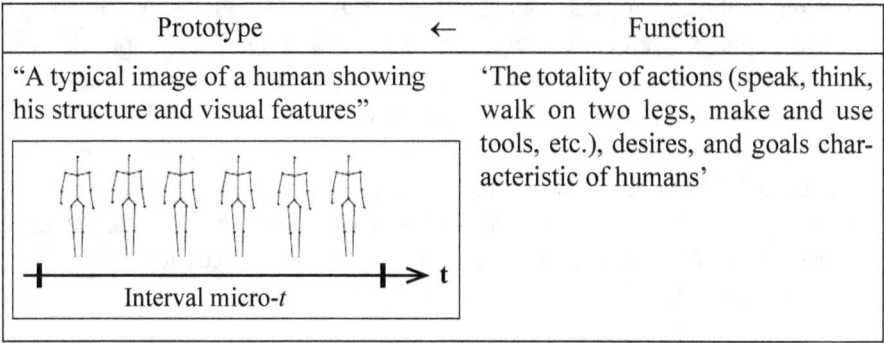 Interval micro-*t*	'The totality of actions (speak, think, walk on two legs, make and use tools, etc.), desires, and goals characteristic of humans'

2.4.3. The formation of a motor concept (action). The motor concept IS RUNNING (the main concept) is an object-motor protoconcept X-IS RUNNING **generalized according to the Agent**. It defines, on the interval micro-*t*, a class of visually similar actions (the run of a human, ostrich, penguin, dinosaur, etc.) with a common function 'move to another location'. The point is to abstract the concept **X-IS RUNNING** from the concrete shape of X (Agent). For that, the shape of the Agent must be generalized—not to a maximum (any X) but to a degree when X's run is still recognizable as such. And it is recognizable when it is a bipedal run, that is, when X is a bipedal creature. In a general case, therefore, we get the motor concept IS RUNNING maximally generalized according to the Agent, or the protoconcept **BIPEDAL CREATURE-IS RUNNING** generalized according to the Agent's structure (a semisphere is running on two legs):

(19) Motor concept **IS RUNNING** =

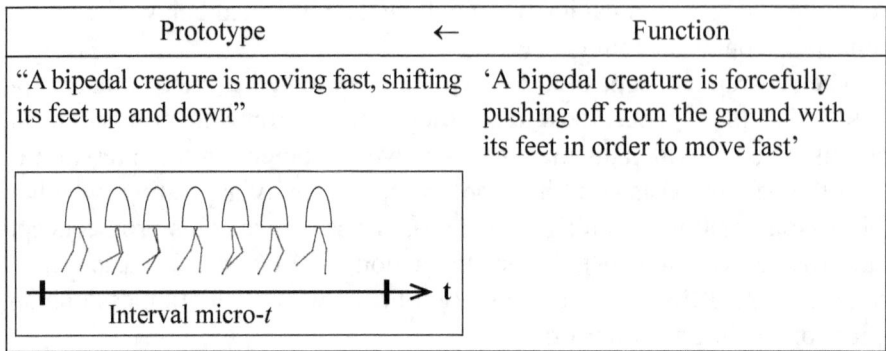

Prototype	←	Function
"A bipedal creature is moving fast, shifting its feet up and down"		'A bipedal creature is forcefully pushing off from the ground with its feet in order to move fast'

Note. Concepts (18) and (19) are cognitive (non-verbal) definitions of the main meanings of the noun *person* and the verb *is running*. It follows from them that these meanings are qualitatively homogeneous and possess isomorphic dual structure. In particular, the main meaning of the noun is defined not at a 'point' but on a time interval, i.e. it possesses a generalized processual feature, while the main meaning of the verb, at first sight not related to the doer of the action (object feature), is defined according to the recognizably generalized doer. Concepts (18) and (19) may also serve as cognitive templates for defining the main meanings of nouns and verbs as parts of speech—for a discussion of linguistic meanings, see Koshelev (2017: 91–108).

2.4.4. The formation of a predicative relationship. Simultaneously with the division of a protoconcept into concepts a role relationship of **merging** appears (←), indicating that an object concept merges with a motor concept in space-time on the time interval micro-t. Such a merge is error-free since both concepts have similar dual structures. Apart from the relationship of merging, these concepts are connected by a predicative relationship designated by the sign '+'; both relationships are designated by the sign '←+'. This is where the differentiation stage ends.

Subsequently, both concepts are integrated into a dual predicative system:

(20)   BOY ←+ **IS RUNNING**.

This system occupies a special place in the situation. It is an **elementary proposition** (assertion). Considering the current linguistic tradition, we hold the concept BOY in (20) to be dependent and the concept **IS RUNNING** to be

2.4. The development of protoconcepts into systems of object...

the main concept. Let us agree to call a dual system of concepts a **biconcept**, and (20) a **predicative biconcept**.

A brief clarification of the contents of the predicative relationship "←+" is in place here. To this end, let us consider how a picture of a man running with his dog is perceived (see figure 5). A number of protosituations can be singled out here:

1) MAN-IS RUNNING;

2) MAN-IS LOOKING-AT-DOG;

3) MAN-IS SWINGING-ARM;

4) MAN-IS HOLDING-LEASH;

5) DOG-IS RUNNING, etc.

Fig. 5. A man is running with his dog

From among these protosituations an observer instantly singles out a situation he believes to be the main one, that which spontaneously attracts his attention. It seems reasonable to assume that Agent is singled out first, since it is Agent that defines the locus of the protosituation. We will call such an Agent the main Agent. For example, Agent MAN in the picture defines one specific locus for the situation development, while Agent DOG defines another. Then, the main action of the main Agent is singled out; it determines what exactly is happening at this locus. Suppose MAN becomes the main Agent to the observer, and from the range of his actions (running, looking, holding the leash, etc.) RUNNING becomes the main one. The resulting pair constitutes a predicative biconcept MAN ←+ IS RUNNING.

Another observer, looking at the same picture, might form a different elementary proposition—a predicative biconcept DOG ←+ IS TRAMPLING-GRASS.

Thus, the left argument in the predicative relationship (20) is the **main** Agent in the perceived real-world situation (it defines the locus of action in the situation), and the right argument is the Agent's **main** action.[15]

---

[15] When a hearer hears a sentence, he has to, first of all, localize the situation described by the sentence in space, and to understand who the main agent in this situation is. Perhaps, that is why in most languages basic word-order begins with the subject (SVO or SOV).

It follows from this line of reasoning that the arguments in a predicative relationship are interdependent with regard to their content; each one of them is superordinate to the other in one respect and subordinate in another. Such an understanding of a predicative relationship corresponds to how it is understood in the former grammar tradition, where the nominal subject and the predicate verb are viewed as interdependent (Kasevich 2011: 104; Testelets 2001: 89, 408).

Along with the main action, the Agent may be involved in other actions as well. As an example, consider the situation described by the sentence:

Beguŝij   ***Ivan**   **mašet***   mne   *rukoj.*
Running-PrP   Ivan   wave-PRES   me-DAT   hand-INS
'Ivan, who is running by, waves to me'.

Here, the predicative nucleus *Ivan mašet* 'Ivan wave-PRES' represents a predicative biconcept IVAN ←+PRED-**WAVES**, while the expression *beguŝij Ivan* 'running Ivan' represents a non-predicative biconcepts **IVAN** → BEŽIT ('IS RUNNING') in which IVAN is already the main component and BEŽIT ('IS RUNNING') is its processual feature and, therefore, a supplementary component.

To emphasize again, the main concept **BEŽIT** ('IS RUNNING') defines running as the Agent's main action, while the supplementary concept BEŽIT defines the same action as not the main action, that is, as a property of the Agent.

2.4.5. The stage of conceptual integration. Let us consider the predicative relationship "←+". It indicates that the concepts are merged, i.e. the prototypes of the arguments are mutually specified: the shape of a person specifies the general shape of a running bipedal creature, while the shape of the creature's action (the bipedal run) specifies an undetermined action of the human shape on the interval micro-*t*. At the same time, the functions of concepts are also mutually specified. This mutual specification of concepts is illustrated in figure 6.

Simultaneously, the functions of concepts also merge.

Note. As may be seen, the legs of the runner become one of the main features of the motor concept IS RUNNING. The ability of infants to take this feature into account at an early age was discovered experimentally. It was found that at 14 months infants are in some cases more sensitive to the separate parts

2.4. The development of protoconcepts into systems of object...

or details of an object than to the object's shape as a whole. It was demonstrated by Rakinson and colleagues (Rakison, Butterworth 1998; Rakison, Cohen 1999) that infants at 14 months often built their categorical judgements based on the most salient features of objects (such as legs and wheels) rather than on the overall shape. For example, when shown toy cows with wheels instead of legs they categorized them as vehicles rather than animals and, conversely, vehicles with cow legs were categorized as animals rather than vehicles.

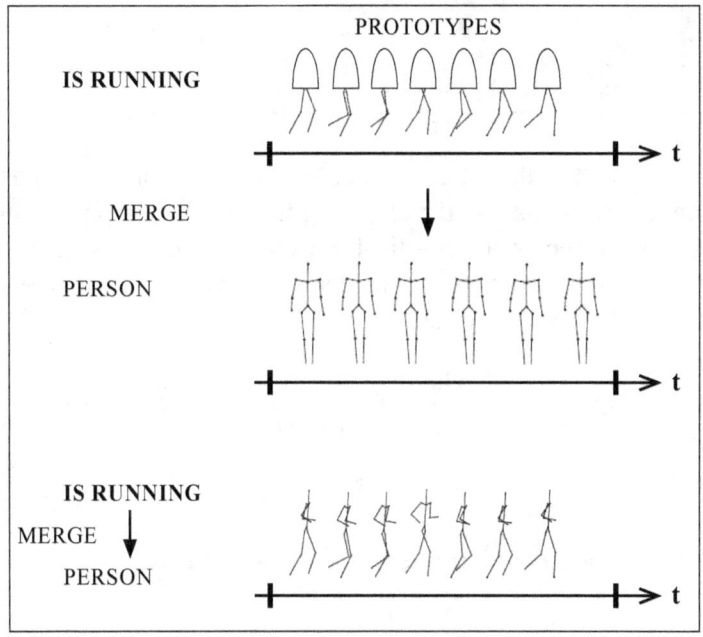

Fig. 6. Mutual specification of concepts

The supplementary protoconcepts SURFACE-LIES and GOAL-EXISTS are differentiated in a similar way. But their processual features are undetermined and do not affect the situation (for example, a surface may move itself as in the case of a walkway), and therefore they will be omitted. Thereby these generalized protoconcepts become the concepts SURFACE and GOAL.

The relationships '–On→' and '–To→', which connect them with the main concept IS RUNNING, are defined similarly to those in (7) and (8). As stated before, their prototypes consist of prototypical arguments, and their functions of the functions of the arguments. As an illustration, let us define the relationship '–On→' with the generalized concept IS MOVING:

Role relationship —On→ (**IS MOVING** —On→ SURFACE) =

Prototype	←	Function
"Object is moving, being in **physical contact** with the surface" 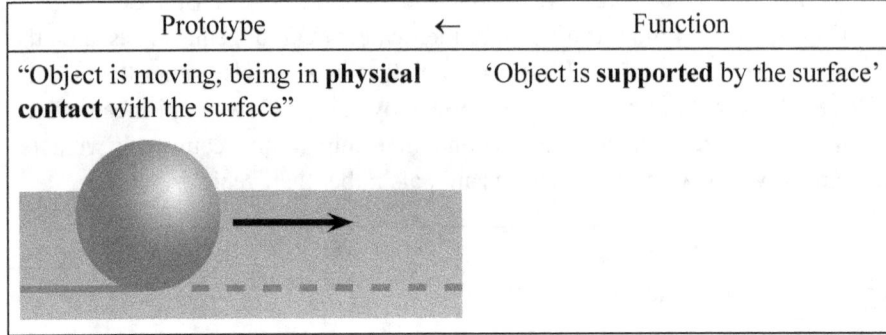		'Object is **supported** by the surface'

Thus, as a result of the differentiation of protoconcepts followed by their integration into systems, the development tree, (16), is supplemented with a level of new elementary units—the basic concepts PERSON, IS RUNNING, SURFACE, etc. For clarification, consider these two levels with the sublevel of specific protoconcepts omitted:

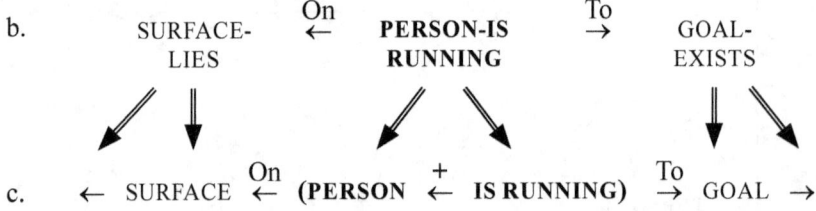

As before, a double arrow (⇓) designates the relationship "Whole—part," and a single arrow (←) a role relationship that shows that the supplementary argument merges with the main argument in space on the time interval micro-t.

2.4.6. The conceptual level of a development tree. Let us open the brackets on the conceptual level (c). The concept **IS RUNNING** becomes the main concept for the concepts SURFACE and GOAL as well. As a result, a **conceptual situation** emerges:

(21c)

$$\text{SURFACE} \xleftarrow{\text{On}} \text{PERSON} \xleftarrow{+} \textbf{IS RUNNING} \xrightarrow{\text{To}} \text{GOAL}$$

2.4. The development of protoconcepts into systems of object... 103

Let us agree to call it a **basic proposition** (assertion)—a system of biconcepts which includes the predicative biconcept PERSON ←+ IS RUNNING.

Finally, the development tree of the situation (16) is supplemented with a conceptual level, (c):

(21)

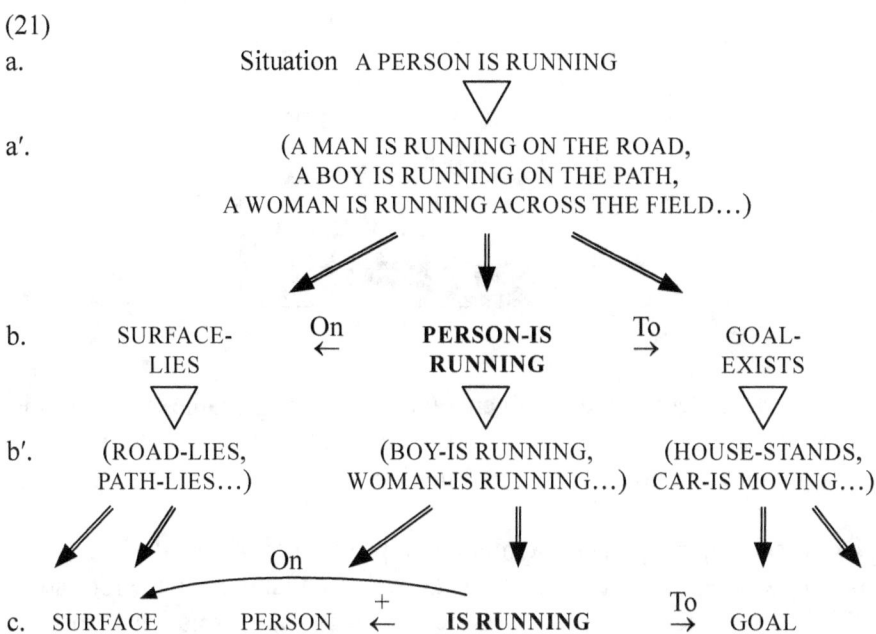

The conceptual situation (21c) is authentic with the whole situation (21a) PERSON IS RUNNING. Its formation is a crucial event in the child's cognitive development: **human notions**—concepts, as well as **a predicative relationship** and **propositions**—conceptual situations of the type shown in (21c) (see section 2.5), appear in the child's memory **for the first time** and practically simultaneously.

To continue our analysis, let us consider the following picture as a visual spatial representation of the situation in (21c) (see p. 104).

As soon as the conceptual situation (22)/(21c) appears in the tree (21), that is, in the child's long-term memory, the child begins to use it instead of the protosituation (11b) in subsequent identifications of observed situations of a bipedal run. For example, it is already this conceptual situation that is associated with the picture of a running boy (*) in the process of its identification. To emphasize: the main component of the situation—the concept

(22)/(21c)

(*)

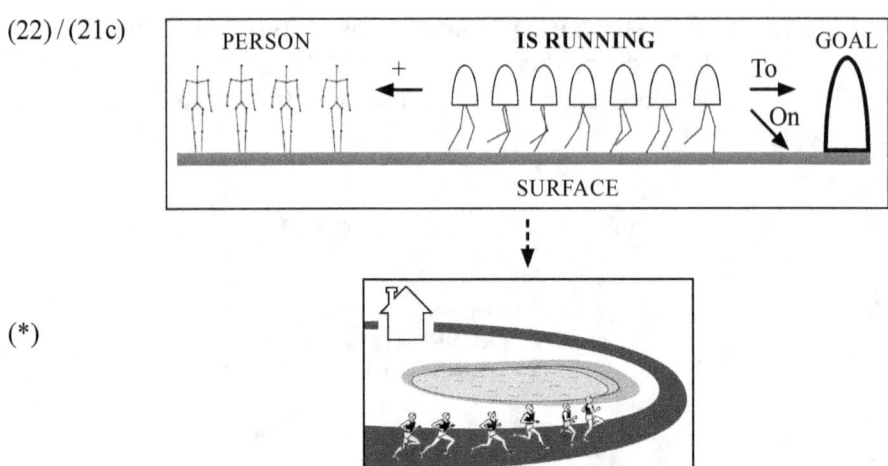

IS RUNNING—defines the most general but still recognizable characteristic feature of the entire class of situations of bipedal runs, this feature not depending on the specific shape of the running Agent.

2.4.7. Specific concepts. Differentiation of protoconcepts into the basic concepts PERSON, IS RUNNING, SURFACE, etc. is the first stage in the formation of the level of concepts. Then comes the next stage—the formation of specific varieties of basic concepts, or specific concepts.

As the conceptual situation (22)/(21c) is repeatedly used in identifying various situations of running, for each basic concept a set of its **specific concepts** is formed. The storage for the concept IS RUNNING is filled with various types of bipedal run: IS RUNNING-TYPICALLY, IS RUNNING-MINCING, IS RUNNING-JOGGING, IS RUNNING-SPORTILY, etc.;[16] the storage for the concept PERSON is filled with its varieties: MAN, WOMAN, BOY, etc. As a result, the predicative protoconcept **A PERSON-IS RUNNING** develops as follows.

---

[16] The website (http://www.biomotionlab.ca) shows many different modes of human walking. They may easily be recognized, which means that they belong to different specific protoconcepts: walking may be fast or slow, the person walking may be a man or a woman, happy or sad, stout or skinny, relaxed or nervous, etc.

2.4. The development of protoconcepts into systems of object...   105

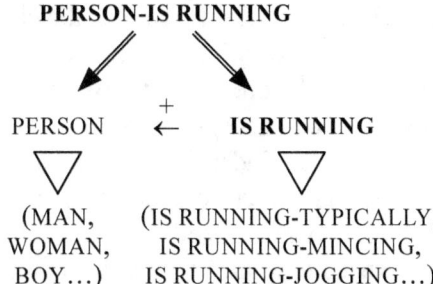

Specific concepts for the basic concepts SURFACE and GOAL are formed similarly. Together, they constitute the sublevel, (21c′), of the level (21c)— compare with the formation of specific protoconcepts in (21b′). Finally, the development tree, (21), is supplemented with the level of specific concepts, (c′):

(23)

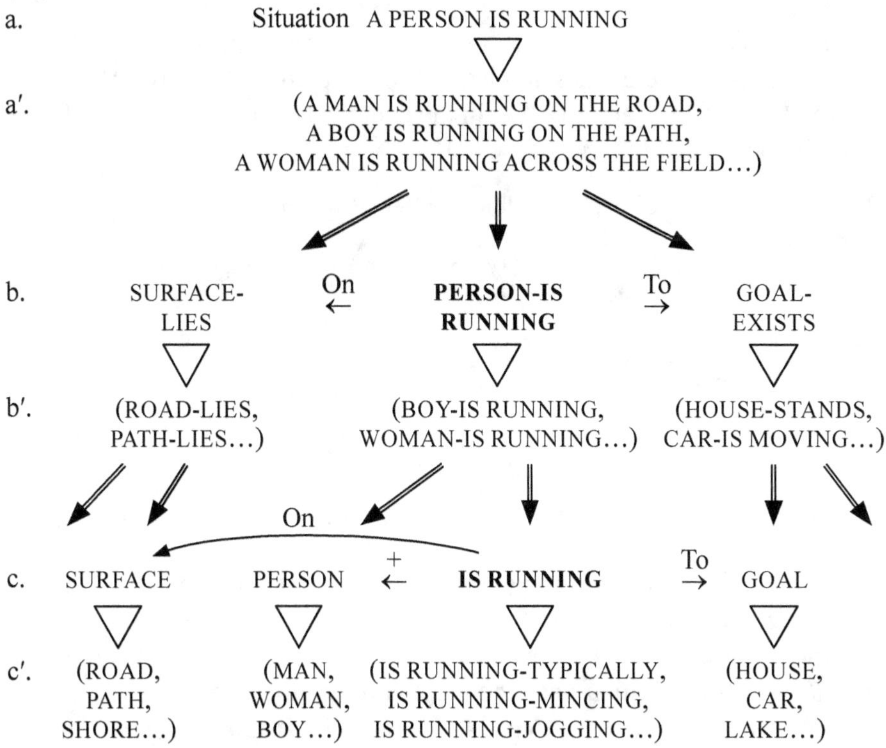

a. Situation A PERSON IS RUNNING
    ▽

a′. (A MAN IS RUNNING ON THE ROAD,
     A BOY IS RUNNING ON THE PATH,
     A WOMAN IS RUNNING ACROSS THE FIELD...)

b. SURFACE-   On   PERSON-IS   To   GOAL-
    LIES   ←   RUNNING   →   EXISTS
    ▽   ▽   ▽

b′. (ROAD-LIES,   (BOY-IS RUNNING,   (HOUSE-STANDS,
     PATH-LIES...) WOMAN-IS RUNNING...) CAR-IS MOVING...)

                        On
                                +   To
c. SURFACE   PERSON   ←   IS RUNNING →   GOAL
    ▽   ▽   ▽   ▽

c′. (ROAD,   (MAN,   (IS RUNNING-TYPICALLY,   (HOUSE,
     PATH,   WOMAN,   IS RUNNING-MINCING,   CAR,
     SHORE...)   BOY...)   IS RUNNING-JOGGING...) LAKE...)

The tree level (23c′) considerably extends the child's abilities. Using specific concepts and role relationships, the child can form, from the conceptual situation (23c), a variety of more concrete **specific situations** of a human run which reflect its various characteristic features. As a matter of fact, the specific concepts of level (c′) are independent. For example, jogging can be done by a man, woman, boy, etc.; therefore, any combination of specific concepts of different types yields a viable specific situation. Thus, the specific concepts of level (c′) may be used to build 81 specific situations ($3 \times 3 \times 3 \times 3$).

2.4.8. Clarifying the identification process. Let us illustrate how the new level (c–c′) of the tree (23) works. As noted above, in identifying the picture of a running boy the conceptual situation (22)/(21c) is correlated with the picture. The concepts from this situation are correlated with the parts of the picture: first, the manner of movement of the Agent is correlated with the general concept IS RUNNING. Then, other participants are identified: the running Agent is interpreted as PERSON, the black strip as SURFACE, and the image of a house as GOAL. After this, sublevel (21c′) is involved in the process. Basic concepts are substituted by appropriate specific concepts that are the closest to the images singled out in the picture: IS RUNNING-TYPICALLY, BOY, ROAD, and HOUSE. In the end, the tree, (23), is reduced to the following identification tree:

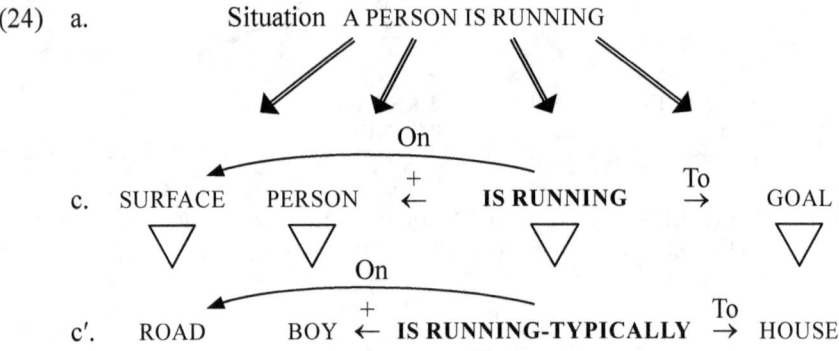

Now the picture of a running boy, (*), is interpreted by means of a system of specific concepts, (25). Such a representation is much more detailed than the representation in (17b′) in which specific protoconcepts are used, or in (22)/(21c) in which basic concepts are used. For example, the specific concept IS RUNNING-TYPICALLY provides a quite concrete image of the run.

2.4. The development of protoconcepts into systems of object...

A spatial representation of level (24c′) looks as follows:

(25)/(24c′)

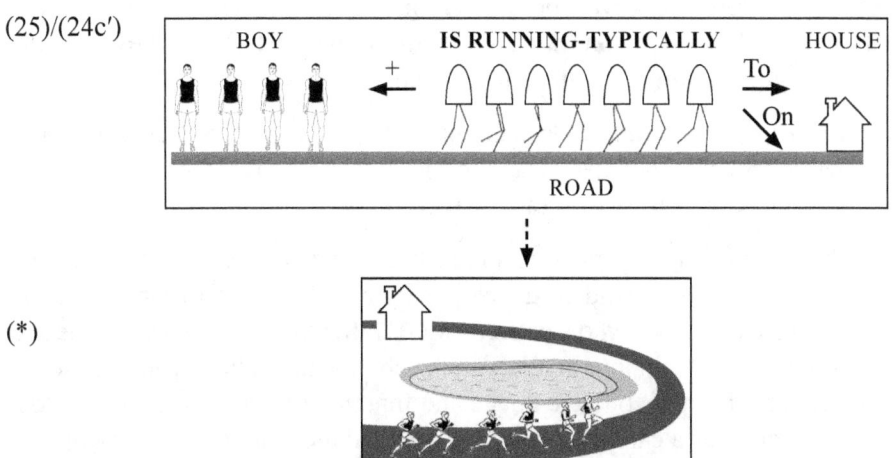

(*)

2.4.9. The formation of conceptual situations of actions. So far we have considered situations of locomotion. However, at the age of 14 months infants also begin to differentiate protosituations of visually observed actions. For example, as was demonstrated by Casasola and Cohen (2002), at 14 months infants distinguish between the actions of 'pushing' and 'pulling'. Song et al. (2006) describe infants at 13–15 months who successfully differentiated certain categories of unusual actions performed, for example during aerobics exercises in a classroom. Infants were tested for their ability to distinguish between such actions and the doers of these actions. Infants at the age of 10 to 12 months were unable to make this distinction.

As was demonstrated by Waxman (2008), it is at about this age that infants begin to identify the type of a simple **action** (waving a balloon), differentiating it from the **object**—the balloon waved by the experimenter (see subsection 2.4.1).

One kind of evidence that children form role relationships connecting the action and the participants in a situation at an early age is acquisition by Russian-speaking children of all six nominal cases, including the dative, instrumental, and locative, by the age of 24 months (Lepskaia 2013: 65–66; Voeikova 2015: 143–144; Tseitlin 2009: 168, 169, 175). According to Koshelev's (2017: 91–92) analysis, this becomes possible because of the advanced development in children of grammatical meanings of the said cases (the corelates of role relationships for which the child then acquires external expressions).

In conclusion, let me illustrate my approach with two concrete examples. As Pinker (2007) observes, both an empiricist who believes in the compositionality of concepts and a not-so-extreme nativist who believes in the non-compositionality and innateness of concepts

> would be satisfied with the claim that most of these concepts are built out of more elementary units—perhaps *mother* is mentally represented as "female parent," perhaps *kill* is conceptualized as "cause to become not alive" (p. 93; original emphasis).

The logic of my argument is somewhat different. The idea of "mother," which is one of the first ideas developed by a child, is most probably represented in the brain by a whole concept, MOTHER, which expresses the role and properties of the main intermediary in the child's interactions with the world. This concept has the concrete image and function of the female who is closest to the child as a caregiver and who is called the child's mother by others. Later, the concept MOTHER is differentiated into properties (a female who has given birth to the child, breastfed it, cared for it, etc.). Yet this concept is not naturally (in the course of the child's development) decomposed into simpler concepts (see subsection 2.8.1). For example, the idea of "parent" is a more abstract notion developed by the child much later. Therefore, one would be more likely to assume (and a thorough analysis is needed here) that, to the contrary, the concepts MOTHER, FATHER are primary components of the idea of "parent." Then the child would have the **inferred** knowledge that a mother is "a female parent." As for the meanings of *stepmother*, *surrogate mother*, *adoptive mother*, *foster mother*, *biological mother*, *donor mother*, etc. (for an analysis, see Lakoff (1987: 76), Wierzbicka (1996: 154–155), they are all metaphors making use of the properties of the whole concept MOTHER—the main meaning of the word *mother*—which appear later.

The idea of "kill" is not an object but a motor concept **KILL**—the main participant of a whole situation PERSON X **KILLS** PERSON Y WITH OBJECT Z (supplementary participant). This situation takes place on the time interval micro-t (up to 10–15 seconds). Therefore, it does not include such borderline cases as death from poison or a wound on the day following the day of poisoning or wounding. In this situation, X and Y are in one "local space" (the child sees both). X, holding Z in his hand, performs a certain purposeful action towards Y (strikes him with a sword or a knife, or aims a gun at him and shoots), as a result of which (causation) Y falls and becomes motionless and not alive. It should be emphasized that the relationship "causation of killing" must be quite concrete: it must contain a prototypical constituent—a promptly

2.4. The development of protoconcepts into systems of object... 109

identifiable action performed by X towards Y—for the whole situation to be easily identified. The relationship "cause to become not alive" is a much later abstraction. Later this whole situation does transform into a basic proposition—a system of participants and relationships that connect the participants. As the child's experience increases, each participant generates its specific concepts in the child's memory. Thus, concept Z generates specific concepts SWORD, DAGGER, ARROW, PISTOL, and so forth, which are later generalized into a functional concept, WEAPON, which does not have an unequivocal prototype but which has a single function. Thereby the child acquires inferential knowledge that killing is usually done with a weapon.

Later, the motor concept X KILLS Y—the main meaning of the verb *kill*—is metaphorically transferred onto similar situations: sniper X kills Y (X and Y have different loci), X kills Y by misadventure, Z kills Y on X's order (metonymy), etc. Clearly, depending on the child's experience of observing homicide situations, the initial whole situation may vary, but in any case it will be concrete enough to be promptly identified.

As a conclusion, I would like to refer to Givón's (1998: 1) proposition that the evolutionary growth of the visual information processing system plays a crucial role in supporting human language.

2.4.10. The outcome of the third cycle in the child's development. Beginning at 14 months, children learn to represent observed situations using basic and specific concepts that, compared to protoconcepts, are more fragmentary and more abstract cognitive units. Although the number of basic concepts seems to be less than the number of basic protoconcepts by an order of magnitude, children are able to use them in building a great variety of new representations of agentive situations. Every such representation provides a more detailed (structurally and functionally) description of the situation.

This is where the development of mental representations of situations ends, because the conceptual level is the last level on which predicativity—the main characteristic of an observed situation—is preserved. Single concepts do not feature predicativity, therefore their later development is not related to the development of situations (their mental representations).

For the description of the stages in a child's cognitive development to be complete it is necessary to define the initial level of the first cycle, whose outcome are the child's mental representations of agentive situations.

Let us agree that this initial level is formed, during the first months of life, by the infant's syncretic mental state in which the infant experiences himself and the world as a whole, without differentiating this whole into self and external real situations. As noted by Vygotsky (1986), two features distinguish the mentality of the newborn: "first, the child does not yet separate not only himself, but also other people from the merged situation that develops on the basis of his instinctive needs; second, for the child there is still nothing and no one at this period; more likely, he experiences *states* rather than specific objective content" (p. 232; emphasis added).

Consider the pivot table of the three levels of development trees determined by the child's three developmental cycles.

Levels of situation development tree	Age (months)	Elementary units (mental representations)
0. Start	Before 7–9	Syncretic state
1.	9–11	Whole situations (primary units)
2.	11–13	Protoconcepts—parts of situations
3.	14–17	Concepts—parts of protoconcepts

Table 1. The levels of a situation development tree. On each subsequent level more fragmentary elementary units appear—the components of elementary units of the previous level

2.5. Matrices of concepts, propositions, and language

As has already been said, appearance of the conceptual level (c–c′) in situation trees of the type shown in (23) is a crucial neoformation in a child's cognitive development. Human concepts, role relationships (the stage of complete differentiation of protoconcepts), and basic propositions made of these concepts and relationships, appear almost simultaneously in the child's memory. Practically at the same time some of these concepts receive names and become lexical meanings. Generalizations of these meanings become the initial part-of-speech meanings, while the role relationships which connect these names (or their correlates) take the form of syntactic relationships expressed in language (see subsection 2.5.4). Words of human language could not appear on the previous level of protoconcepts and protosituations because protoconcepts are not human concepts and cannot, therefore, become lexical meanings. True, children begin to speak 2–3 months earlier, at the beginning of their second year. However, many researchers concur that single-word utterances are not words; they are holophrastic and refer to whole situations. Later, these designate protoconcepts (see the analysis above).

To continue our line of reasoning, it may be assumed that the first two levels in development trees of the type shown in (23) reflect pre-human-specific stages in the child's development, while the third level—the level of concepts and propositions—marks the **first stage** in the child's **human development** proper. This conclusion allows us to formulate, with certain reservations, the following **evolutionary hypothesis**: the first two levels of type (23) development trees indirectly reflect two successive stages in the evolution of pre-human animals, while the **third level correlates with the level of cognitive and linguistic development of the first *Homo*.**[17]

2.5.1. Conceptual classification of the visible world. Conceptual matrix.
Two important varieties of cognitive units appear in the child's long-term memory: notions (basic concepts) and conceptual situations (basic propositions).

Let us take a closer look at these, starting with a basic concept. It has the structure "Prototype ← Function." Its function bears on the inner world of a human individual and is an elementary independent component of this world. It is because of this that a concept is an elementary independent unit (see subsection 1.3.8). The prototype of a basic concept bears on the visual world. It describes the appearance of the part of this world that can actualize the function (cause it to happen in real time in the child's functional world). Thus, the functions of basic concepts—independent components of an individual's inner (functional) world—are projected onto the phenomenal world by means of prototypes. They divide this world into parts that resemble the prototypes and, therefore, correspond to their functions. An **elementary human classification of the visible world** emerges—a totality of categories (pairs "Classical category (defined by Function) → Prototypical category (defined by Prototype)," see subsection 1.5.1)—which divides this world

---

[17] The problem of recapitulation (to what extent ontogeny replicates human evolution, and linguistic ontogeny the evolution of language) is discussed, for example, by Bickerton (1990), Givón (1998), and Slobin (2004). Slobin's generally negative attitude to various recapitulation issues seems to reflect his unwillingness to separate the child's thought and language (cf. Slobin 1996). A similar position is held by Chomsky (see subsections 2.5.3 and 2.6.2).

(by prototypical categories) into a variety of independent and functionally different classes of visible parts.

Let us introduce into our analysis a conceptual matrix: the matrix of concepts stored in the child's (human individual's) memory. Each matrix cell has three levels and contains an assortment of concepts. Consider the cell <BANANA>. It stores the developed three-level concept BANANA (30) (see chapter 1) along with other related concepts. On its first level is the basic concept (14) BANANA with its motor component (EAT-BANANA) (for the full definition of a basic concept, see chapter 1 subsection 1.3.2). Also stored on this level is its life cycle (42) (see chapter 1) and its common name *banana* (not all concepts in the matrix have a name). Moreover, the first level of the cell also stores specific concepts, their life cycles, and names. For example, the cell <TREE> contains the concept itself, its life cycle (see (17) and (40b) in chapter 1), the common name *tree*, the specific concepts APPLE-TREE, BIRCH, BAOBAB, etc. with their names and life cycles. Let us go back to the cell <BANANA>. On its second and third levels are found the adjectival, (30b), and partitive, (30c), systems correspondingly, both for the basic concept BANANA and its specific concepts with their names (see subsections 1.4.2 and 1.3.6). Additionally, this cell also stores typical metaphorical meanings of the word *banana*—though these will not be discussed here.

All of the above applies to motor concepts as well. For example, the appropriate cell stores the basic motor concept BEŽIT 'IS RUNNING', its life cycle (the run of a child, adolescent, youth, adult, senior, or an old person), the name *bežit* 'is running', as well as specific concepts (IS RUNNING-JOGGING, IS RUNNING-MINCING), their names (*jogging, mincing*), and life cycles (a jogging child, youth, adult, etc.).

Thus, the conceptual matrix is a separate storage of objects and actions assimilated by a person, as well as their semantic, that is, inherent features (see subsection 1.5.4). Similarly arranged are the matrix cells for special concepts such as CARBURETTOR, TROMBONE, or ADZE—a developed concept of Langda stonecutters (see subsection 3.2.6 in chapter 3). It should be remembered that all the components of the assortment of concepts stored in the cell are defined on time intervals; therefore, the concept BANANA, for example, is naturally combined with the motor component EAT-BANANA.

The conceptual matrix is stored in long-term memory and is, apparently, outside the zone of actual consciousness of the native speaker. This raises the question of how its cells—for example, the cell <BANANA>—are actualized, and what are the cell's points of entry. There are two such points.

2.5. Matrices of concepts, propositions, and language

Firstly, it is the prototypical image of a ripe banana (one or two pictures). In contrast with the concept's prototype, these images may be defined not on a time interval but 'at a point in time'. Secondly, it is the concept's name, *banana* (though many concepts do not have names). Therefore, the cell has a two-component structure:

Cell entry	→	Cell
Typical image and name	→	<BANANA>

Every point of entry to the cell <BANANA> (the image and the name) is, apparently, in the zone of actual consciousness of the native speaker, that is, it is the explicit manifestation of the cell. When a native speaker perceives one of the entry points, a cell instantly becomes active in his mind. It follows, in particular, that to describe the meaning of the word *banana* it is enough to describe the typical image of a ripe banana—see such descriptions in chapter 1, section 1.1 (of course, such descriptions are of use only to native speakers familiar with bananas and how they are used). The point of entry to a motor concept, such as <RUN>, is arranged similarly. To emphasize: a single-frame picture unambiguously points to the prototypical action extended in time. As has been argued elsewhere (Koshelev 2019: 59–60, 173–175), a simple visible action is instantly identified by its typical "frame." The neurobiological mechanism of transition from a picture (point of entry to the object or motor concept) to a matrix cell is described in Koshelev 2019: 152–156, 166–177.

2.5.2. Propositional classification of the visible world. Propositional matrix. Now let us consider a basic proposition of the following type:

(23c)

$$\text{SURFACE} \xleftarrow{\text{On}} \text{PERSON} \xleftarrow{+} \textbf{IS RUNNING} \xrightarrow{\text{To}} \text{GOAL}$$

It has the structure of a role situation, or a role component (see (7e) in subsection 1.2.5), and comprises three biconcepts which emerge at the stage of partial integration:

IS RUNNING +→ PERSON,
IS RUNNING –On→ SURFACE,
IS RUNNING –To→ GOAL.

Each supplementary participant—PERSON, SURFACE, and GOAL—adds its function to the function of the main participant **IS RUNNING**, so that the resulting function of the proposition (23c) coincides with the function of the initial whole situation. This happens because, in accordance with the role relationship, the prototype of each supplementary participant is positioned relative to the prototype of the main participant such that their functions are added up. The functional concept GOAL does not have a prototypical shape but it occupies its prototypical position—ahead of the main participant in the direction of movement.

The basic proposition (conceptual situation (23c)) contains the predicative concept PERSON ←+ **IS RUNNING**. Because the basic proposition is also a pair "Prototype ← Function" with a separate function (see subsection 2.3.12), it defines the propositional category of the visible world: "Classical category (defined by the predicative Function) → Prototypical category (defined by the compositional prototype)." This category is similar to the conceptual category, differing from it only in that it is a category of predicative parts of reality insofar as the predicative function of the proposition is projected on them.

Let us introduce into our consideration a **propositional matrix**—an assortment of all of the three-level trees of the type shown in (23) which are stored in the child's memory. Each cell of this matrix stores a separate three-level tree of situation development with all three sublevels of specific units. Obviously, the propositional and conceptual matrices are connected: each basic concept of the third level of the propositional matrix has a reference—the entry to its cell in the conceptual matrix. It may be assumed that entries to the cells of the propositional matrix are arranged similar to cell entries in the conceptual matrix. For example, entry to the cell <PERSON IS RUNNING> looks as follows:

Cell entry	→	Cell
Typical image and name		Cell
a person is running	→	<PERSON IS RUNNING>

2.5. Matrices of concepts, propositions, and language

A proposition may not have a linguistic name.

Thus, on the "surface" level of a native speaker's consciousness his classification of the visible world consists of two sets of entries: (a) images of object and motor conceptual prototypes and (b) images of propositional prototypes. Some of these images have names (words and simple sentences). The first set of images correlates with the conceptual matrix and the second set with the propositional matrix.

As was demonstrated above, it is whole basic situations that are the infant's primary cognitive units. From these, basic propositions are formed as a result of two cycles in the child's development. Therefore, the classification defined by the propositional matrix is the **primary human classification of the visible (phenomenal) world**.

This conclusion disagrees with the generally shared view developed in well-known works by Wittgenstein (1953), Zadeh (1965), Brown (1958; 1965), Rosch (1973; 1975a; 1975b; 1978; Rosch et al. 1976), Berlin (1976; Berlin, Kay 1969), Mervis (1984), Lakoff (1987) and others; according to their view, the initial level in the child's classification of the world is the level of basic concepts (Lakoff 1987: chap. 2). The grounds for such a view are clear: basic concepts are primary human notions ("basic-level categories are functionally and epistemologically primary" (Ibid.: 13). They are the first to appear in children and the first to receive lexical names. However, the arguments given above allow me to claim that, from the point of view of the child's development, the primary cognitive units in the child's representation of the world are whole situations, that is, merged predicative units that appear between the ages of 9 to 11 months. Basic propositions crown their cognitive development. They emerge practically simultaneously with basic concepts. Moreover, there is no doubt that concepts receive their names as participants of basic situations; in this respect, concepts are secondary.

The primacy of basic propositions seems to be related to their predicativity. Predicativity does not simply fix changes (motor concepts) or objects (object concepts); it fixes **relevant changes happening with objects** whose prompt comprehension is vital to the child.

After 36 months, the child begins to add other, supplementary propositions to the basic proposition (which becomes the main proposition). This is when the child's speech begins to feature utterances with complex syntactic structures (embedded constructions and the like) such as *The boy took the apple which lay on the table.*

The proposed **two-level** (propositional and conceptual) **classification of the visible world is inherent in humans**. It clearly shows how differently the world is viewed by humans and anthropoids, with their essentially different inner world (variety of functions). After all, according to the evolutionary hypothesis (see the beginning of this section), the development of anthropoids stops at the level of protoconcepts. True, their protoconceptual 'thoughts' possess one hierarchical level (strictly speaking, this differs from Chomsky's thesis mentioned in subsection 2.1.1 but is close to it substantially). Yet the syncretism of protoconcepts radically narrows down the variety of such 'thoughts'.

2.5.3. The conceptual language of thought. Thought procedure. The language of thought was introduced in chapter 1 (subsection 1.4.7), where it was pointed out that the nodes of developed concepts (three-level tree-like structures of the type BANANA, see (30), chapter 1) may be viewed as the 'lexicon' of the child's language of thought, while the set of 'part-of-speech' classes of these concepts (object, motor, adjectival, and adverbial) as well as the relationships which connect them—case relationships (predicative, object, etc.), the relationships "Object $\Rightarrow$ Property" and "Part $\Leftarrow$ Object"—constitute the main component of its grammar. In this, the propositional matrix is a subset of typical 'utterances' (complete thoughts) in this language. The functional components of these propositions are predicative functions that reflect, in their totality, the inner (functional) world of the child. The procedure for building such propositions may be called **thought**. How this procedure works was demonstrated, from different perspectives and with various examples, above (the formation of biconcepts from concepts, and propositions from biconcepts). I will only add that, firstly, input to the thought procedure is provided by some holistic function foregrounded in the child's inner worldview (it is the child's mental demand), while output is a proposition with the same function, represented systemically, and with the prototype that realizes this function. Secondly, the formed proposition receives an interpretation (contextual understanding) as its predicative function (the functional constituent with its functional components) related to a corresponding part of the child's inner (functional) world.

> **Note.** It may be assumed that the process of thinking takes place in the area of random-access memory where thought procedure stores the concepts and relationships it needs, retrieving them from the conceptual and propositional matrices. For concepts retrieval, it uses their points of entry—images and words. This explains the well-known notions of "image thinking" and "verbal thinking."

2.5. Matrices of concepts, propositions, and language 117

The language of thought outlined above is an adjustment of the common idea of what thought is. For example, its lexicon (the conceptual matrix) is much richer than the lexicon of any human language, while its propositions are formed solely by binary relationships. Moreover, this language of thought is closely connected with more basic levels of situation representation—the levels of whole situations and protosituations. It must be stressed that, initially, the language of thought is represented in the propositional matrix. In this matrix, the conceptual elements and the relationships which connect them are given as a **systemic unity**. Chomsky (2010) questions the existence of an independent or prior "language of thought" (LOT): "Note that postulation of an independent or prior 'language of thought' LOT raises all the problems of evolution of language, but with the extra difficulty that we have almost no idea what LOT would be, independently of linguistic evidence" (p. 226, footnote 24). Therefore, discussing the problems in the study of human thought, he points to difficult questions such as "which aspects of thought might be language-independent, including questions of argument structure (so-called 'theta-roles'), the status of propositional attitudes, determination of event structure, and much else" (Ibid.: 56).

Based on the propositional and conceptual matrices, it may be stated that all these aspects of thought (propositions, their argument structure, event or situation structure) initially appear in children before and independently of their mother tongue in the process of constructing mental representations of observed agentive situations. In particular, the conceptual matrix may well be viewed as a subset of Chomsky's set of word-like atoms (for details, see subsection 2.6.2).

2.5.4. The linguistic matrix as an initial stage of the child's language. The appearance of levels of concepts (c–c′) in development trees of the type shown in (23) serves as a basis for the child's acquisition of the lexicon and elementary grammar of the child's mother tongue. Indeed, the concepts BOY, ROAD, HOUSE, BANANA, IS RUNNING, IS EATING, etc. which appear on this level are the primary meanings of words in the child's language. Therefore, to learn a new word, such as *mal'čik* 'boy' or *bežit* 'is running', it suffices for the child to understand which specific concept on level (c′) of the matrix this word designates and then use this word as a name for the concept (place it in this basic concept's matrix cell).

In this, the child is assisted by two circumstances. Firstly, the referents of the child's words allow for ostensive definition: they may be pointed at with a gesture, glance, or nod. It is just such an ostensive definition that the child receives hearing his mother speak, because the child involuntarily focuses his attention on that situation with its particular components (participants and their relationships) which he observes and describes (Tomasello 2008: 107–108; Butterworth, Harris 1994: chap. 7).[18]

Secondly, the typical referent of the word—a member of the classical category defined by the basic concept—is identified by its outward appearance regardless of the context. The child does not need any additional knowledge for its identification. Therefore, based on the prompts from the acts of reference performed by the people around him, the child connects the word—by association – with the basic concept stored in the child's conceptual matrix. Thereby the word (its vocalization) acquires its primary meaning.

This process was vividly described by St. Augustine:

> For I was no longer a speechless infant, but a speaking boy. This I remember; and have since observed how I learned to speak. It was not that my elders taught me words (as, soon after, other learning) in any set method; but I, longing by cries and broken accents and various motions of my limbs to express my thoughts, that so I might have my will, and yet unable to express all I willed, or to whom I willed, did myself, by the understanding which Thou, my God, gavest me, practise the sounds in my memory. When they named any thing, and as they spoke turned towards it, I saw and remembered that they called what they would point out by the name they uttered. And that they meant this thing and no other was plain from the motion of their body, the natural language, as it were, of all nations, expressed by the countenance, glances of the eye, gestures of the limbs, and tones of the voice, indicating the affections of the mind, as it pursues, possesses, rejects, or shuns. And thus by constantly hearing words, as they occurred in various sentences, I collected gradually for what they stood; and having broken in my mouth to these signs, I thereby gave utterance to my will (Saint Augustine 2002: book 1).

Very soon and in a similar way the child begins to form grammatical meanings and their linguistic expressions—word forms, prepositions

---

[18] As Isenina's (1986) research showed, at 4.5 months, infants already develop an early correlate of this ability, 'the function of appropriate interaction' with their mother; it ensures development of the pre-speech language of facial expressions, gestures, and vocalizations. From then on, this function continues to develop, by stages, up to 18 months.

2.5. Matrices of concepts, propositions, and language

(postpositions), etc. As a matter of fact, role relationships also have prototypical components, therefore they (or their correlates) may be acquired through ostensive definitions just like lexical meanings (see subsections 2.4.4–2.4.5, Koshelev 2017: 91–96). As a result, certain concepts from development trees, and their relationships (predicative, objective and other case relationships, partitive, etc.), receive names and other forms of expression in language.

As an example, let us consider a part of the tree in (23) with basic concepts as nodes named by morphological words and with the role relationship named "–On→":

(26) a′.

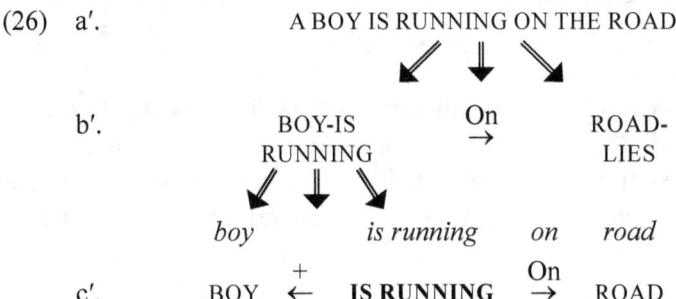

This yields a sentence, (27), which designates the proposition (c′):

(27) *Mal'čik bežit po doroge* 'A boy is running on the road'.

In this sentence the word forms are connected by the relationships of syntactic dependence—correlates of the corresponding role relationships. The word form *bežit* 'is running'—the apex of the syntactic tree (the name of the basic concept)—is connected by the predicative relationship correlate ←+ with the word form *mal'čik* 'boy' and by the object relationship correlate –On→ with the word form *doroge* 'road-LOC' (cf. Greenfield 1991: 532–233, figures 2 and 3). Moreover, all the word forms are arranged in a basic order characteristic of the given language.

Let us now ask, "How does the child come to have binary syntactic relationships?" In the syntactic dependency theory (cf. Testelets 2001: 70–76) explaining their significance is a problem. Testelets (2001) speaks of the "manifestations of intuition" (p. 65). Mel'čuk (2016) holds that syntactic dependencies are "purely abstract entities that cannot be grasped mentally or sensorily" (p. 173). Following my line of reasoning, it is reasonable to assume that syntactic dependencies are induced by binary role and partitive relationships which connect the meanings of dependent words. At the same time, it is explained how the child learns syntactic dependencies. Moreover this line of reasoning indirectly illustrates Humboldt's thought: "4. Es kann auch die Sprache nicht anders, als auf einmal entstehen, oder um es genauer auszudrücken, sie muß in jedem Augenblick ihres Daseins dasjenige besitzen, was sie zu einem Ganzen macht" (Humboldt 1905) "Language cannot arise otherwise than all at once, or more precisely, in every moment of its existence it must possess that which makes it the whole" [translation S. Zhigalkin]).

Let us now touch on the issue of part-of-speech meanings. Level (c–c') of the propositional matrix defines the classes of object and motor concepts that are in themselves the initial versions of the part-of-speech meanings of nouns and verbs, while some role relationships are the basis for the initial meanings of prepositions.

The role component (26c')—an outcome of the twice repeated development cycle of the whole situation (26a)—has a hierarchical structure which is isomorphic to the structure of the syntactic component (see Note and a role structure (7e) in chapter 1, subsection 1.2.5). Therefore, it is reasonable to assume that, similar to syntactic dependencies, the syntactic component (27) is induced by the role component (26c') which appears earlier. Thus, it may be assumed that syntax, believed by some linguists to be the crucial evolutionary development in human language (Givón 1979; 1898; Bickerton 1990; 2009; Chomsky 2010; Jackendoff 2010; Berwick, Chomsky 2016), is a direct reflection of the corresponding achievement in the evolution of human thought, in particular, evolution of mental representations of situations.[19]

Let us agree to call the denominated part of the propositional matrix a **linguistic matrix** (it includes, in particular, the denominated proposition (26c')). In contrast to the conventional view of language as a trinity of relatively independent components—lexicon, grammar, and lexical-syntactic interface—the linguistic matrix determines the initial stage of language **as a systemic unity of these components**. It must be pointed out that this language stage does not emerge independently; it is based on the third level (c–c') of the child's situation development trees.

2.5.5. Distinguishing between general-cognitive and language-specific processes. Initial stages in language evolution. As theoretical issues, the

---

[19] In contrast to this conclusion, Everaert et al. (2017: 570) reiterate Chomsky's earlier observation that "all examples we know point to thought structured by syntax, not the reverse."

2.5. Matrices of concepts, propositions, and language

division of cognition into human cognition and animal cognition on the one hand and human cognition into general-cognitive and language-specific on the other require special attention (cf. Hauser et al. 2002; Pinker, Jackendoff 2005). Here, only some very preliminary conclusions will be touched on, based on the situation tree (26) and its denominated level (c'). As could be seen, many crucial components of the sentence in (27)—its meaning (the proposition (26c')), lexical and part-of-speech meanings of the words in the sentence, the syntactic relationships between them, and the structure of the syntactic constituent—are not independent components of language in contrast to the opinion of N. Chomsky (Chomsky 2010; Berwick, Chomsky 2016). They are derived from, and induced by, an independently emerging cognitive structure—proposition (26c').

It is reasonable to ask, What are the linguistic components proper in sentence (27) which are independent of this cognitive structure? Here is a very brief and purely declarative answer: the linguistic components proper are lexical names, linguistic expressions of syntactic relationships, and the specificity of their meanings (correlates of role relationships), as well as word order (SVO or some other). As a totality, these are the means that allow the child to express an independently formed proposition (26c') in sound form—that is, in Chomsky's terms, these are the means of externalization of hierarchical expressions by the sensory-motor interface (Berwick, Chomsky 2016: 11–12, 101–102; see also subsection 2.6.2).

Let us now touch upon the initial stage in the evolution of man and human language. Let us ask the question, What factors affect the singularity of language components listed above? According to the evolutionary hypothesis formulated earlier, level (c–c') of the tree (26) determines the thought and language of the first people (early *Homo*). It is then reasonable to assume that the components in question were predetermined by the features of the worldview characteristic of the first tribe ("a 'primitive group' with barely discernible elements of language and culture," according to Sapir (2008: 147)). These tribe-specific representations determined which of the emerged basic concepts were most relevant and must, therefore, receive names, to what extent the content of role relationships must be embodied in the syntactic relationships connecting these names, and which parts of a proposition were the most informative (their names must come first in the word order. If, for example, for a particular tribe the subject (S) was the most informative situation participant, its name opened the word order). If, for example, for a particular tribe the subject (S) was the most informative situation participant, its name opened the word order, etc. This reasoning is consonant with Sapir's thesis that during the initial period of the existence of a tribe the development of its language depended on the development of its culture (Sapir 2008: 148, see subsection 3.3.9).

It may also be assumed that, at a still earlier time, when the first communities of people had representations of the world which did not differ substantionally, their languages did not differ substantionally either. Some reflections of this period may be found in the initial stages of the child's speech. Thus, the syntactic structures of the child's first expressions reflect, quite directly, the role relationships between situation participants. Comparing two-word phrases in the speech of children speaking different languages, researchers point out their inter-language similarity and universal syntax (Slobin 1979: chap. 2; Pinker 1994: 268). There are also grounds to believe that the word order SOV is the most natural, initial word order. For example, it is this word order that Russian speaking children often use in their first expressions, cf.: *Baba kasa varit'* 'Granny kas(h)a boils', *Mama nis'ka citat'* 'Mummy book read' (Tseitlin 2000: 86–87), although they have no auditory exposure to such an order. A little later or even at the same time they begin to use the SVO word order characteristic of the Russian language.

Let us now touch on the issue of gradual *vs.* leap-like language evolution. According to one view, human language appeared "at once," in one leap (Humboldt 1905; Müller 1885; Chomsky 2010: 59). Others believe that language emerged gradually from protolanguage—a system of communicative signs between animal signal systems and human language (cf. Bickerton 1990; Jackendoff 2010). According to Bickerton (2007; 2009; 2010), human language had a precursor: asyntactic protolanguage which combined "words together like beads on a string, A + B + C" (Bickerton 2009: 188) without forming hierarchical syntactic structures (Bickerton 2014: 105 ff).[20] Jackendoff (2010) believes that such a protolanguage itself could go through several evolutionary stages. According to Givón's (1998: 12–13) approach, protolanguage possessed proto-grammar.

My evolutionary hypothesis does not admit the possibility of a lexical protolanguage in a community of anthropoids that evolutionarily precedes the first *Homo*. Their cognitive development stopped at the level of protoconcepts and protosituations, (23b–b'). There are no human notions on this level yet;

---

[20] One can agree with Slobin's (2004) position shared by Bickerton (2014: 189–193) that protolanguage should not be analogized with the language of children at 18–24 months; starting with their first two-word expressions, this language possesses syntax.

2.5. Matrices of concepts, propositions, and language

therefore, words as names of such notions cannot appear. This thought has been reiterated by Chomsky (2010): word-like atoms are a crucial innovation in human evolution (cf. Berwick, Chomsky 2016: 112). Other animals do not have such notions—as, for example, an analysis of gesture 'words' and their combinations learned by a chimpanzee named Nim demonstrated in the Project Nim Chimpsky (cf. Berwick, Chomsky 2016). At the same time, Chomsky does not concede that early *Homo* might have a protolanguage in its initial stages, referring, among other things, to the lack of direct evidence that such languages did exist: "Note that there is no room in this picture for any precursors to language—say a language-like system with only short sentences. [...] and there is of course no direct evidence for such 'protolanguages'" (Chomsky 2010: 72; for more detail, see subsection 2.6.2).

Thus, in accordance with level (c–c′) of the trees in (23) and (26), it may be assumed that the language of the first *Homo* was a **syntactic protolanguage**—human language in its initial evolutionary stage; it possessed (a) an elementary lexicon which consisted of nouns, verbs and, possibly, prepositions and the particle *not*, and (b) a hierarchical syntax of simple two-part sentences with the possible addition of imperative and negative constructions. During the next development cycle of *Homo*, object and motor concepts of the third level of the trees (23) and (26) are decomposed into properties—adjectival and adverbial concepts (see subsections 1.4.2, 3.3.1, and Koshelev 2019: 217–219). Thereby their protolanguage was supplemented by adjectives and adverbs as well as some other lexical and syntactic expressions—pronouns, interrogative constructions, etc.—and entered the next stage in its evolution. In certain respects this protolanguage was like the language of two-year old children (for a discussion, see Bickerton 2014: 189–193). The stadial language evolution hypothesis (cf. the description of the four stages in the development of ABSL in subsection 3.2.7) is an alternative to Chomsky's hypothesis about a mutation which led to the emergence of human language in a single leap; cf.: "the generative procedure emerged suddenly as the result of a minor mutation" (Berwick, Chomsky 2016: 70; see also Chomsky 2010, and, for more detail, subsection 2.6.2).

2.5.6. Rapid growth of the child's lexicon. As Hauser et al. (2002: 1576) observe, "the rate at which children build the lexicon is so massively different from non-human primates that one must entertain the possibility of an independently evolved mechanism." This leads them to a conclusion that "human children may use domain-general mechanisms to acquire and recall words"

(Hauser et al. 2002). This is contested by Pinker and Jackendoff (2005: 215) who argue: "But words are not just names for things [...] They also are marked for a syntactic category (verb, preposition, and so on), for obligatory grammatically encoded arguments (agent, theme, path, and so on)…"

Recourse to situation development trees of the type shown in (23) allows for claiming that the speed of lexicon acquisition is determined by the speed of growth of their third level (c–c'), on which many nodes at once receive their names—word forms. Two kinds of human mechanisms merge inseparably in this process: language-specific (giving names to tree nodes and forming syntactic relationships between names) and general-cognitive (forming basic lexical and grammatical meanings).

Now, using the concept of protolanguage as defined above, my approach to human thought and language may be contrasted with those of Aristotle and Chomsky.

2.6. Aristotle and Chomsky on thought and language

2.6.1. Aristotle's approach. Aristotle treats language as an instrument of thought (a universal component, because humans think alike):

> No real distinction, such as some people pro-pose, exists between arguments used against the word and those used against the thought; for it is absurd to suppose that some arguments are used against the word and others against the thought, and not the same in both cases (Aristotle 1962: 53).

According to Aristotle, only lexical polysemy may be the source of divergence between the thought and the word; therefore, it requires special attention. Contrasting different languages, Aristotle comes to the following conclusion:

> As writing, so also is speech not the same for all races of men. But the mental affections themselves, of which these words are primarily signs, are the same for the whole of mankind, as are also the objects of which those affections are representations or likenesses, images, copies (Ibid.: 115).

Thus, according to Aristotle, (a) sentence structure in language corresponds to (b) the structure of human thought and (c) the structure of facts in the phenomenal world. To my thinking, this implies the correspondence between thought and reality because, to Aristotle, language is just a sound form that preserves the structure of the thought and does not have any content

2.6. Aristotle and Chomsky on thought and language

of its own. An expert on ancient teachings about language, Perelmutter (1980) characterized Aristotle's view of language as follows:

> The internal semantic structure of all languages is, according to Aristotle, the same; at the same time, this structure contains nothing or almost nothing language-specific, it is fully adequate [...] to the structure of reality [...]. Aristotle assumes that languages differ only in the sounding of their words, that the internal semantic structure of all languages is the same, that, by and large, this structure exactly matches external reality and our representation of it [...]. In his view, linguistic relations necessarily must reflect the relationships in external reality. Exploring relationships between phenomena, Aristotle always pays attention to relationships between the names of these phenomena; he often starts with the nature of relationships between names to discover the nature of real relationships between phenomena (p. 164; 166; see also Zubkova 2015: 101–102).

Aristotle's approach may be visually illustrated by figure 7. In this figure, all three levels are separated and correlated: sentence structure, (a), thought structure (proposition (b)), and part of reality (the image of a running boy, (c)). From my line of reasoning it follows that, firstly, the sentence designates a proposition and, basically, does not possess its own content apart from the content of the proposition; secondly, the part of reality, (c), is structurally isomorphic to the proposition, (b).

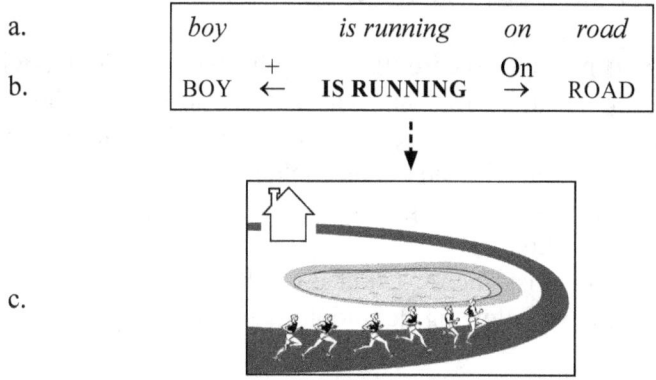

Fig. 7. Mutual correlation of the sentence, (a), the proposition designated by this sentence, (b), and the image of a part of reality, (c), which corresponds to the proposition

However, it also follows that the structure of the image (c) does not have an independent status. It is induced by the structure of the propositional prototype, composed of the prototypical arguments of the proposition—the concepts BOY, IS RUNNING, and ROAD. Strictly speaking, only the prototypical proposition (b) corresponds to the image. As for the functions of the proposition and its arguments, they are brought into the image by the speaker based on its structural similarity to the prototype; that is, they are attributed to the image hypothetically (for a discussion of reference, see subsection 1.4.6).

It must be pointed out that the above correspondences are preserved only for the basic meanings of linguistic expressions which meet the requirement of semantic compositionality: the meaning of a linguistic expression is a function of the meanings of its parts and the manner of their syntactic combination (Weinreich 1966; Partee 1984; Paducheva 2004). This principle does not apply to derived (metaphorical and metonymical) meanings because, in order to 'compute' these meanings, one must know or observe their referents. This is clearly revealed in children's reactions to such expressions: "Especially often children are critical of expressions in which motion verbs are used […] in their derived meanings: '*The milk is overrunning. Milk cannot overrun, for IT DOESN'T HAVE LEGS!*'; '*The road is running down the hill. Why, does it have LEGS?*'" (Tseitlin 2000: 199–201). A child cannot 'compute' the meanings of such expressions because the verbs in them are used not in their basic but in their derived meanings and the referents of these metaphors and metonymies are unknown to the child.

2.6.2. Chomsky's approach. According to N. Chomsky and R. Berwick (2016), language—or, rather, Internal language—is an instrument of thought, a mental system, while its sound form, on which externalization of mental objects depends, is practically devoid of any content. Moreover, Chomsky's theory covers only the subset of linguistic expressions which satisfy the principle of compositionality.

Leaning on his Minimalist Theory, Chomsky (Chomsky 2010; Berwick, Chomsky 2016) gives the following definition of Internal language, or its basic feature:

(28) a language is a finite computational system yielding an infinity of expressions, each of which has a definite interpretation in semantic-pragmatic and sensorimotor systems (informally, thought and sound) (Berwick, Chomsky 2016: 1).

The two crucial components of language (as a computational system) are (a) a set of "word-like atoms" (lexicon) and (b) a recursive generative

2.6. Aristotle and Chomsky on thought and language

procedure which generates structured expressions from these atoms (Berwick, Chomsky 2016: 104). Therefore, to explain language evolution, three problems must be solved, according to Chomsky: (1) sorting out the word-like atoms (of which, Chomsky thinks, there are 30 to 50 thousand), (2) understanding how the generative procedure works, and (3) defining the two interfaces of mental objects with language-external systems: the system of thought which enables the interpretation and understanding of expressions built by the generative procedure on the one hand and the sensorimotor system which externalizes these expressions in sound form on the other (Chomsky 2010: 66, 69).

Chomsky goes on to acknowledge that solving these tasks turns out to be more daunting than it first appears. As a matter of fact, so far only an explanation of the generative procedure has been offered by reducing recursion to the two-argument operation Merge, which builds new hierarchically structured expressions from word-like atoms (Berwick, Chomsky 2016: 10). As for the other two problems – the origin of word-like atoms and the operation of two interfaces—they remain yet to be solved. The situation does not seem to have changed (cf. Chomsky 2010: 62).

All in all, Berwick and Chomsky (2016: 87) briefly reiterate:

> [Let us just summarize briefly] what seems to be the current best guess about the unity and diversity of language and thought. In some completely unknown way, our ancestors developed human concepts. At some time in the very recent past, apparently some time before 80,000 years ago if we can judge from associated symbolic proxies, individuals in a small group of hominids in East Africa underwent a minor biological change that provided the operation Merge—an operation that takes human concepts as computational atoms and yields structured expressions that, systematically interpreted by the conceptual system, provide a rich language of thought [...] At some later stage, the internal language of thought was connected to the sensorimotor system.

Contrasting Chomsky's approach with ours, it is easy to see that all components of the Internal language (28) have correlates in the protolanguage which emerges on the third level of development trees (23)/(26). Indeed, the array of word-like atoms (lexicon) is determined by the matrix of basic (object and motor) concepts; the operation Merge correlates with the operation of assembly of biconcepts from concepts and propositions from biconcepts; hierarchically structured expressions correlate with propositions of the type shown in (26c); they are externalized by sentences of the type shown in (27), and their semantic-pragmatic interpretation consists in relating their predicative function with the corresponding part of a functional representation of reality, for it is this relationship that ensures a context-dependent comprehension of a proposition. Finally, the computational system correlates with the above introduced thought procedure which composes—from concepts, biconcepts, and role relationships—propositions extended over the interval micro-t, similar to dynamic 3D puzzles (short videoclips).

Thus, it is clear that Chomsky's model of thought and language, (28), is fully isomorphic to my model. The fact that these models were developed by using totally different approaches such an isomorphism seems to confirm (in general) the adequacy of Chomsky's earlier model and the adequacy (in certain details) of my model.[21]

Both approaches also share, firstly, the conclusion that word-like atoms and the operation Merge (Berwick, Chomsky 2016: 111–112, 120–121) (object and motor concepts and the operations of merging concepts into biconcepts, and biconcepts into propositions) were the main innovations in human evolution, secondly, the provision that objects external to language do not exist outside human consciousness because they contain components of the human mind (functions—see subsection 1.4.6 in chapter 1) and, thirdly, that propositions—just like expressions—have a hierarchical structure and are indifferent to linear order (Ibid.: 8–10, 114–120). Unlike expressions, however, propositions may contain elements with names.

Let us now list the differences between the models.

1. As was demonstrated above, all the listed components of my model emerge in the process of human evolution. Thereby, in the framework considered here, the problems (1)–(3) pointed out by Chomsky, receive their primary solution.

2. Chomsky sees the Internal language, (28), as a generative computational system which forms expressions based on its internal principles without any external input (Ibid.: 56, 91). My model of thought and language is not a generative one. To the contrary, the thought procedure in this model forms propositions that meet the demand from the functional representation of the world (see subsection 2.5.3). Moreover, in accordance with its functions (see above, and subsection 3.2.4), this model is closely associated with the wide scope of human activities.

---

[21] Clearly, the model offered here is the simplest case of the general model. However, it allows us to tell a lot about this model (see In lieu of a foreword, section 1).

3. Protolanguage (the initial stage of human language) appears in the first *Homo*, that is, over 2 million years ago. At the same time, the first *Homo* develop first human concepts, propositions, and sentences which express them (externalizations)—see section 2.5 on the evolutionary hypothesis.

To emphasize: some concepts receive lexical names almost at once and become words. Moreover, according to this theory, the number of atom-like elements is not 30–50 thousand as Chomsky proposes, it is larger at least by an order of magnitude. Finally, being the arguments of role relationships, concepts acquire their roles ('syntactic' properties) at once.

Chomsky stresses that word-like atoms are syntactic objects. However, if these atoms (or some of them) appeared, as he claims, before the operation Merge,[22] it remains unclear how they acquired syntactic properties, that is, how they became syntactic objects.

4. All these innovations appear as a result of the next cycle of development, from protoconcepts and protosituations intrinsic to higher anthropoids, and not as a result of a mutation. Chomsky's saltationism—non-human animals do not have language, while humans do—makes unexplainable the presence, acknowledged by Chomsky, of developed thought in other animals (Berwick, Chomsky 2016: 139–140). According to this view, human thinking appears to be as detached from animal thinking as language is from animal communication systems. By contrast, the discrete gradualness of my model demonstrates the presence in higher animals of initial forms of hierarchical thought—protoconcepts and protosituations, early correlates of concepts and propositions. Thereby the continuity of human evolution is preserved (cf. for example Greenfield 1991: 549–550). Accordingly, in the early stages of a child's development, practical thinking emerges prior to language and develops independently of it. This conclusion is close to Vygotsky's (1986) thesis that, initially, practical thinking and speech develop in children independently.

5. Many vocal designations of propositions appear simultaneously with the appearance of propositions and not at a later stage, like Chomsky's sensorimotor system.

6. As the first *Homo* continued to evolve, the thought and speech model became more complicated with every stage until it fully acquired all its properties in *Homo sapiens sapiens*.

---

[22] "It's easy to speculate that at least some of these elements existed prior to Merge, since otherwise there's nothing for Merge to work…" (Berwick, Chomsky 2016: 149), see also Bolhuis et al. 2014.

7. In the definition of the internal language, (28), the sensorimotor component plays a secondary role, cf.: "These facts at once suggest that language evolved as an instrument of internal thought, with externalization a secondary process" (Berwick, Chomsky 2016: 74). And this is quite understandable because what Chomsky calls 'internal language' are basic structures of thought. The issue of the function of language as an instrument of thought is resolved in the same way:

> …language evolved for thought and interpretation: it is fundamentally a system of meaning. Aristotle's classic dictum that language is sound with meaning should be reversed. Language is meaning with sound (or some other externalization, or none) […] Externalization at the sensorimotor level, then, is an ancillary process, reflecting properties of the sensory modality used, with different arrangements for speech and sign (Ibid.: 101).

By means of externalization, language can also be used for the purpose of communication. But, according to Chomsky, this is by no means its main function. In the context of the above line of reasoning, these issues are resolved in an essentially different way. I adhere to the traditional understanding of language as an 'external' tool, that is, a means of voicing thoughts, not so much for the purpose of communication as for the unification and development of mental representations of reality by the speakers (see subsection 2.6.3). And from this point of view, which separates language and thought, the sensorimotor interface is, contrary to, the main rather than the secondary mechanism. By virtue of this, Aristotle's classic dictum appears to be quite adequate.

2.6.3. On the purpose of language. Suppose the thought procedure performs its function: it forms propositions in the human mind which correspond to a given predicative function. Let us ask, What is the point of their externalization? To many, the answer would be self-evident: for the purpose of communication. In my opinion, however, language (protolanguage) has a more needful task: the unification of a child's private basic concepts, their convergence with adult basic concepts. It is important to understand that, in the absence of language, the basic concepts of children with different experience may differ considerably. Although all such concepts are based on visual (perceptual) images of the world, the degree of differentiation of these images (and their functions, respectively) is not preset—compare, for example, the different degrees of concretization of a prototypical basic concept and its specific concepts.

2.6. Aristotle and Chomsky on thought and language

Consider another example. In the English language the trivial action *jump* is differentiated into 5 classes of jumps by basic concepts: HOP, JUMP, SKIP, BOUNCE, LEAP (see figure 8). In Russian, this action is defined by one basic concept PRYGAT' 'JUMP-Imp' and its specific concept SKAKAT' 'SKIP-Imp'. Thus, the variety of jumps receives one unified taxonomy in the representation of the perceptual world by speakers of English and another, essentially different, taxonomy in the Russian language.

Fig. 8. The English taxonomy of jumps—*hop, jump, skip, bounce, leap* (adapted from Longman 2009: 949)—essentially differs from the Russian one: *prygat', skakat'*

This is also true of role relationships—compare, for example, the different systems of spatial relationships in different languages, see Pinker 2007: 141–147; Boroditsky 2009.

Famous neurologist H. Jerison wrote:

We model "reality" linguistically just as we model it visually or tactilely. Languages may be media for communication because different human brains construct essentially the same "reality." And we can share that reality because it is already shared in the linguistic structures we have in common and in the linguistic factors that are part of our fundamental image of the real world. Speech and reading, in this sense, provide a genuine shared consciousness for members of the human species, given a common cultural background. [...] the origins of language were as likely in the pressures to create a better model of a real world, that is, in perceptual and cognitive development, as in the pressures toward being able to communicate with one's fellows (Jerison 1973: 430, 432).

Note that Jerison connects the creation of a better model of the world only with the development of perception and imagery (Ibid.: 410), since his book is about the evolution of the perceptual world. In my terminology, it is basic concepts—cognitive units which have, along with the prototypical component, the functional component. Basic concepts form a unified perceptual model of the tribe's world. The names of basic concepts are called sensory words (Koshelev 2019: 58).

The second purpose of language, which is no less important, is to support and develop the tribe's functional representation of the world (Koshelev 2017: 427). This representation is made up of functional concepts—cognitive units which are more abstract than basic concepts and which have a function but no visible (perceptual) prototype: SORNJAK 'WEED', XIŜNIK 'PREDATOR', DRAČUN 'BRAWLER', GLUPYJ 'STUPID', KRASIVYJ 'BEAUTIFUL', VOSPITIVAET 'BRINGS UP', UPRAVLJAET 'RULES / MANAGES', RABOTAET 'WORKS', and the like. The abstract character of such functions is manifested in the fact that they can be carried by objects of very different shapes. For example, plants categorized as weeds do not share any common visual features. This is also true of objects described as beautiful. A person can be beautiful, as can a house, a basketball throw. The names of functional concepts constitute the functional lexicon of a language.

The 'natural' manifestation of the function of a basic concept is its prototype—the 'hook' on which this function 'hangs' in the memory of a native speaker. A functional concept (that is, function) does not have such a manifestation. Instead, a manifestation, the 'hook' that holds it in semantic memory, is a linguistic label—the word which names this function. A name allows the native speaker to crystallize and unify the function. And without a name it cannot validly exist.[23] Therefore, without a functional lexis humans would not be able to develop a unified functional representation of the world.

Finally, there is another important function of language: its involvement in the development of new, professional kinds of activities, that is, the

---

[23] Cf. also notions of a "week" (Jackendoff 1996), "number" (Wiese 2003), "justice of the peace," "treasurer" and others (Pinker, Jackendoff 2005).

2.6. Aristotle and Chomsky on thought and language

progress of the tribe. As is demonstrated in subsections 3.2.4–3.2.6 in chapter 3, such progress is impossible without the involvement of language.

Let us sum up our arguments. Language is instrumental in the development and unification of a tribe's mental representation of the world (see subsection 3.2.4, fig. 1b)—a basis for mutual understanding among the members of an ethnogroup. This is also true about professional groups and their representations.

> **Note.** Let us touch on the composition of a native speaker's mental representation. Firstly, it includes denominated concepts (basic and functional) that are common to native speaker's. Secondly, personal mental representations include concepts without names, both object and motor. These are various specific kinds of objects and actions generated by a person's experience: specific kinds of chairs, sofas, tables, cups, clocks, houses, facial expressions, human gestures, movements, etc. Having no names, they remain personal and differ from speaker to speaker. Note that their number, in comparison with named concepts (words), is larger at least by an order of magnitude, cf. subsection 2.3.11 and 2.4.7. It is clear that, out of this variety of concepts only those that are most important for the group receive names (and, therefore, become generally valid). Thereby a tribal mental representation becomes ethno-specific, reflecting the "folk spirit," according to Potebnia, or the "spiritual power of the nation," according to W. von Humboldt, see the quote from A. A. Potebnia and W. von Humboldt in subsection 2.6.4. It follows from the above that a set of **nameless** word-like atoms, postulated by Chomsky as inherent in all native speakers (cf. subsection 2.6.2), does not exist. Instead, each tribe has its own set of **notional words** (sensory and functional)—named (basic and functional) concepts from which "structured expressions" of a given language are generated.

Further, along with lexis, grammar plays an important role in the formation and development of mental representations of the ethnogroup; regarding some of its features (word order, meanings of syntactic relationships, etc.) it is also ethno-specific (cf. subsection 3.3.9). Thanks to the speech expressions the child hears from the people around him, his representation of the world is supplemented by more complex, compositional cognitive units which describe situations and other cognitive structures (Bloom 1994; Pinker, Jackendoff 2005; Boroditsky 2000; 2009; Corballis 2017; 2019). First and foremost, these structures are shaped by folklore—fairy tales, riddles, folk legends, songs, proverbs and sayings, fables, and so forth. In the course of repeated exposer to folk tales the child's mental representation of the world is supplemented by folk stereotyped reasoning, value criteria, examples of heroic or, conversely, shameful conduct, etc. Thereby an ethnic specificity becomes more complete in the child's representation of the world, develops their "folk spirit," in the terminology of Potebnia.

In the same vein, the child is influenced by the moralistic discourse which reflects the domestic culture of the child's immediate environment: speech formulae for rules of conduct, prohibitions and prescriptions, encouragement and punishment, etc. For example, if a boy wants to cross the street where there is no crossing, his American father will probably say: *Son, this is **unlawful***, while his Russian father might say: *Son, this is **dangerous***.

> **Note**. Let us touch on the linguistic relativity hypothesis (cf. Pinker 2007: 124–148; Boroditsky 2009; Gleitman and Papafragou 2012). It is reasonable to assume that, in the sphere of everyday life, a person's native language affects his thought (his system of concepts and common logic of reasoning). However, we should not forget about the initial formative influence that the ethnicity specific representation of the world and folk culture have on language (cf. subsections 3.1.2 and 3.3.9 in chapter 3). Because of this, language should not be treated as a separate system independent of the ethnic group in which it originated. The above given line of reasoning allows us to claim that the influence of language on thought is induced by the anticipatory effect that folk representations of the world and folk culture have on language.

Now let us return to the communicative functions of language. I agree with R. Jackendoff, I. A. Mel'čuk (Jackendoff 2007: 69–70; Mel'čuk 2016: 1–2) and scores of other researchers who think that this function is more important than that of language as an instrument of thought. As a matter of fact, because of the ever-increasing complexity of world representations and the growing diversity of human actions, to predict and interpret human behavior becomes much harder than to predict and interpret other animals' behavior. For example, a dog or cat eats to satisfy hunger and runs to move quickly from one place to another (these are basic actions). Humans, however, apart from basic actions can also perform derived actions which have the same shape but a different function: eating even when full so as not to offend the hostess or, to be good company, taking a bite after a shot, testing a dish, etc. An athlete may run not because the main goal is 'to move to a different place' but to exercise, a PE teacher to show the students the running technique, and a ballerina to express by means of a run some aesthetic idea or a feeling.[24] A person "may smile, and smile, and be a villain" (Hamlet), while a beast cannot fawn wishing to bite. Therefore, without linguistic communication members of a community would simply not understand each other's actions and their goals.

Finally, language also considerably contributes to thinking, but not so much to the organization of the process of thinking as to the formation of a set of mental concepts. As was demonstrated above, it is because of language that humans are able to form a universal set of elementary mental units—the denominated basic (object and motor) and functional concepts that make up mental structures. About other functions of language see, for example, (Zubkova 2016: 563–568).

2.6.4. Why are there languages, and so many of them? In conclusion, let us consider two questions made by Chomsky to be most important: "First, why are there any languages at all, evidently unique to the human lineage […]? Second, why are there so many languages?" (Berwick, Chomsky 2016: 53, 84). An answer to the first question directly follows from the arguments given above: language is a necessary component, firstly, of coordinated cognitive development of and interactions among members of a ethnogroup, and, secondly, of the ethnogroup's progress. Without language, further evolution of the early *Homo* would be impossible. It is also clear why only humans have language: if a species lacks a third stage of development and the range of concepts and propositions generated at this stage this obviously prevents the emergence of language (lexical protolanguage). Yet the presence of such a protolanguage itself decides little. Emergence, in the case of early *Homo*, of the third and subsequent evolutionary stages was accompanied by the synchronous and **interconnected** development of a whole complex of subsystems: the cognitive system, the systems of protolanguage and hierarchic attention, the anatomical system (speech apparatus, auditory analyzer, the wrist, upright posture, etc.), the systems of brain substrates, kinds of activity, and so forth, which **support one another** (cf. Givón 1998). For all that, not

---

[24] In the case of humans, an action is represented by a motor concept, i.e. a dual system "Action's Shape ← its Function" whose components are independent and may change. In the case of other animals, I believe, an action is represented by a syncretic protoconcept in which the shape and its main function are merged; therefore, such changes are not possible.

only protolanguage but the entire complex of neoformations did not give early *Homo* a decisive advantage—all their species are now extinct. Only *Homo sapiens sapiens* turned out to be successful. Thanks to the complex of neoformations developed at this stage, the progress of activities (extension of the kinds of activities—see section 3.2, chapter 3) allowed this species to gradually populate the entire planet and successfully master practically **all its niches**, becoming the dominant species everywhere.

In this context, the following question is often raised: What is the evolutionary advantage of human language? Within the framework of our research logic, it would not be quite correct to discuss evolutionary advantages given to humans by a single subsystem of the above-mentioned complex, be it thought, language, or anatomy. One can speak only about the specific contribution made by this subsystem to the overall activity of an ethnogroup (see subsection 3.2.4).

An answer to the second question (why are there so many languages?) also follows from the above argumentation. As could be seen, the key features of a language take shape, mostly, during the initial period of the ethnogroup's evolution and express the specificity of its representations of external reality. Therefore, the great variety of languages reflects the initial diversity of ethnic groups. This conclusion agrees with Sapir's (2008: 147) position discussed in chapter 3, subsections 3.1.2 and 3.3.9, and Potebnia's (1999) observation (with reference to Humboldt[25]) that "the variety of structures of languages appears to depend on features of the folk spirit and should be explained by them" (p. 35).

According to Sapir (2008: 148), this great variety later expands under the influence of the progress of the ethnic group—the civilization component of its culture (see subsection 3.3.9 To the obvious objection, why in two

---

[25] "Müssen wir als das reale Erklärungsprinzip und als den wahren Bestimmungsgrund der Sprachverschiedenheit die geistige Kraft der Nationen ansehen" (Humboldt 1848: 38). ("...should we consider the spiritual power of nations as the real principle explaining variety of languages, as true foundation defining this variety..."; translation S. Zhigalkin.) Cf., a century earlier, in 1746, É. B. de Condillac wrote: "§143 Just as the government influences the character of nations, so the character of nations influences that of languages. [...] Thus everything confirms that the language of each nation expresses the character of the people who speak it. [...] This character must form the character of the language by multiplying the turns of phrase that express the prevailing taste of a nation" (Condillac 2001: 184, 188).

neighboring African villages that appear quite similar in their lifestyle and level of civilization the languages may be absolutely different, the answer is as follows. Their distant ancestors' worldviews were essentially different, which resulted in the difference between their languages. And the convergence of their worldviews, which came later, was unable to cause a change in the initially established structural features of their languages (word order, etc.). Still, there is an objection to this, too: why, then, did the English language, originally strictly inflectional and with free word order, turn, over a thousand years, into a language with a fixed word order and few inflections? (Pinker 1994: 235) My answer is as follows: because, over this thousand years, English civilization progressed immensely, and it was this progress that resulted in such astonishing changes in language (cf. subsections 3.2.7 and 3.3.9).

2.7. Appendix. Does a child's language affect his formation of concepts?
(supplement to subsection 2.3.6)

A child begins to speak at roughly at 12 months. This naturally poses a question, Are word meanings formed independently, or is this process affected by language?

There are some experimental data on the more general issue of how the child's language affects the formation of concepts. In a series of experiments with children between 13–16 months, Kol'tsova and Antakova-Fomina studied the factors that accelerated the development of speech (Kol'tsova 1967: 100–106). Briefly, their results were as follows:

(1) Intensified verbal communication with children practically did not have any noticeable stimulating effect on the development of their speech.
(2) Activization of motility (the children were encouraged to engage in motor activity, they could crawl freely, walk over a large area of the floor, etc.) **almost doubled the speed** of growth of the range of vocal reactions.
(3) Stimulation of fine motor skills—subtle fingers movement training (assembling pyramids, fingering beads, stringing buttons on a wire, and the like)—**increased** the intensity of vocal reaction development **several times** compared to activization of motility.

An indirect inference from the first experiment is that intensification of verbal communication does not lead to the formation of new lexical meanings or their correlates. Otherwise, the development of children's verbal activity as a result of extended verbal communication would follow. As the other two experiments demonstrated, the development of general motility and, specifically, fine motor skills, by contrast, stimulates (both directly and indirectly) the formation of new concepts and, consequently, the development of verbal activity. These conclusions are supported by the well-known fact that "the child begins to give names first of all to the objects he handles (cup, spoon, doll, etc.) and the parts of these objects which he touches more often" (Kol'tsova 1973: 131 [translation A. Kravchenko]).

Let us note in connection with this that one of the important objectives of cognitive linguistics is to explain how children acquire so-called relational terms—words like *bežit* 'is running', *idët* 'is walking', *v* 'in', *na* 'on', and others which refer to the participants of dynamic situations and the relationships between them. In this context, the central thesis of some contemporary research about the primacy of the formation of initial (pre-linguistic) components of situations becomes crucial (Gentner, Boroditsky 2001; Golinkoff et al. 2002; Gentner, Bowerman 2009; Pruden et al. 2013). As was noted above, without their advanced appearance in the child's long-term memory, acquisition of relation words which describe these situations (first of all, verbs and prepositions) would not be possible. Later, as the child acquires a relational lexis, primary conceptual components are lexicalized by children in different ways depending on the specific features of their mother tongue (Jackendoff 1983; Mandler 1992; 2004; Hespos, Spelke 2004).

Clearly, under the influence of linguistic differences, children may focus on various such components (Pruden et al. 2008: 163; Göksun et al. 2017: 34). However, they **do not lose the ability** to perceive and classify fundamental components not expressed lexically in their language (Munnich et al. 2001; Norbury et al. 2008). In other words, according to Göksun et al. (2017: 38), the child's sensitivity to fundamental constructions is universal in two respects: (1) children detect these constructions (non-linguistic situation components) regardless of the linguistic environment in which they are brought up, and (2) infants notice fine-grained distinctions between events even though they are not codified in their mother tongue (Hespos, Spelke 2004; Göksun et al. 2008).

Let us now consider a more specific hypothesis. Throughout this book (see also chapter 3) I have tried to demonstrate that a new word—the name of a thing, action, or property—is acquired by the human child only when **there is already**, in long-term memory, a primary concept close to the

2.7. Appendix. Does a child's language affect his formation of concepts?

meaning of this word, namely, a somewhat independent mental representation of the class of similar things, concrete actions, or properties. Merging with this concept-meaning (the relationship of merging "name ← meaning"), the name becomes a word. Therefore, the main question is whether, when the child observes referential uses of an unfamiliar word by others, such uses can prompt the formation of this word's meaning. The answer, which will be substantiated below, is this: if the correlate of the new word's meaning is not yet formed in the child's long-term memory, its formation cannot begin based solely on observed referential uses of the word (its sound form) by others. However, if the child already has some primary correlate of the concept-meaning, referential uses of the word accelerate its formation. Thereby acquisition of this word by the child is also accelerated. In particular, language can **accelerate the formation** of protosituations which are already taking shape that is, can single out the participants (protoconcepts) in the situation, but it **cannot initiate their emergence** (the beginning of differentiation of protoconcepts).

This hypothesis is supported by some experimental data. As some research projects have shown, infants display a close connection between naming and categorization not only at 12 months, but also at 6 and even 4 months (Xu 2002; Waxman, Braun 2005; Fulkerson, Waxman 2007; Waxman 2008). More specifically, if the toys an infant is handling are given names at the same time, object categorization (what I call 'formation of object-motor protoconcepts') goes faster.[26] Building on this fact, some researchers (S. Waxman, F. Xu) began to speak of a decisive role of speech development in the cognitive development of children: "words serve as *invitations* to form categories" (Waxman 2008: 103; original emphasis). However, some data attest to the independent, non-linguistic nature of child categorization. Arguing against the decisive role of names, Pinker cites some experimental work (Hauser 2000; Santos et al. 2002) done on monkeys (rhesus macaques) which established that 1 year old monkeys form categorical classes: "The monkeys were surprised when, after a carrot and a squash took turns emerging from behind the screen, only one or the other was there when the screen was

---

[26] Infants showed faster categorization even in the case when nonce words (sound complexes devoid of meaning) were used to name objects. By contrast, they failed when both objects were named by the word *toy*, or by two different sounds of the same pitch, or by two different emotionally colored (but non-verbal) exclamations (Waxman 2008; Xu 2007: 403).

removed—just as twelve-month-olds, and you and I, would be surprised. But monkeys, of course, don't know a word of English" (Pinker 2007: 137).[27]

Waxman (2008) demonstrated that the word *purple* cannot promote the formation of a category based on the color the word denotes in the same way that a concrete noun promotes the formation of a category based on the shape it denotes. Neither at 12 nor at 14 months could infants form classes of purple objects, as was discovered in the same series of experiments. And this is despite the fact that, while discerning objects, infants of 12 months paid attention to purple objects when they heard the adjective *purple* and used color distinctions (Wilcox 1999: 157).

This fact allows us to make the following two assumptions. First, in the mental representations that infants have at this age, Color is not yet differentiated from the syncretic mix of an object's properties; therefore, there can be no conceptualization of specific colors. Second, in such conditions (without the primary strictly cognitive differentiation), lexical items—adjectives perceived by the infant—cannot prompt the infant to single out respective properties and begin to form a new (adjectival) category (see subsection 3.3.4). The perceived words can only speed up differentiation of those properties whose isolation has already begun as a consequence of the infant's strictly cognitive development.

From what has been said above it follows in particular that, at 12 months, language does not take any substantial part in the formation of protosituations. Therefore it may be assumed, with certain reservations, that protosituations are the child's **universal** mental representations.

2.8. Conclusion

2.8.1. On the indecomposability of concepts into elementary concepts.
The above discussion clarifies the way humans form concepts and the relationships and propositions which connect them. Firstly, concepts are not innate; their actualization depends only on the child's accumulated experience. They emerge from the child's pre-conceptual mental representations in the course of their development by stages. For example, the object concepts ČELOVEK 'PERSON', BEŽIT 'IS RUNNING', DOROGA 'ROAD' and the role

---

[27] And in a later article (Ferry et al. 2010: 473), Waxman agreed with the proposition that children formed primary categories independent of the acquisition of their names.

2.8. Conclusion

relationships which connect them appear at an early age as a result of development of mental representations of whole locomotive situations. Language is practically not involved in this process.

It also may be concluded that the child's culture-specific concepts appear in a similar way, although much later. The concept CARBURETTOR is formed by decomposing a variety of automotive situations in which it participates; TROMBONE is the result of the decomposition of a variety of music situations in which it participates. Language plays a secondary part in this process; it accelerates but does not determine the formation of concepts.

Secondly, the emerging concepts possess complex structure. On the one hand, they all contain an observable (perceptual) and a non-observable (functional) component, which are merged together at the initial stages of the child's development. On the other hand, these concepts are decomposed into more fragmentary components: properties and parts that belong to successive levels in the development of basic concepts (see subsections 1.3.5 and 1.4.2). They are not, however, decomposable into universal semantic primes—more elementary concepts of **the same level** of the concept development tree. This was convincingly demonstrated above: whole situations do not reduce to simpler situations, protoconcepts to simpler concepts, or concepts to simpler concepts.

Insisting that "the meaning of a word can and must be described in terms of simpler meanings—that is, decomposed," Mel'čuk (2016: 88) appeals to similarities in the physical world, rightly observing that molecules are decomposed into atoms, atoms into elementary particles, etc. (see subsection 2.1.1). But let us note that **molecules are not decomposed into simpler molecules**. They are decomposed into atoms—**more fragmentary components** (parts of molecules). Similarly, atoms are decomposed not into simpler atoms but into elementary particles as parts of atoms.

Therefore, using our results and the above analogy, it may be claimed, contrary to the proposals of A. Wierzbicka, I. Mel'čuk, and others (see subsection 2.1.1), that lexical meanings (basic concepts) are not decomposed into semantic primes (elementary basic components). It is not concepts that are decomposed into semantic primes but their approximations, rough correlates given in definitions. For example, the widely used definition of the Russian word *kreslo* 'armchair' is 'chair with armrests' (see (34b) in chapter 1). Thus it appears that this meaning is decomposed into two simpler meanings: 'chair' and 'armrests'. However, as was demonstrated in subsection 1.5.1, the definition in question is not adequate. It gives a very rough correlate of the exact meaning (basic concept KRESLO 'ARMCHAIR' (35)), thus making decomposition possible. For rigorous definitions of the meanings of the Russian words *stul* 'chair' and *kreslo* 'armchair' such a decomposition is wrong because the psycho-physical state of a person sitting in an armchair is not composed of the holistic state of the person sitting in a chair and the state of his arms (elbows) supported by the armrests (see also subsection 1.5.1 for an analysis of the meanings of the English words *chair* and *armchair*).

One could raise an objection: why, then, is the holistic state 'armchair' (state of a person sitting in an armchair) decomposed into its parts—specific states 'seat', 'back', 'armrests', and 'legs'? The fact is that these specific states together with their relationships emerged directly from the state 'armchair' as a result of decomposition of its neurobiological code into specific codes and relationships between them. Therefore they are in exact "alignment" with one another. And if the state 'armchair' is decomposed into 'chair' + armrests', the state 'chair' does not emerge from the state 'armchair' it is not a part of it. It emerges independently and, as a whole, is not embedded in 'armchair'. The integrity of a situation and its indecomposability into elementary situations has a similar explanation, regardless of the fact that the situation is decomposed into separate participants and the relationships between them.

Interpretations are not exact definitions;[28] they play a different role. Using interpretation as an informative point of entry, one can quickly find in his memory the exact concept (a cell with the corresponding concept in the conceptual matrix) and thereby understand it. For example, upon reading an interpretation of the word *kreslo* 'armchair'—'chair with armrests'—a native speaker at once imagines a prototypical chair, adds to it prototypical armrests, and gets the prototype of an armchair—a point of entry to the cell <ARMCHAIR>. Once there, he spontaneously moves to the function of the armchair and its other characteristic features. Thus, the native speaker instantly understands the exact meaning of the word *kreslo* 'armchair' (see (35), chapter 1) and receives the (false) impression that the interpretation is exact. More details on the status of interpretation are given in subsection 1.5.1; an exception from the stated position is given and explained as well: an example of an accurate interpretation of the English word *armchair*.

---

[28] This agrees with Chomsky's (1987) position that dictionary definitions are far from being descriptions of lexical meanings. Pinker (2007) holds that dictionary definitions may be incomplete; unlike such definitions, semantic representations of lexical meanings (conceptual structures in the language of thought) must be more explicit.

2.8. Conclusion

To conclude, concept **decomposition** and concept **interpretation** must be strictly distinguished.

2.8.2. Leaps in the child's cognitive development. Let us demonstrate that the child develops by leaps—genetically conditioned transformations. According to the traditional view, also shared by Chomsky (Berwick, Chomsky 2016: 120), one of the species-specific features of humans is the presence of concepts and thought which operates on these concepts. The analysis offered in this book is pursuant with this position. One cannot build assertions from the protoconcepts MAN-IS RUNNING, TREE-STANDS, and the like (see subsection 2.3.5), because every protoconcept is already a syncretic proto-assertion. At the same time, using human concepts such as PERSON, TREE, IS RUNNING, STANDS, children are able to form various assertions (propositions): PERSON ←+ IS RUNNING, PERSON ←+ STANDS, TREE ←+ STANDS, and so forth.

In accordance with section 2.4, concepts are **components of decomposed** protoconcepts, i.e. elementary units of a lower (in terms of the degree of fragmentation) level of representation of the visible world, not unlike atoms—components of molecular decomposition. There are not any intermediate concepts (decomposable components) between them. Just like atoms for molecules, concepts are qualitatively more abstract than protoconcepts. For them to be singled out, serious analytical work is required. It cannot be done by the child's mind. It is reasonable to assume that transition to concepts is genetically conditioned: the child develops an ability to distinguish objective components in protoconcepts, the Agent and the Agent's action—while, say, the child of an anthropoid does not develop such an ability. Therefore, it is only reasonable to describe the transition from protoconcepts to concepts (from the level (23b) to the level (23c) of the situation development tree (23), see p. 131) as **a leap**. Then comes the next transition, from basic concepts to specific concepts (from (23c) to (23c′): PERSON ▷ (BOY, WOMAN…); IS RUNNING ▷ (RUNNING-MINCING, RUNNING-JOGGING…). It is similar to the transition from an atom in general to the atoms of chlorine, hydrogen, etc. Specific concepts are conditioned by external reality as they are based in the child's perceptual experience of concrete situations and their participants. They emerge gradually as the child's experience grows. It is reasonable to call such a transition **gradual**. Thus, the child's stage of concept formation consists of two successive transitions: one a **leap** (from basic protoconcepts to basic concepts) and the other **gradual** (from basic concepts to specific concepts).

The previous stage in the child's development appears to also be a two-step transition. First, the child makes a leap to basic protoconcepts—decompositional components of basic situations, cf. the transition from (23a) to (23b). From these then more concrete, specific protoconcepts gradually emerge: PERSON-IS RUNNING ▷ (WOMAN-IS RUNNING...), cf. the transition from (23b) to (23b′). This is also true of the subsequent stages. Thus, the child first acquires basic properties—COLOR, SHAPE, etc., which are the products of decomposition of concepts. And from these specific properties are formed: COLOR ▷ (GREEN...), SHAPE ▷ (ROUND...), cf. (5) and (5′) in subsection 3.3.1, chapter 3. Finally, during the subsequent decomposition of the concept SHAPE into parts, common parts—HANDLE, BLADE, etc.—appear first, and then they are subdivided into concrete instances—DOOR / HAMMER HANDLE; KNIFE / AX BLADE, and so forth (see Koshelev 2017: 389–390).

We end up with the following:

(29) Stage in the child's development = leap-like transition (to decompositions of elementary cognitive units) + gradual transition (to their specific instances).

It follows from this analysis that the genetically conditioned tree (23) is the beginning of a **tree of decomposition of elementary units** for the representation of the visible (phenomenal) world. From the concepts of the everyday world it develops in two opposite directions: a) upward, to the scientific concepts of the macrocosm: the planetary system and its variations (solar system and others) and b) downward, to the scientific concepts of the microcosm: atom (nucleus and electrons) and its variants. This means that the tree (23) predetermines the tree of decomposition, including its scientific parts. In particular, it explains why decompositions of an atom, planetary system, and situation are isomorphic and have the structure of the role systems (7e) and (31) (see chapter 1).

The tree of decomposition of elementary units clearly illustrates the fundamental limitation of the scientific cognition of the phenomenal world.

2.8.3. Spatial actions. Koshelev (2017) demonstrated close mutual influence of the child's actions and his representation of the world. Let us note, briefly, how the emergence of concepts contributes to the extension of the child's range of actions. Entering his second year, the child begins to actively learn a wide range of goal-directed actions related to moving objects in space (grab, pass, fetch, throw, pick, drink, eat, etc.) and causing physical changes

2.8. Conclusion

in objects (tear, smash, break, rip off, etc.). Bernshtein (1947: 82–84) distinguished the totality of such actions as a separate class—"level *C* of the spatial field." According to Bernshtein, "the entire second year of the child's life is the year of entering the spatial field array and mastering locomotions" (Bernshtein 1947: 168). The most important support for the child ("key afference") is provided by the **physical space** already taking shape at this time—"objectivized," "homogeneous," "unmovable" (as the child moves or turns around, he is already convinced that it is **he who is moving** while the **surrounding space** with the objects that fill it is **motionless**—in spite of all his receptors telling him the opposite) (Ibid.: 82).

But it is at this time that the child begins to decompose perceived situations of motion and visible actions into concepts (object and motor) and combine them into conceptual situations with the help of role relationships (see above, section 2.4). Without such a conceptual leap, full-fledged formation of the child's physical space and his mastery of spatial actions in it would be unattainable. The child would not be able to imagine a 'required future' for his action (Bernshtein 1966: 281).

Chapter 3

The effect of culture on language: The case of the Amazonian tribe Pirahã [1]

The central theme of this chapter is the effect of culture on language. In section 3.1, it is argued that the development of civilization within a society contributes to the development of the content component of its language—the expansion of its lexical and grammatical meanings. Everett's hypothesis about the influence of culture on language is discussed. In section 3.2, three-component models of the development of human activity are proposed, with Activity as the main component and Thought and Language as auxiliary components that ensure the successful realization of activities. The models are illustrated with examples of some concrete societies, concluding with a discussion of the final stage in the evolutionary development of human civilization. In section 3.3, in light of these models, some uncommon properties of the Pirahã language are analyzed, including the absence of color terms, numerals, and passive voice. It is argued that these properties are preconditioned by the Pirahã tribe being at an initial stage of civilizational development; it may be hypothesized that these properties would disappear with the tribe's transition to the subsequent stages of development. Finally, in section 3.4, the immediacy of perception principle (syncretic perception) and the mediated perception principle (systemic perception) are discussed and the notion of 'exotic linguistic property' analyzed. With Pirahã as a case study, it is argued that 'exotic linguistic property' is a relative concept that may not be used unconditionally in characterizing any linguistic feature.

3.1. Introduction

3.1.1. On the Pirahã language: does culture affect language? According to the research conducted by Daniel Everett, the language of the Pirahãs—a small community of hunter-gatherers living on the banks of the

---

[1] This chapter is based on the previously published papers: Koshelev 2018a; 2018b.

Maici River (a tributary of the Amazon)—possesses a number of uncommon lexical and grammatical features, such as the absence of numerals, color terms, grammatical number, passive voice and recursion, and poverty of lexical markers for time, kinship, and so forth (Everett 2005; 2008; 2009; Futrell et al. 2016). Everett believes that these features, which set the Pirahã language apart among human languages as most exotic, are conditioned by the community's no less exotic culture.

In the well-known documentary about the Pirahã tribe, *The Grammar of Happiness* (2012), Everett speaks of his goal to prove that culture affects not only the lexicon of a language but also its structure. This thought is also advanced in his book:

> Like most linguists today, I once believed that culture and language were largely independent. But if I am correct that culture can exercise major effects on grammar, then the theory [...] that grammar is part of the human genome and that the variations in the grammars of the world's languages are largely insignificant—is dead wrong (Everett 2008: 238).

Not surprisingly, Everett's views on language have undergone a lot of criticisms from researchers who are partial, in various degrees, to generative theory. For example, in the aforementioned documentary, Steven Pinker points out the general rule to which many linguists subscribe: the differences between the world's languages have nothing to do with the cultural differences of the peoples speaking these languages. For example, Pinker argues, in some languages the object follows the verb, as in *John was eating sushi*, while in other languages it precedes the verb, as in *John sushi was eating*. And this has nothing to do with culture (for more criticisms, see Nevins et al. 2009a; 2009b).

Thus, the controversy over whether culture does or does not affect language has again become an issue in contemporary linguistics. Since the purpose of the present work does not allow for even a brief detour to outline the historical background of this issue, I will discuss only the views of Edward Sapir and Jan Baudouin de Courtenay, as they bear on the view developed below.

3.1.2. Sapir and Baudouin de Courtenay on the effect of culture on language. In order to consider Sapir's views, our approach to the concept of culture must first be clarified. According to Sapir (1999: 50), "culture [...] may be briefly defined as civilization in so far as it embodies national genius," that is, "culture may be defined as *what* a society does and thinks" (Sapir

1921: chapter 10; original emphasis). In such an understanding of culture it is important to distinguish between two components: the invariable component, "national genius", and the component that varies over time, "civilization" ("*what* a society does"). Speaking of language in the context of discussing the issue of whether culture effects language, Sapir draws a distinction between the content, the lexicon that reflects the cultural background of a given society, and the grammatical system. As for the effect that the culture of a ethnic group might have on its language, Sapir hypothesized that during the initial stage in the formation of such a group (that is, when it is a 'primitive group' with hardly discernible elements of language and culture) language (both its content and grammatical system) develops in parallel with culture:

> [T]hey will parallel each other somewhat closely, so that the forms of cultural activity will be reflected in the grammatical system of the language. In other words, not only will the words themselves of a language serve as symbols of detached cultural elements, as is true of languages at all periods of development, but we may suppose the grammatical categories and processes themselves to symbolize corresponding types of thought and activity of cultural significance (Sapir 2008: 147).

As the group continues to develop, the cause-and-effect relationship between culture (with its rapidly changing civilizational constituent) and language (with its much slower change of form) remain, but become fuzzy and hard to detect. Cf.:

> Though the forms of language may not change as rapidly as those of culture, it is doubtless true that an unusual rate of cultural change is accompanied by a corresponding accelerated rate of change in language. If this point of view be pushed to its legitimate conclusion, we must be led to believe that rapidly increasing complexity of culture necessitates correspondingly, though not equally rapid, changes in linguistic form and content. [...] I am not inclined to consider it an accident that the rapid development of culture in western Europe during the last 2000 years has been synchronous with what seems to be unusually rapid changes in language. Though it is impossible to prove the matter definitely, I am inclined to doubt whether many languages of primitive peoples have undergone as rapid modification in a corresponding period of time as has the English language (Ibid.: 148).

It should be noted that over time Sapir became more uncompromising on this issue. The quotation cited above is from a talk given at the end of 1911. In a paper published in 1933, however, he states:

3.1. Introduction

The tendency to see linguistic categories as directly expressive of overt cultural outlines, which seems to have come into fashion among certain sociologists and anthropologists, should be resisted as in no way warranted by the actual facts. There is no general correlation between cultural type and linguistic structure (Sapir 2008: 513).

Baudouin de Courtenay, on the subject of linguistic changes, observes that "they are constant and perpetual because their causes are constant and perpetual" (Boduen de Kurtene 1963, I: 249). Among the general causes of linguistic change he names the "subconscious abstraction, the desire to discriminate and differentiate" (Ibid.: 102)—which, as will be demonstrated, is a major driving force of language change.

Baudouin thought that, along with vacillating changes, it is in the nature of language to move in one direction predetermined by the "objective progress of man as a link in the chain of nature" (Ibid.: 349). Baudouin calls this motion **language progress**. The crucial "inherent feature of this progress is the ever-growing abstractedness of language" which, in its turn, leads to the "ever-growing spiritualization of language" (Ibid.: 236, 262).

Our position may briefly be characterized as follows. The culture of a society substantially affects its language. However, the effect of culture on language is quite selective and bears mainly on the level of civilization of the society and the content of its language. Namely, the civilizational component of culture, which changes with the progress of society, preconditions the development of the content of language (which in our view includes both lexical and **grammatical meanings**). As I will attempt to show, the main criterion of societal progress is the constant expansion of the kinds of activity the society engages in. Thereby the number of professional sublanguages related to new kinds of activity also keeps growing. Certain concepts and terms from these sublanguages diffuse into the representations of the world and the language of the society, acquiring simplified, generally comprehensible interpretations. Due to this process the content part of language is enlarged with new lexical and grammatical items, abstract, metaphorical, and metonymical meanings, and the view of the world characteristic of a given society becomes ever more differentiated and systemic. This process will be described in detail below, using the Pirahã tribe as a case study. It will be demonstrated that the absence, or poverty, of many lexical and grammatical tools in the language of the Pirahãs is related to the **non-differentiated (syncretic) character of the corresponding aspects of their representation of the world. Such**

syncretism, in its turn, is preconditioned by the extremely narrow scope of the kinds of activities the Pirahãs engage in, which is an indicator that the tribe is in an initial stage of civilizational progress.

Further on, in section 3.2, a general-theoretical basis for the proposed view is laid out, and in section 3.3 its main points are illustrated by an analysis of the Pirahã culture and language. Section 3.4 is devoted to the immediacy of perception principle (syncretism) and mediated perception (systematicity), and to an analysis of the notion exotic (unique) linguistic feature. With Pirahã as a case study, it is demonstrated that 'exotic' has only relative status and is not an inherent characteristic of any linguistic feature.

3.2. Models of activity development for individuals and ethnic groups

3.2.1. The uniform progress of an ethnic group. Let us introduce the key concepts used in this chapter. I will refer to a group of people united by a common language, culture, and a range of **ordinary** (everyday) activities as an **ethnic group** (I do not consider here the issue of ethnic identity as a criterion for identifying tribal communities because it is not directly related to the goals of this article).

The **level of progress** of an ethnogroup is determined by the qualitative diversity of activities characteristic of the group. The initial level of progress is characterized by a homogeneous group that lacks specialized or what might be called **professional activities** (for example, pottery as an industry). Such activities are performed by particular individuals who collectively use a specialized professional sublanguage. Common (non-professional) activities are carried out by all members of the ethnogroup who use **ordinary** (universally understood) language. The Pirahã tribe is an example of a homogeneous ethnogroup. An ethnogroup that cultivate professional activities I shall call **heterogeneous.**

The concepts introduced above are closely connected with some concepts of Lewis Morgan's theory of the single path of the progress of human societies (Morgan 1944). This theory, which had its heyday in the late 19th century, is seldom mentioned in contemporary research. Nevertheless, it contains some "grains of truth," and some of its positions seem to be quite productive (it should be remembered that the theory was based on an analysis of ethnographic data on many tribes that populated different continents, and that some of these tribes were discovered in Morgan's times and were still in a primitive state).

3.2. Models of activity development for individuals and ethnic groups 151

A note on terminology. Many of the ideas in Morgan's theory of the periods of progress ethnogroups undergo have been adopted by the scientific apparatus of contemporary anthropology, however Morgan's terminology is hardly ever used. This is partly due to its derogatory connotations ('savagery', 'barbarism') attributed to many archaic tribes. Later periodizations were based on other criteria, and the emphasis shifted from the social structure of communities to their material culture, much more easily reconstructed on the basis of archaeological data (the Paleolithic, Mesolithic, Neolithic, etc.). However, Morgan's systematics are much more useful for our objectives than the classifications accepted in contemporary social anthropology. Therefore, while eliminating terminology with undesirable connotations, I utilize many of Morgan's concepts.

In Morgan's theory, three periods are distinguished in the progress of ethnogroups: 'savagery', 'barbarism', and 'civilization', each representing a distinct condition of society and distinguishable by a mode of life peculiar to itself (Morgan 1944: chap. 1). Of special interest to us are the first two periods, whose characteristics will be used in our further exposition:

1) 'savagery', the earliest period in the progress, characterized by the absence of private property and the equality of all members of the community;
2) 'barbarism', the next period of progress marked by the emergence of the pottery industry, agriculture, cattle husbandry, private property, and social hierarchy.

The concepts of homogeneous and heterogeneous ethogroups introduced above correspond to the periods classified by Morgan: the stage of 'homogeneity' corresponds with the state of 'savagery', and the transition of a tribal group to the stage of 'heterogeneity' corresponds to the state of 'barbarism'. On the basis of Morgan's analysis, the following inference can be made: the turning point that marks a qualitatively new stage in the progress of a ethnogroup is its transition from a homogeneous to a heterogeneous state. A heterogeneous ethnogroup is characterized by specialized, professional activities that involve only certain collectives within the tribal group. A homogeneous community is characterized by the absence of such activities: all kinds of activities at this stage bear on everyday life, that is, are accessible to any member of the group.

Among the professional activities that cause a shift in the structure of an ethnogroup, Morgan considered making pottery to be of primary importance. At first sight, this thesis appears to be odd. Why would pottery be so important as to radically change the status of the group? Morgan supported the well-known proposition that, as far as its effects and consequences go, the greatest event in the history of human experience was the beginning of iron production.

Some clarification is needed here. First, the beginnings of pottery in themselves were a remarkable achievement of mankind. It gave humans heat-resistant utensils for cooking food, which had previously been done primitively in clay-plastered wicker baskets and skin-lined pits. Cooking itself was done with the help of preheated stones. Pottery began by plastering wooden utensils with a kind of clay ('a good finger thick') to protect them from fire; only later was it discovered that clay alone could serve the purpose (Morgan 1944: 30–31).

Second, and this is of paramount importance, according to Morgan (Ibid.) pottery was the first kind of activity engaged in by only a small group out of an entire tribe. This was the pivoting point, when the originally homogeneous community started to turn into a heterogeneous community due to its social and professional differentiation.

3.2.2. The Pirahã tribe and pottery. Everett's analysis of everyday tribal life shows that the Pirahã tribe has a homogeneous status: all its members are equal and there is practically no private property. The Pirahãs have weapons (bows and arrows) but lack either pottery or any other kind of professional activity that requires specialized skills, knowledge, and language which would make it inaccessible to all members of the tribe.

Hunting, fishing, gathering, cooking food in aluminum pots, making wicker baskets, hand spinning (almost every family has "an indigenous handheld cotton spinner" (Everett 2008: 80)), resting by the fire—all these are common activities accessible to all the members of the Pirahã tribe, not only to adults but to growing children, who get used to these activities from an early age. Members of every family hunt, fish, gather fruits and roots in the jungle, do wickerwork, take part in building a new hut, etc.

The homogeneous status of the Pirahã tribe is reflected in their language which does not have, as has been mentioned above, a whole range of common lexical and grammatical units: numerals, color terms (analogue expressions are used instead, such as 'it is bloodlike' for the color red, 'it is not ripe' for the color green, etc.), lexical indicators of time such as *yesterday, today, tomorrow, morning, evening, week, month*, and passive voice. Below,

3.2. Models of activity development for individuals and ethnic groups 153

in section 3.3, it will be argued that the absence of such linguistic expressions is preconditioned by the absence of relevant activities among the Pirahãs. The Pirahãs do not use counting in their ordinary activities; specific colors do not possess identifying functions similar to the colors of traffic lights, for example; their lives are not divided into the usual time cycles we call *morning, evening, yesterday, tomorrow*, etc. (they sleep at odd moments at day and at night); there are no activities in their routine life which would require passive voice to refer to, and so forth (Everett 2005; 2009).

I believe that the emergence of new practices in the life of the Pirahãs may have served as a direct cause of the development of their language. To illustrate a possible way for the Pirahã language to develop the above-mentioned lexical and grammatical elements, let us imagine that some members of the tribe have started, for the first time, to practice a certain professional activity. Let us suppose that a large Pirahã family begins to master pottery. First of all, the family and their close community begin to be involved in a whole range of new interconnected activities such as procuring a suitable kind of clay, collecting shells, making a mixture of clay and crushed shells, plastering wooden and wicker utensils with this mixture, drying out these utensils in certain conditions (including their periodic watering and the like), counting and storing the finished utensils, receiving orders, exchanging finished products, etc. In practice, all these activities must be carried out by daylight. Therefore, the entire family begins to live in a time mode different from that of the rest of the community: they work during the day and sleep at night. With time, the range of manufactured products grows and products of various shapes and sizes appear; paints are obtained from traveling traders and the manufactured utensils are painted in various colors, etc.

Clearly, all these activities become an important external stimulus for the conceptualization of the categories of number, color, size, and time. For the family and the members of the tribe involved in their activities, a need arises for new lexical classes—names for specific product sizes and shapes (*large, medium, small*; *round, flat, deep*, etc.), quantities (*one, three*, etc.), colors (*green, red*, etc.), time of production (*yesterday, tomorrow*) and so forth.

Certain kinds of work, being carried out over a prolonged duration, cease to meet the immediacy of perception principle characteristic of the Pirahã's way of life ('here and now', see subsection 3.3.7)—the outcome develops slowly and cannot be directly observed. Moreover, it is often unknown or unimportant to know who is producing the work—it is important to know the current state of the production process, its intermediate or end result. Consequently, the need for the passive voice may arises: *Your order is being processed*; *The bowls will be finished tomorrow*, etc. Thus, conditions arise under which the immediacy of perception principle loses its dominating role in the life of the Pirahãs.

It is evident that through some such sequence of events a number of previously absent practices may develop, and with them emerge the linguistic means necessary for their description.

3.2.3. Activities: crossing the Rubicon. Even the above cursory analysis shows that the production of pottery may exert a direct and multifaceted influence on the life and language of potters. But it may also affect, in a similar fashion, other members of the tribe who choose the color and size of the products they purchase and learn to utilize them. Their perception of different time intervals within a day may become more differentiated. Influenced by the language the potters use the language of the community may also expand, adding the most frequently used terms, expressions of politeness practically missing in Pirahã (see, however, Kibrik 2018), etc. (this process is described in more detail in subsection 3.2.6). In this way, diversification of activities in a ethnogroup directly contributes to the development of both its language and its representations of the material world.

The emergence of professional activities in a ethnogroup is, to use a metaphor, like crossing the Rubicon in that it effects a qualitative change in the ethnogroup's mental representation of the world. Prior to the emergence of such activities, the progress of the ethnogroup consisted only in the expansion of the range of ordinary activities, knowledge of these activities, and the language used to describe them. Therefore, all members of the ethnogroup shared a similar view of the material world, its opportunities and hazards. Now, on the other hand, through the development of pottery production and other kinds of professional occupations characteristic of a period of heterogeneity, separate collectives are formed that add, as it were, a new, analytical representation of some aspects of the generally shared representation of the world. This analytical representation reflects their experience of enhanced interactions with these aspects, on account of which new elements emerge in their image of the world that are absent in that of the other members of the ethnogroup. And this is important societal growth.

3.2.4. The minimal model of human activity development. In light of the above, I will consider language and thought (principally, human mental representations of perceived reality) not separately but as forming a single

3.2. Models of activity development for individuals and ethnic groups

whole with a third component, human activity. As will be shown below, human activity, or, rather, the totality of all the specific kinds of activity in which humans engage, is the most important driving force in the development of human thought (where thought is defined as mental representations of the knowledge of the world) and language. In other words, our focus will be on the system: 'thought (world representation)—**types of activity**—language', where 'types of activity' is the main subsystem, and 'thought' and 'language' are supplementary subsystems that facilitate successful implementation of specific types of activity[2] (on the interaction between these subsystems in children in the course of their development, see Koshelev 2017: 16–37). Since none of these subsystems can evolve and develop without interacting with the other two, they should be studied only in the framework of a single system.[3] This ternary system will be referred to as the **minimal model of human activity development** (hereafter simply the model), and is shown in figure 1a. It allows us to study human society as an integral system of activities in the process (at a particular stage) of its development. The model is minimal because it ceases to be a model of the man in the above sense without any of its subsystems.

The model for a ethnogroup (figure 1b), consisting of the models of its individual members, has a quite similar structure. In it the types of activity represented in the community are comprised of the types of activities of its individual members and the representation of the world and language are the group averages—prototypes of the corresponding subsystems for individual members of the tribal group.

---

[2] It may be objected that, in this model, thought should be viewed as the main component, because it is thought (discoveries and inventions made by individuals) that ensures the expansion of activities. To counter this objection, let us point out that, in the end, such inventions and discoveries are realized primarily in human activities. It is human activities (the qualitative diversity of types of activity) that serve as a unified criterion of a society's progress. In this respect thought, just like language, is a supplementary system that ensures the diversity and efficiency of human activities.

[3] See also Steven Pinker's evolutionary theory (Pinker 2013: ch. 13), cf.:
"I have sketched a testable theory, rooted in cognitive science and evolutionary psychology […] According to this theory, hominids evolved to specialize in the cognitive niche, which is defined by the triad of reasoning about the causal structure of the world, cooperating with other individuals, and sharing that knowledge and negotiating those agreements via language" (p. 362).

(1)

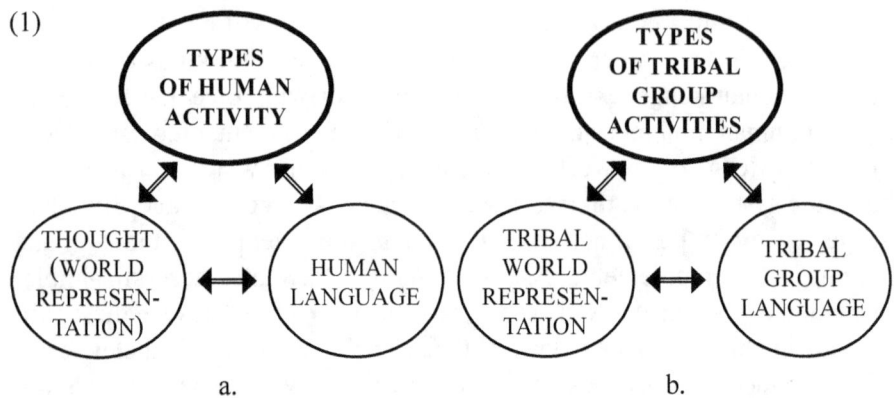

Fig. 1. Minimal models of activity development of (a) human individuals and (b) ethnogroups. Two-sided arrows stand for the interconnections between the subsystems

Note. The models in figure 1 share certain features with the approach of N. Marr (1936), who considered phonic language in conjunction with thought and material production. Without going into a detailed analysis of Marr's approach, the following quotations are characteristic:

"Language is the creation of a collective engaged in production. There is not a single word, form, sound or linguistic phenomenon that bypassed consciousness created and regulated by the collective and, later, mass production" (Marr 1936: 271)

"[...] not only thought and word, i.e. language and thinking, but both of them, together with production, constitute a unity" (Ibid.: 459).

"It is self-evident that [...] just like language, thinking and its technique are related to production" (Marr 1933: 280).

Concerning the linear, or manual (gestural and mimic) speech that first arose and existed for "hundreds of thousands of years," Marr emphasizes that over this long period of time prerequisites emerged for the creation of phonic speech which "at the beginning was also just a part of the work process, a work language. It was only gradually that phonic language became spoken language, its oldest stock representing a translation of manual speech" (Marr 1933: 280; see also Marr 1936: 129, 200–203).

3.2.5. The model of human activity development: basic concepts. Using the models in figure 1, let us discuss homogeneous and heterogeneous groups

3.2. Models of activity development for individuals and ethnic groups

in more detail. All members of a homogeneous ethnogroup are involved in **ordinary activities**—a conventionally established set of activities necessary to sustain daily life. These ordinary activities provide for the community's necessities, such as food, abode, safety, rest, entertainment, etc. This type of activity spans the entire range of common everyday activities and their associated emotional experiences and physical exertions. I will call the totality of mental representations that a member of a ethnogroup has and that are related to everyday activities (their goals, order and manner of implementation, intermediate results, etc.), an **ordinary world representation, or ordinary knowledge**.

Hereafter it will be important to distinguish between two types of knowledge about an activity: (a) practical (or procedural) knowledge based on the actual experience of engaging in this activity and, because of such an experience, allowing for **understanding** of the activity, and (b) theoretical knowledge, or mental representations of how this activity is carried out, that is not supported by actual experience (akin to declarative knowledge), cf. Squire 1986. An example would be theoretical knowledge about how to ride a bicycle ('mount it, push from the ground and start turning the pedals, using the handlebars to choose a direction') versus the practical knowledge of riding a bicycle that a cyclist has. The cyclist has a subliminal sensory-motor, or "embodied," understanding of the cycling activity that a person with theoretical knowledge of cycling does not have. As is clear from the above, ordinary knowledge belongs to the domain of practical knowledge.

Directly connected to ordinary knowledge and ordinary activities is the language that describes them. Let us agree to call this language the **ordinary language** of a ethnogroup. It is adequately used and understood by all members of the community.[4] Thus, the ordinary life of each member of the group is carried out according to the interaction of the thought (knowledge), activity, and language components of the model, (1a). It is understood that all members of the group have similar models.

Ordinary activity is contrasted by specialized, or **professional**, activity. This is carried out by a particular collective, set apart from the rest of the group, who use a specialized **professional** sublanguage and specialized concepts unknown outside of the collective.

---

[4] For space considerations, I will not compare our concept of 'ordinary language' with the well-known (and rather ambiguous) notion of 'ordinary language' in philosophy (cf. Ryle 1960: 108–127).

For example, having wine at dinner is part of the life routine in our society. The process is well familiar to people from different walks of life. However, wine tasting by sommeliers, discussing merits and demerits of a particular wine and deciding which wine is good with what dish, is already a specialized activity which requires knowledge of traditions, special terms to differentiate different flavors and aromas, etc. Such discussions by sommeliers would hardly make sense to the average wine-lover not versed in the art of wine tasting.

Those involved in professional activities possess **professional** knowledge and practical experience. Thus, typologically the knowledge of the professional group is analogous to the ordinary knowledge of the whole tribe. Engaged in their professional activity, a collective of professionals develops, on the basis of the ordinary language, a professional sublanguage. Consequently, just as for ordinary life, the professional life of the collective is carried out through the interaction of the same three (but in this case professional) components: knowledge, activity, and language. Having knowledge and activity experience, members of the collective adequately understand one another when communicating through the professional language.

3.2.6. Case example: medical activity and its effects on the language and thought of an ethnogroup. To clarify the development of the model shown in (1b) and the interaction of its components, let us consider the role of language in the activities of a professional community. Take, for example, the medical language of a community of professional doctors and medical researchers. Every member of this community speaks the ordinary language of the ethnogroup to which he belongs, as well as the medical language. The latter is a specialized language that has the structure of the ordinary language but a specialized lexicon that includes terms concerning the structure and function of the human body, diseases, medications, etc., as well as certain specialized syntactic constructions. In addition to this professional sublanguage members of the medical community possess a stock of medical knowledge that supplements the ordinary human representations of the world, as well as the skills necessary for particular medical practices.

It should be stressed that a community of doctors cannot exist and develop in the absence of even one of the components that make up the model for medics similar to (1a)—"medical representation of the human world—**medical activity**—medical language." Even more, not one of the system's components can exist and develop independently, separated from the other two.

3.2. Models of activity development for individuals and ethnic groups

For example, if a medical researcher obtains new knowledge about the human organism (= development of medical representations), this new knowledge will receive a description in the medical language that may involve new terminology (development of the medical language) and will quickly become the domain of the medical community. This, in turn, brings to life new methods of treatment (= development of activity), thereby stimulating progress in the medical community. If, on the other hand, for one reason or another, certain kinds of medical activity deteriorate (due to religious bans, withdrawal of funding, etc.), the terms and medical notions related to such activities fall out of use and are forgotten, and the medical community begins to regress.

It is clear from this example that the main component in the medic's model is medical activity. Through the implementation of these activities neural codes are formed in the long-term memory of a medical professional, a surgeon, for example, for specific types of medical practices; these codes are used to store motor, sensory, and mental experience (for more details on these codes, see Koshelev 2019: 146–149). Such neural codes are not formed in the memory of the surgeon's assistant, who helps in the operation process but does not take part in the operation itself. Therefore, the surgeon possesses professional knowledge (medical representations of human organisms, or declarative knowledge) and sensory-motor knowledge, or an 'embodied' understanding of the operation process (experience of the medical activity, i.e. a synthesis of declarative and procedural knowledge), while his assistant has only professional knowledge.

It should be emphasized that the ultimate goal for any existing medical community is successful medical activity. With this in view, the other two components of the model are supplementary. Thought is the second most important component; it paves the way to new kinds of activity. Medical language is third in importance. It is actively involved in the formation of the first two components, supporting collective thought and collective activities.

A most important function of language should be noted, without which the progress of medical thought would be impossible. Suppose a medical researcher discovers a new disease whose symptoms are varied (such as AIDS, for example). He uses a new term to name it and, using medical language, begins to elucidate its meaning (the nature of the disease) to his colleagues. Thus, the new term becomes generally comprehensible in medical circles. Without such a term, the newly introduced concept—'AIDS disease'—could not possibly be understood by other doctors because direct reference to the symptoms would not help in this instance. For this reason it is the term itself

160   Chapter 3. The effect of culture on language...

that 'contains' the concept and gives it its generally applicable status. Note that in the initial stage of the development of the medical community, when all diseases might, relatively speaking, be called 'sensory', i.e. manifested to medical thought by their observable symptoms, the role of language is not critical. It becomes so with the appearance of 'functional' diseases, that is to say diseases that cannot be identified by their symptoms alone.

What has been said above may be illustrated visually by how professional activity, thought, and language interact in the case of Langda stonecutters, a tribe living in a village located on a small mountainous plateau on the island of New Guinea (Stout 2002; 2005). To till their land the Langda use skillfully made stone adzes shown in figure 2a. Taking a blank, an experienced stonecutter divides it into several parts that must be shaped in a particular way using special techniques. Each part has its terminological name, as can be seen in the diagram in figure 2b (in essence, this is a developed concept STONE ADZE). Following this schema step by step, the stonecutter knaps an adze from the stone.

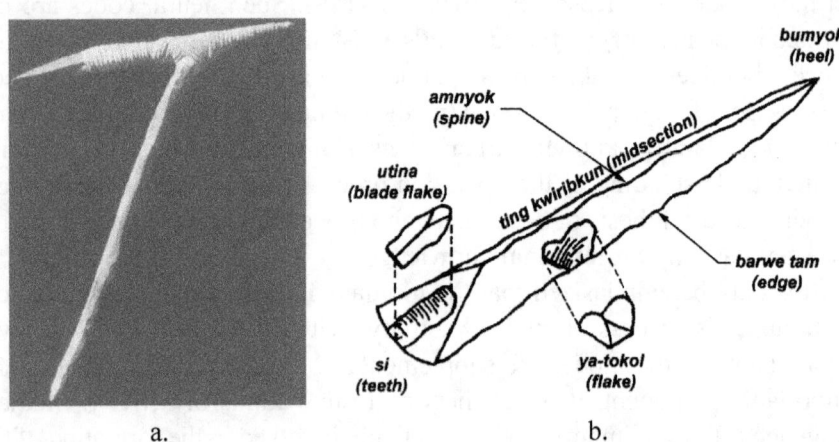

Fig. 2. A stone adze (a) and a diagram (b) of its parts
(adapted from Stout 2002: 703)

As noted by Stout, many of the terms used to refer to the different parts of an adze and to various kinds of chips are anatomical metaphors, their English equivalents being *spine* (sharp crest of the blank's upper side), *teeth* (large sharp edges), *flakes* (small chips). Moreover, "a well-developed terminology exists to describe particular knapping techniques and strategies" (Stout 2002: 703). It is quite obvious that a stonecutter's work, thought, and professional language are very closely interconnected.

3.2. Models of activity development for individuals and ethnic groups

Let us now touch on the issue of the influence professional groups have on other members of an ethnogroup (both professionals in other areas and 'non-professionals'). Let us look at the group of medics again. They directly interact with other members of the ethnogroup in the course of ordinary life and when engaged in medical activities; their influence is therefore multifaceted.

In the first place, the lexicon of the ordinary language expands. Some of the medical terminology diffuses into it, acquiring **pseudo-professional** (simplified) meanings that are easily understood. These include diseases (*flue, tonsillitis, tuberculosis*, etc.), medicines (*drops, tablet, pill, mixture*, etc.), treatment procedures (*take a medicine, use a plaster cast, go to hospital for a medical examination*, etc.). Importantly, the verbs that name such activities acquire new, 'medical' meanings heretofore absent in everyday speech. For example, the Russian verb *prinjat'* 'take' is used in the medical meaning 'insert through the mouth a medicine for treatment'. Thus, it is correct to say, in Russian, *prinjal porošok / tabletku / miksturu* 'took a powder / pill / some mixture', but one cannot say **prinjal stakan vody* 'took a glass of water', *prinjal obed 'took dinner', **prinjal tabletku, čtoby protestirovat' eë* 'took a pill to test it'. Similarly, one can say *naložil povjazku na šeju* '(he) put a bandage on his neck' but not **naložil šarf / galstuk na šeju* '(he) put a scarf / tie on his neck'. Healing can be done (such as in a religious context) by *naloženiem ruk*, lit. 'by the laying on of hands', but not by **priloženiem / *prikladyvaniem ruk*, lit. 'by holding-PF / holding-IMP hands to'.

The expression *ložit'sja na*, lit. 'lie (down) on' acquires a new meaning and becomes an idiom. One can say *ložus' na gemodializ / na ximioterapiju / na operaciju / na obsledovanie* '(I'm) going in [to hospital] for hemodialysis / chemotherapy / an operation / an examination'. But it is not appropriate to say **ložus' na tatuirovku / na solnečnye vanny* '(I'm) going in for a tattoo / sunbath'. One does not say * *ložus' na massaž* lit. '(I'm) lying down for massage' in reference to a one-time massage while at a spa, for example. However, it would be correct to say so in reference to a course of massotherapy. Similarly, the expression *ložus' na gipnoz* '(I'm) lying down for hypnosis' is correct with reference to therapeutic hypnosis but inappropriate when it refers to a demonstration of hypnosis technique. Also, new metaphorical expressions arise, for example: *Revmatism ližet sustavy i gložet serdce* 'Rheumatism licks at the joints and gnaws at the heart'.

Secondly, some syntactic structures and grammatical meanings become part of ordinary language. For example, it seems natural to assume that the expression 'if and only if' came from mathematics and logic, the formula *I will speak the truth, the whole truth and nothing but the truth* from jurisprudence, and formulae of the type *Take before meals three times a day for two weeks* from medicine.[5] This new content component of language (let us call it **pseudo-professional**) has an independent status. It is typologically different both from general ordinary language and medical language.

The other components of the model (1a), knowledge and activity, expand along with language. Knowledge of professional terms and expressions that "took root" in ordinary language enlarges the layman's knowledge of medical situations. Let us call such knowledge **pseudo-professional knowledge**. In contrast to practical knowledge (both ordinary and professional), pseudo-professional knowledge is theoretical knowledge not supported by carried out by professionals. Correlating superficially with professional knowledge, it is individualized and may vary from person to person. For example, some know one way of treating the flue or quinsy, some another, and some practically nothing about it.

Lastly, expansion of the set of medical notions leads to the growth and finer differentiation of activities related to these notions: diagnosing a disease by its outward symptoms, identification of medicines by their color, shape, type of substance (powder, tablet, drops, mixture), how they are taken (including the time, regularity, and length of treatment), analysis of their effect, etc.

Thus, all components of the model (1a) of members of a heterogeneous ethnogroup are supplemented by pseudo-professional constituents:

(2) Activity = ordinary + pseudo-professional activity

(3) World representation = ordinary + pseudo-professional knowledge

(4) Language = ordinary + pseudo-professional language

For professionals, such as doctors for example, professional constituents are added to the part on the right in (2)–(4).

---

[5] Such examples reveal the mechanism (via new professional languages) by which the **progress of a society** (expansion of its professional activities) **leads to linguistic progress**, i.e. development of the content component of its language—its lexical and grammatical means. These examples also illustrate Baudouin de Courtenay's thesis that the progress of a language is manifested in the growth of its abstractedness (cf. subsection 3.1.2).

3.2. Models of activity development for individuals and ethnic groups   163

Further progress of a heterogeneous ethnogroup—the development of various kinds of professional activity—leads to growing individualization of the pseudo-professional components of the model. Because of this, outside of ordinary activity and ordinary language individuals understand one another less and less because their pseudo-professional knowledge is theoretical and individualized (for more details, see Koshelev 2017: 469–473).

Therefore, the main criterion for the progress of a ethnogroup is expansion of the kinds of activities it engages in. This expansion is supported by the other two components, thought and language, which also develop along with it.

3.2.7. Case-study: stages in the development of Al-Sayyid Bedouin Sign Language, ABSL. Naturally the question arises, what exactly are the forms of linguistic expression, and in what order, that develop during the transition from one period of societal progress to another? In order to answer this question I consider a concrete example, ABSL, as all its developmental stages have been described in the literature.

Al-Sayyid is a village in the Negev desert in the south of Israel that has a Bedouin population of about 3,500. A high percentage of deaf children are born in this community for generations. About 80 years ago, an elementary sign language emerged among deaf children in this community that subsequently evolved rapidly, becoming more complex with almost each successive generation (Padden et al. 2010; Sandler et al. 2011; Sandler 2013). Presently, being in the fourth stage of its development, ABSL has reached a state comparable to phonic human language. Dronov (2016) describes all four stages in the evolution of ABSL, from initial to contemporary:

> Researchers were lucky to find the first users of this language alive, so they were able to document four age strata differing from one another in the ever-growing complexity of morphology and syntax. [...]
> 1) simple structures effected with arms and hands (an example would be a story told by a person from the first generation of ABSL users; short, one- or two-word phrases—symbolic signs—were used, accompanied by pantomime, that is, iconic embodied signs);
> 2) the subject and object are singled out, and the theme and rhema are marked (by movements of the head);
> 3) complex sentences, expression of illocutionary force (facial expressions, positions of arms and body and gesture reiteration as analogs of prosody),

introductory words, embedded structures, emphatic stress analogs, emergence of new grammatical markers (head movements, facial expressions);
4) embedded clauses and embedded structures within such clauses, opposition of two referents, emergence of new grammatical markers (body movements and postures, leading hand *vs.* supporting hand) (Dronov 2016: 321–322).

This rapid evolution of ABSL, virtually occurring over a single life-span, seems mysterious. Our hypothesis that the level of progress of a ethnogroup crucially affects the development of its language provides a simple explanation: over the past 80 years (since the late 1920s / early 1930s) the societal progress of Bedouins populating the southern part of Israel has been no less rapid. In just a few leaps it transitioned from the stage of homogeneity to that of a contemporary civilization, thus causing excelleration in the development of ABSL.[6]

A historical digression: milestones in the social progress of Bedouins. For thousands of years Bedouins lived a nomadic life, occupied by raising livestock (goats and sheep). This nomadic state may be viewed as corresponding to the stage of homogeneity, insofar as it is impoverished compared to tribal life at a more advanced stage of societal / civilizational development (such as that of the Pirahã tribe, for example). In the 1930s, during the rapid growth of kibbutzim, their organizers began to recruit Bedouins as agricultural laborers. Through this work the Bedouins began to be involved in entirely new types of activities and also gained access to some of the advancements of modern civilization (travel to nearby cities for shopping, medical aid, etc.). When the State of Israel was established in 1949, Bedouins became Israeli citizens. Israeli policy aimed to transition Bedouins from nomadic to settled life. Many Bedouins began to take part in elections, supporting the Kibbutz Movement, and young Bedouins began to serve in the Israeli army (in tracker units).

By 1974, many settlements (town-like housing developments) had been built in the Negev desert and tens of thousands of Bedouins had moved into these settlements for permanent residence. Al-Sayyid was one such settlement. Most young Bedouins living in these settlements began to change their traditional occupations to modern professions. Many received a college education and started their own businesses. As a result of all such changes, the level of societal progress in Bedouin settlements has shown an unprecedented rise and may

---

[6] The social and linguistic progress of Bedouins is very clearly shown in the documentary *Voices from El Sayed* (cf. https://www.youtube.com/watch?v=kBjIIcVMdRQ).

3.2. Models of activity development for individuals and ethnic groups 165

be described now as a synthesis of contemporary civilization and old Bedouin traditions (sheep are kept in annexes to modern houses; young Bedouins largely preserve their traditional perception of the desert they are accustomed to—by hardly noticeable signs Bedouin trackers identify mined areas, the pathways of terrorists and possible places of ambush, etc.).

On the whole, it can be said that, from the of homogeneous stage characteristic of Bedouin communities in the late 1920 / early 1930s, subsequent generations, moving to settlements in the Negev desert, had transitioned by the early 2000s to contemporary civilization. It may be assumed that the community of deaf Bedouins using ABSL (about 200 people) is at the same level of societal development. It is not separated from the surrounding language: thousands of Bedouins with unimpaired hearing use ABSL to communicate with their deaf compatriots. The latter are thus involved in the social life of the larger community (Kisch 2008; 2012).

Let us go back to the four stages in the developmental of ABSL mentioned above and the comment given by Dronov (2016: 322): "[i]t is quite possible that similar complexification took place in the case of 'phonic' languages; then, Pirahã would be an example of a language 'frozen' at the stage that corresponds to the second stage in ABSL development." What has been said above supports this hypothesis and provides the basis for the following interpretation of it. The first developmental stage of ABSL corresponds to the middle stage of the homogeneous period in the societal evolution of Bedouins and the second stage to the highest level of progress in that period, so it is at this level that ABSL resembles Pirahã. The third stage corresponds to the first stage of the heterogeneity period, and the fourth to the developed stage of a heterogeneous community. It should be noted that recursion appears only at the third developmental stage of ABSL and becomes fully developed (featuring embedded clauses) at the fourth stage (cf. also Padden et al. 2010).

3.2.8. The final stage of human civilization. The increasing differentiation of a heterogeneous community into separate groups identified by their professional activities shows a paradoxical tendency. The higher the progress of a ethnogroup in accumulating knowledge of the world, that is, the greater the number of professional groups, the less individual members of the tribe understand one another outside of the domain of their ordinary life. All the members of a homogeneous ethnogroup understand one another very well as they know well both the surrounding world, to which they are accustomed, and their ordinary language; they are continuously involved in ordinary daily activities described by ordinary language. The knowledge of the world possessed by the members of a contemporary (heterogeneous) ethnogroup is much broader and includes, along with ordinary knowledge, pseudo-professional knowledge (see (3), subsection 3.2.6). However, this rapidly growing knowledge is passive by nature. It is superficial, not grounded in real activities, and becomes more and more individualized, differing from one individual to the next. Correspondingly, their languages also differ (primarily lexically—see (4), subsection 3.2.6). Therefore, in communication today, when conversing on topics that lie outside the scope of their ordinary knowledge, people do not understand each other as well as, for example, the Pirahãs, who lack pseudo-professional knowledge and, consequently, corresponding individual linguistic idiosyncrasies.

This process may be illustrated well by an analysis of how a community of professionals develops. For example, a group of medical professionals within a community at the initial stage of its existence would exemplify a homogeneous professional social group in which no other specific kinds of activity are present. In this respect such a social group would be similar to a homogeneous community, such as the Pirahã tribe, and develop in a similar way—by expanding the kinds of medical activities, medical notions, and medical language understandable to all the members of the group. Then, reaching a certain limit in homogeneous development, at which point "everybody still understands everything," such a homogeneous social group would begin to break down into separate professional groups, each group undertaking a deeper exploration of one or another particular problem (oncological diseases, Alzheimer's disease, etc.). Each separate group would develop its own methods of treatment, insights into the disease and its characteristic manifestations, and a special sublanguage. Other medical professionals would now understand their colleagues only superficially and fragmentarily, that is, "pseudo-professionally." Thus, a homogeneous social group of medical professionals becomes heterogeneous, repeating the developmental path of the original homogeneous ethnogroup.

As a heterogeneous social group develops the number of professional (in a broad sense) groups increases, and these groups gradually become more and more removed from each other (intellectually, socially, culturally). Members of different groups cease to understand one another on many issues. The only link that keeps these groups together as a single social group and maintains mutual understanding is the ordinary component of their activities,

3.2. Models of activity development for individuals and ethnic groups

language, and representations of the world. As soon as this component is lost or becomes irrelevant, the heterogeneous ethnogroup loses its unity and disintegrates. Our approach to the socially determined evolution of humans, expounded above, is close in some respect to the teaching of George Gurdjieff. This is what he said a hundred years ago (as presented by Pyotr Ouspensky):

> There are two lines along which man's development proceeds, the line of knowledge and the line of being. In right evolution the line of knowledge and the line of being develop simultaneously, parallel to, and helping one another. But if the line of knowledge gets too far ahead of the line of being, or if the line of being gets ahead of the line of knowledge, man's development goes wrong, and sooner or later it must come to a standstill.
>
> [...] If knowledge outweighs being a man knows but has no power to do. [...] The development of the line of knowledge without the line of being gives [...] a man who knows a great deal but can do nothing, a man who *does not understand* what he knows [...] Understanding is the resultant of knowledge and being. [...]
>
> One of the reasons for the divergence between the line of knowledge and the line of being in life, and the lack of understanding which is partly the cause and partly the effect of this divergence, is to be found in the language which people speak. [...] The language in which they speak is adapted to practical life only. [...] as soon as they pass to a slightly more complex sphere they are immediately lost, and they cease to understand one another, although they are unconscious of it.
>
> It is quite clear that, for proper study, for an exact exchange of thoughts, an exact language is necessary [...] The idea is perfectly clear and every branch of science endeavors to elaborate and to establish an exact language for itself. But there is no universal language. People continually confuse the languages of different sciences and can never establish their exact correlation. And even in each separate branch of science new terminologies, new nomenclatures, are constantly appearing. And the further it goes the worse it becomes. Misunderstanding grows and increases instead of diminishing and there is every reason to think that it will continue to increase in the same way. And people will understand one another ever less and less (Ouspensky 2001: 71–77; original emphasis).

3.2.9. *Homo perfectus.* The increasing progress of contemporary computerized society results in inescapable deterioration of mutual understanding.

Can this tendency be expected to stop? Based on the general theory of development (chapter 1, subsection 1.2.5), a tentative positive answer to this question may be given. In accordance with this theory, the process of differentiation of professional knowledge must, at a certain point, be replaced by a reverse process: integration of professional knowledge, when each member of a certain group will be able to comprehend all the given types of professional knowledge.

I believe that a necessary condition for such integration is an evolutionary leap of *Homo sapiens sapiens* that would ensure an explosive growth of human emotional, intellectual, and agentive abilities, commensurate with the explosive growth of these abilities that marked the transition from anthropoids to humans. Such a leap would transform *Homo sapiens sapiens* into **Homo syntheticus**, or, let us say, **Homo perfectus**. As a consequence of such a leap, every member of this new people would be able to learn and develop not a single specific kind of professional activity but the totality of heretofore separate professional activities, along with the professional knowledge and languages associated with these activities. Subsuming what used to be everyday ordinary activity, this unified multi-professional activity would become the new ordinary activity for all members of the *Homo perfectus* community. Knowledge of this activity would become their new representation of the world (the new representation will be the same for all members of *Homo perfectus*), and the multi-professional language their new everyday language.[7]

---

[7] Outstanding individuals throughout history—scientists, philosophers, and artists, who were encyclopedists and naturalists at the same time—may be viewed as distant prototypes of *Homo perfectus*. Among them were Aristotle (384–322 BC) and Ibn Sina (Avicenna) (980–1037), whose professional interests included medicine, philosophy, logic, geometry, astronomy, mechanics, chemistry, geology, philology, poetry, and music, Leonardo da Vinci (1452–1519)—art, anatomy, medicine, biomechanics, physics, optics, engineering and the art of war, architecture, Mikhail Lomonosov (1711–1765)—natural science, chemistry, physics, mineralogy, optics, history, philology, linguistics, and poetry. The unity of knowledge and activity (being) provided each of these people with a holistic deep understanding (representation) of the world unavailable to the modern ordinary mind. However, because of the finiteness of human mental and emotional spheres, these holistic representations were unavoidably different. Hypothetically, the extended abilities of perfect people might allow them to gain a unified representation of the world.

3.2. Models of activity development for individuals and ethnic groups

Note. In terms of the development cycle (5), see subsection 1.2.5, chapter 1, the computerized human society *Homo sapiens sapiens*, with its many professional activities and their professional languages, can be correlated with the level (5c) of full differentiation into separate components more early homogeneous society (level (5a)), and society *Homo perfectus*—with the final level (5e) of full integration of these components, their system unity. The qualitative leap of *Homo sapiens sapiens* necessary for the onset of integration (5e) distinguishes the evolutionary process from the process of development.

It is hard to offer a well-grounded hypothesis as to what the necessary evolutionary leap in expanding human knowledge might consist of. Keeping in mind the evolutionary leap that led to the emergence of man and human concepts (see sections 2.4, 2.5 in chapter 2), I may only assume that, as a result of such a leap, *Homo perfectus* will possess cognitive units much more abstract than human concepts—let us say, superconcepts—which he will use to build a representation of the world qualitatively more global and holistic than the current human representation of the world. For example, it can be life cycles of objects (life cycles of a tree (40b), banana (42), see subsection 1.5.2, chapter 1) expanded into a four-dimensional space. Cf.:

Let us imagine the internal motion of a body in the course of which its molecules, having retreated from one another, do not approach one another again, but the distance between them is filled up with new molecules, which in their turn move asunder and make room for new ones. Such an internal motion of a body would be its growth, at least a geometrical scheme of growth. If we compare a little green apple just formed from the ovary with a large red fruit we shall realise that the molecules composing the ovary could not create the apple while moving only in three-dimensional space. They need in addition to this a continuous motion in time, a continuous deviation into the space which lies outside the three-dimensional sphere. The apple is separated from the ovary by time. From this point of view the apple represents three or four months' motion of molecules along the fourth dimension. If we imagine the whole of the way from the ovary to the apple, we shall see the direction of the **fourth** dimension, that is, the mysterious fourth perpendicular—the line perpendicular to all three perpendiculars of our space and parallel to none of them […] The outline of a tree gradually spreading into branches and twigs is, as it were, a diagram of the fourth dimension (Ouspensky 1931: chap. 2; original emphasis), see also Hinton 2004.

In four-dimensional space **the entire life cycle of a tree**, including all its age concepts, from the first sprout to the half-rotten stump (see figure 7, chapter 1), **can be perceived at once**.[8] This is what Aksënov (1896) wrote about perception of four-dimensional space and its objects:

> If we had access to the fourth dimension, if we could see in the direction of this dimension, could behold the four-dimensional space with its objects, we would discover that [in three-dimensional space] we perceive not the whole objects but only their cross-sections in the direction perpendicular to the fourth dimension, that is, that we perceive not the real world, not real objects, but only the ideal (subjective) world and the ideal (subjective) objects—we would discover that the real object will be obtained only if we take the object of our perception in all the moments of its existence and sum them all up... Then, in particular, we would discover that what we call a "human being" is something ideal (subjective), partial and that the real human being comes out only if we take him along his entire stretch on the line of time (Aksënov 2011: 107) [translation S. Zhigalkin].[9]

While imagining a four-dimensional object (tree, banana) as extending along the fourth coordinate axis, it should be kept in mind that all the age concepts that it is made up of are consecutively positioned in the same domain of three-dimensional space (cf. the description of an apple in Ouspensky's quote).

The life cycle of a three-dimensional object perceived at once (i.e. all its age concepts are perceived simultaneously) shall be called an **integral**

---

[8] As one of Mozart's biographers wrote, Mozart could hear his entire symphony in one second.

[9] Human perception of the third dimension is likewise astonishing. We automatically reconstruct a three-dimensional object from its two-dimensional projection. What we directly perceive is the world of two-dimensional images (Bower 1974: chap. 4). The third dimension (depth) is "computed" and gradually added in the visual cortex of the brain: "Visual information is initially represented as 2D images on the retina, but our brains are able to transform this input to perceive our rich 3D environment [...] spatial representations gradually transition from 2D-dominant to balanced 3D (2D and depth) along the visual hierarchy" (Finlayson et al. 2017: 507).

3.2. Models of activity development for individuals and ethnic groups

concept. An integral concept defines the category of four-dimensional objects. For example, similar to the age concept (39) TREE (chapter 1) which defines the category of three-dimensional trees, the integral concept TREE defines the category of four-dimensional trees.

It is reasonable to assume that the basic meanings of *tree* and *banana* (cf. (41) and (43) in subsection 1.5.3) will also broaden and become integral concepts in the language of *Homo perfectus*.

But the most important acquisition of *Homo perfectus* will be his liberation from the dictates of the physical body, which, in accordance with its needs and desires, directs the emotions, thoughts, and actions of *Homo sapiens sapiens*.[10] Like a monk convinced of his faith or a perfect yogi, *Homo perfectus* will cease to be a machine in the sense of Gurdjieff and will gain true freedom of will. His desires and actions will obey thought.

The emergent community of perfect people would again **become homogeneous**, similar to the homogeneous Pirahã tribe (see section 3.2), and its members would gain **complete mutual understanding**. On the basis of a common understanding of the goals of the harmonious development of mankind, the collective thinking of *Homo perfectus* will become the main factor ensuring their achievement.

To conclude this brief analysis, I would like to express a hope that the practically forgotten issue of *Homo perfectus* will again draw the attention of academia and become a subject matter of a wide transdisciplinary discussion. In this connection, I would like to quote Pyotr Ouspensky, who wrote about a century ago:

> [...] popular wisdom has never regarded man as the crowning achievement of creation. It has always understood the place of man, and always accepted and admitted the thought that there can and must be beings who, though also human, are much higher, stronger, more complex, more "miraculous," than ordinary man. It is only the opaque and sterilised thought of the last centuries of European culture which has lost touch with the idea of superman and put as its aim man as he is, as he always was and always will be. And in this comparatively

---

[10] According to G. I. Gurdjieff, man is a machine, cf.: "All the people... are machines, actual machines working solely under the power of external influences [...] functions of the *physical body* govern all the other functions, in other words, everything is governed by the body which, in its turn, is governed by external influences" (quoted by Ouspensky 2001: chap. One; original emphasis).

short period of time, European thought had so thoroughly forgotten the idea of superman that, when Nietzsche threw out this idea to the West, it appeared new, original and unexpected. [...]

Evolution towards superman is the creation of new forms of thinking and feeling, and the abandonment of old forms. [...]

Nietzsche's Zarathustra speaks of this in the following words:

"I teach you the superman. Man is something that has to be surmounted. What have you done to surmount man?

What is the ape to man? A laughing stock or a sore disgrace! And just the same shall man be to the superman—a laughing stock or a sore disgrace" (Nietzsche 1906: 11). [...]

"What is great in man is that he is a bridge and not a goal; what is lovable in man is that he is an over-going and a down-going" (Ibid.: 13).

These words of Zarathustra have not entered into our usual thinking (Ouspensky 1931: chap. 3).

In a recent TV interview (05/13/2019, https://www.youtube.com/watch?v=mS4gzAozJ5A), to the question of the correspondent Vladimir Pozner: "What will you say to the Almighty when you meet with Him," Chomsky answered: "Why did you do such a crappy job?" [reversed translation A. Kravchenko]. If we assume that humanity is not the final stage of the evolution of hominids, then in response Chomsky could hear: "*Homo sapiens sapiens* represents the initial stage of the creation of *Homo perfectus.*"

3.3. Systematization of mental representations and conceptualization of linguistic meanings

Let us consider in more detail the close interdependencies between the progress of a society (expansion of its activities), the development of the mental representations of the world held by its members, and the development of its language[11] (the expansion of its linguistic units).

---

[11] As was mentioned in subsection 3.1.2, the term **language progress**, introduced by Baudouin de Courtenay, refers to the formation of new linguistic units caused by the progress of the civilizational component of the culture of a ethnogroup.

3.3.1. Two principles of development. In our further analysis a role of great importance is played by the general theory of development that stems from Spencer's seminal work (1864) and is presented in a number of later works (Sechenov 1952: 272–426; Solov'ëv 1988: 140–148; Werner 2004; Chuprikova 2007; Koshelev 2011). This theory is based on two principles. According to the first principle, the development of a particular integral whole (ethnogroup, living organism or its integral component, etc.) consists in a transformation of this whole into a system of its interconnected components. Such a transformation takes place in two steps: first the whole is differentiated into several independent components, and then these components are integrated into a system functionally identical to the initial whole, see section 1.2, chapter 1. According to the second principle, such development is preconditioned by two interacting factors: intrinsic (genetic) and extrinsic or environmental (influence from without). As Sechenov (1952) put it in his *Elements of Thought*, where this principle was developed and minutely illustrated, "always and everywhere life is made up by the cooperation of two factors, a specific but changing [nervous] organization and an influence from without" (Sechenov 1952: 288).

To demonstrate how these principles work, let us take as an example the two-stage development of a syncretic representation of an object[12] into a hierarchical structure of its features and their meanings. The first, genetically conditioned, stage consists in the elementary development cycle (designated as ◊) that differentiates the syncretic representation of an object into separate features (basic adjectival concepts), such as COLOR, SHAPE, WEIGHT, etc. Each feature is, in itself, a syncretic set of undifferentiated meanings; the feature COLOR is not yet differentiated into a palette of prototypical colors, for example.

At the second stage, conditioned by the child's personal experience—his practical and vocal activities—each feature is differentiated into a range

---

[12] The term 'syncretism' is used to refer to the undifferentiated mental representation of an object, when it is not divided into separate components (properties or parts). It could be compared to how Bower (1974: chap. 5) describes the inherent primitive unity of a child's sensory modalities that allows the child to perceive objects as undivided wholes, when visual properties are not differentiated from their tactile properties. Later on in the process of the child's cognitive development separate sensory properties begin to be singled out from the syncretic representation of an object—its shape, color, size, etc. (Bower 1974; Sechenov 1952: 272–426).

of separate meanings (concrete properties, or concrete adjectival concepts). The feature COLOR is differentiated into the values GREEN, RED, etc., the feature SHAPE into ROUND, CUBIC, etc., the feature WEIGHT into LIGHT, HEAVY, and so forth (to distinguish features from their values, the latter are given in capitals). The relationship between a feature and its values will be viewed as a genus–species relationship and designated by ▷: COLOR ▷ (GREEN, RED, etc.) (for more detail, see Koshelev 2019: chap. 5, § 2). As a result, the mental representation of an object (the concept OBJECT) takes the form of a three-level hierarchical structure:

(5) a. Syncretic (whole) concept   OBJECT

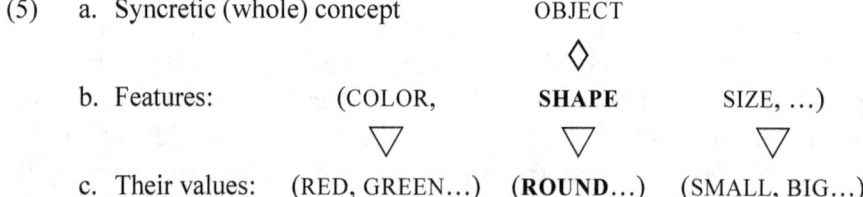

b. Features: (COLOR,   **SHAPE**   SIZE, ...)
                       ▽   ▽   ▽
c. Their values: (RED, GREEN...) (**ROUND**...) (SMALL, BIG...)

In this structure, on the first level (5a) a syncretic representation of object is given, on the second level (5b) its representation as a system of features (basic adjectival concepts): OBJECT = (COLOR, **SHAPE**, SIZE, etc.), and on the third level (5c) each feature is represented by a set of concrete values (specific adjectival concepts, see (28b), chapter 1) through which it is manifested.

Thus, the syncretic representation of an object transforms into a hierarchical system of its features and their values. And because concepts of concrete objects become the main values of concrete nouns, the whole structure (5) illustrates the steps in the development of these meanings during childhood.[13]

There is evidence that the differentiation of representations of objects into features begins before 18 months, as it is roughly after 18 months that children distinguish object shapes, that is, the different values of the feature Shape (Landau et al. 1988; Markson et al. 2008: 204) as well as the values of other features—size, weight, texture, etc. (Bower 1974: chap. 5, 6). The evidence that specific object shapes appear in children's mental representations is provided by a tendency known as the **shape bias** (Landau et al. 1988). It may be found in children at 18-months of age and has been described as follows: "[w]hen children learn the name of a novel object, they tend to extend that name to other objects similar in shape—a phenomenon referred to as the shape bias" (Markson at al. 2008: 204).

---

[13] On the alternative approaches to lexical decomposition, see Pustejovsky 1991; 2013.

3.3. Systematization of mental representations...

Shape is usually understood as the property of an object that fills some part of three-dimensional space (cf., for example, the description of a child's perception of three-dimensional shapes given by Pereira and Smith (2009: 67)). It is reasonable to assume that, in the totality of singled-out features, **SHAPE** is initially the main feature (highlighted in bold type) that represents a three-dimensional object, while other features supplement it; they are localized in shape, making the representation of an object complete. Thereby a binary relationship of combination (→) is established between the shape of an object and its other features: **SHAPE** → WEIGHT, **SHAPE** → COLOR, etc. This relationship shows that a supplementary feature has the same spatio-temporal locus as **SHAPE**. In light of this, an object is represented as a hierarchical system of its specific properties (the values of its features); as Sechenov (1952: 354) observed, "the combination of all of the sensorily accessible properties or characteristics determines the actual sensory image of any object." This is reminiscent of Moore's (1903: 41) proposition discussed by Vendler (1967: 172) that, unlike predicative adjectives of the *good* type, adjectives like *yellow* denote natural properties from which objects are construed as from parts.

Below is a somewhat abridged illustration that shows a developed structure of the mental representation of a typical banana—the concept BANANA that children acquire after 18 months (level (c) is filled with the prototypical meanings of features from level (b), cf. (28b) and (29), chapter 1):

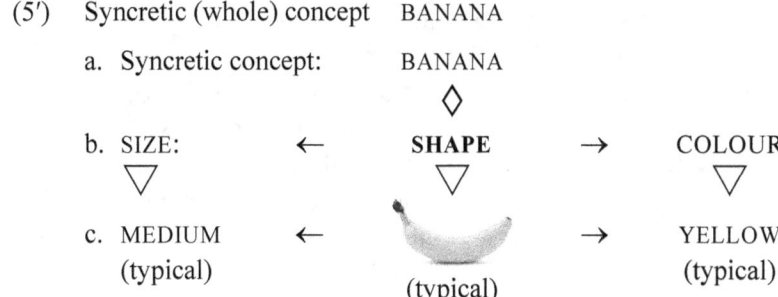

(5')   Syncretic (whole) concept   BANANA

    a. Syncretic concept: BANANA
        ◊

    b. SIZE: ←   **SHAPE**   →   COLOUR
       ▽   ▽   ▽

    c. MEDIUM   ←   →   YELLOW
      (typical)   (typical)   (typical)

After 24 months, during the next stage in the child's cognitive development, one more level appears in the structure (5') as a result of the next developmental cycle. On this level, **SHAPE** is represented as a system of its parts, cf. (30), chapter 1.

Let us now consider some peculiarities of Pirahã and how the Pirahãs perceive the world around them. Our immediate goal is to explain the absence of color terms in Pirahã.

3.3.2. The child's conceptualization of color and other properties. It is necessary to first understand the consistent patterns of adjective acquisition in first-language acquisition. A remarkable paradox may be noted here. Unlike in the case of nouns and verbs, which children learn to use semantically correctly almost at once,[14] the semantically correct use of adjectives comes only with time.

Although adjectives appear in a child's active vocabulary by the age of 18 months, for some time after their use is not based on their meanings but rather imitates the speech of the child's caretakers (Blackwell 2005; Voeikova 2011: 217). At the same time, the primary notion of semantic features, or classes (COLOR, SHAPE, etc.), "becomes apparent earlier than the distinction of homogeneous properties within each class" (Voeikova 2011: 114 ff.; see also Tseitlin 1996). Thus, the child soon ceases to confuse heterogeneous adjectives, such as *sour* and *big*, for example, but continues for some time to confuse homogeneous adjectives, calling a big object small, etc., cf.: "[Philip] can use one color term instead of another […] he can also say *bad* instead of *good* or *big* instead of *small*. In other words, the child would rarely say *bad* instead of *green*, but he can confuse *bad* and *good* or *green* and *red*" (Voeikova 2011: 218; see also: Andrick, Tager-Flusberg 1986; Ebeling, Gelman 1990; Gasser, Smith 1998; Tseitlin 1996).

Children begin to distinguish the colors of objects (their toys) at 18 months (see Rosengardt-Pupko 1948; 1963). However, they require at least another year to learn to use color terms semantically correctly (cf. Andrick, Tager-Flusberg 1986; Tseitlin 1996: 5–7).

Thus, on the one hand, children at the age of 18 months distinguish concrete colors of objects and yet, on the other hand, over the next 12 or even 18 months they seem to be incapable of naming the colors using appropriate adjectives despite repeatedly hearing these adjectives used correctly by adults.

To explain this paradox, I draw on the following general proposition. At the age of 12 months a child has an initial (but fast-growing) model of the world as a system of prelinguistic concepts (for more detail, see Koshelev 2019: 141–145; Waxman 2008: 101). Because of this the child is able to acquire words (lexical meanings) only when the initial correlates of their meanings have already been formed as elements of the model. To acquire a word

---

[14] Some research data indicate that children begin to acquire object categories and names at 12 months, and the categories and names of activities 2–3 months later (Xu, Carey 1996; Xu 2007; Waxman 2008).

3.3. Systematization of mental representations...

the child only has to relate it to a corresponding concept in his model. And this he does based on his observation of particular referential uses of the word by those around him.[15] For example, to learn the meaning of the adjective *red*, the child must have in his model the concept RED—prototypical red color as an independent element separate from other color elements (GREEN, etc.). Then, by observing referential uses of the adjective *red*, the child learns that it is the name of the concept RED. (He already "knows" that concepts in the model have names and he must simply learn them)[16].

The two-stage process of forming hierarchical representations of objects discussed above (see the schema in (5)) describes how the color concepts RED, GREEN, etc. are formed. During the first stage (up to 18 months) the child begins to single out separate sensory features in his (syncretic) representation of objects, such as SHAPE, COLOR, SIZE, and so forth (see level 5b in the schema). From 18 months on the child does not confuse heterogeneous adjectives like *green* and *small*, because their meanings reveal the character of their feature (Color or Size). But the concrete feature specification—GREEN or SMALL—is not yet contained in their meanings, because the meanings themselves are still syncretic, not broken down into concrete components. Therefore, the child may still confuse adjectives such as *green* and *red*, *small* and *big*, and so forth.

Later (during the second stage), based on the child's practical experience and acquisition of lexical names of feature values (*green*, *light*, etc.), within each feature are singled out the separate concepts RED, GREEN, etc., BIG, SMALL, etc.—different visible feature values (cf. level 5c in schema 5). These are now included in the meanings of the corresponding adjectives and children cease to confuse them. According to Voeikova (2011: 217–218), semantic errors in the use of color adjectives in children's speech disappear after the age of 2.5 years (see also Tseitlin 1996). This fact allows us to conclude that, by 2.5 years of age, the child's syncretic meaning of the

---

[15] This is facilitated by the basic ability for shared intentionality the child develops by the end of 12 months; it triggers the processes of joint attention and shared understanding of the current situation (Tomasello 2008: 154–155).

[16] In our view, at the age of 12 months the child's model of the world still lacks many important components found in the adult model, for example concepts of concrete properties. Therefore, at this age, the child is not yet able to understand and learn the names of such properties (for a somewhat different view, see Waxman 2008: 100–101; cf. also section 2.7, chapter 2).

feature COLOR transforms into a palette of concrete prototypical colors, each of which acquires an independent status (on further development of the notions of object properties, and particularly on differentiating separate hues of a concrete color, see Koshelev 2011: 225–228).

These developmental stages apply to the feature SIZE as well. This is indirectly attested by the fact that, while learning the words *big* and *small*, children continue for some time to confuse them just as they confuse color terms (Tseitlin 1996: 5–7). Notably, brain impairment in an adult may lead to regress, when mental representations of certain previously singled out and independent properties are lost. However, the ability to use their earlier developed syncretic correlates is retained. For example, a patient with damage to the cerebral cortex could toss a ball into any of three boxes positioned at different distances, yet he was unable to tell which of the boxes was the nearest and which the farthest (Goldstein, Scheerer 1941). The values of the feature Remoteness (concrete distance to an object), previously differentiated, were lost, but his perception of the distance to the box—a syncretic component of his holistic perception—was retained. Another patient, with damage to the basal temporal lobes, unerringly grasped objects of various sizes but was unable to indicate with thumb and index finger the size of the objects grasped (Goodale et al. 1991).

3.3.3. Does a child's language affect the process of differentiation? This important issue is treated in detail in section 2.7, chapter 2. Based on the research conducted by Waxman (Fulkerson, Waxman 2007; Waxman 2008), Hauser (2000), and others, it is shown that if, in the process of the child's cognitive development, the child begins to form a category—for example, 'globes'—their acquired names (nouns, such as *globe*, *ball*, etc.) speed up the formation process. If, however, the cognitive formation of a category has not started, the words that name the main feature of the category are unable to trigger its formation. For example, acquisition of the adjective *purple* does not trigger the formation of the category 'purple objects'.

3.3.4. Words for color in Pirahã: the role of color in the life of modern industrial societies and the Pirahã Indians. According to Everett (2008), the Pirahã color terms for black, white, red, and green are not simple words:

> More accurate translations of the Pirahã words showed them to mean: "blood is dirty" for black; "it sees" or "it is transparent" for white; "it is blood" for

3.3. Systematization of mental representations... 179

red; and "it is temporarily being immature" for green. [...] They perceive the colors around them like any of us. But they don't codify their color experiences with single words that are inflexibly used to generalize color experiences. They use phrases (p. 119).

Such use of analogy in color naming is not at all unusual. Similar analogous names are not uncommon in European languages, e.g. *bronze, copper*, and the like. What is unusual, however, is that in Pirahã there are no **direct** names for prototypical colors such as 'red' or 'green'. This brings to mind Berlin and Kay's (1969) cross-cultural research of color concepts with its notion of the basic color term—a single-word name for a color (*red, green*, etc.) that designates a basic category for which the prototypical color is the same across different ethnogroup. Summing up Eleonor Rosch's analysis of color terms in the language of the Dani tribe, Lakoff (1987: 41) points out that focal colors have "a special status within color categories—that of the best example of the category."

The absence of basic color terms in Pirahã allows us to assume that the color meanings of the feature Color remain syncretic, undifferentiated in the Pirahãs' mental representations. It would seem they have the same 'best example' of the color red—blood—as speakers of European languages;[17] however, this 'best example' does not seem to have facilitated the formation of a separate, independent prototype for the color red, the concept RED. Therefore, there is no meaning for the basic color term *red*.

Why do Pirahã children not differentiate the syncretic feature COLOR into a color palette, a set of separate color prototypes RED, GREEN, etc. characteristic of children in Europe, especially in view of the fact that the singling out of the feature COLOR does take place? The logical supposition based on the discussion above is that the development of Pirahã children does not include the stage responsible for the singling out of separate

---

[17] Or, to be more precise, *Standard Average European* (*SAE*). This concept was introduced by Whorf (1956) to group the modern Indo-European languages of Europe and includes practically all European languages [this is a problematic statement since it is not the case that practically all European languages are Indo-European languages. If by 'modern Europeans' and 'European languages' you are referring to speakers of Indo-European languages and those languages themselves (which in that case of course include many speakers / languages outside Europe) you would use that specific terminology.]

values of the feature COLOR. The reason for this, it may be hypothesized, lies in the absence of necessary extrinsic factors, above all relevant practices involving color—ordinary daily interactions with separate color meanings.

Children in modern industrial societies are exposed to at least two extrinsic factors that stimulate differentiation of concrete colors. Firstly, children actively engage in choosing objects exclusively by color. Color is extremely informative in a child's world full of randomly colored artifacts. A child may possess a number of similar toys, pieces of clothing, pairs of shoes, sweets, chess pieces, etc., which are only differentiated by color. Often, color can have a conventional symbolic function—for example, as in traffic lights. In addition, when drawing with crayons or watercolors, children are free to choose which color to use. Secondly, color-naming adjectives such as *red*, *green*, etc. are used in the ambient language to name both the colors of objects the child sees and the color patterns of multicolored objects—*red stripes*, *green polka-dots*, and the like.

In the world of Pirahã children everything is different. They are surrounded by a world with its natural invariable (or naturally variable) colors. Artifacts of arbitrary color are very few (the simplest articles of clothing, tools, etc.), and even these are not chosen but acquired or exchanged by chance. Moreover, in those cases when color is informative—for example, green as the evidence that fruit is not ripe—it is usually not the only criterion. While green bananas are sold at grocery stores, the Pirahãs pick bananas only when they are ripe and are not green anymore. And the state of ripeness is assessed by not only the color of the fruit but by other signs as well, such as the smell, color and condition of banana leaves, ripeness of other fruits that ripen at the same time as bananas, and so forth. An additional potential factor in the lack of color terms may be that the Pirahãs seem to lack any inclination for drawing, including the custom of painting their bodies with symbolic patterns—something found in many tribes over the world (Everett 2008: 115). Finally, the second, lexical factor is also absent as Pirahã does not have single-word correlates for the adjectives *red*, *green*, and the like that name colors directly.

Thus, there are grounds to assume that the absence of color-related practices in the ordinary activities of the Pirahãs does not allow their children from differentiating the syncretic spectrum of the feature Color, transforming it into a color palette—a set of separate prototypes as conceptual meanings for basic color terms. This precludes the appearance of the terms themselves.

By contrast, appearance of such practices facilitates formation of prototypes and color-naming words.[18]

The logic of the above argument is attested by the following fact. There are, in European languages, numerous analog designations for various color hues: *amber, amethyst, bronze, carrot, chestnut, chocolate, copper*, and so forth. Clearly, they are quite similar to color designations in Pirahã or, say, in Warlpiri: *yalyu-yalyu*, literally, 'blood-blood', meaning 'looks like blood', *yukuri-yukuri* ('grass-grass', or 'looks like grass after a rain'), and the like (Wierzbicka 2008: 410). It seems reasonable to assume that such designations have a similar explanation: the ordinary life speakers of these languages does not feature practices that would involve such hues; therefore, they have not been conceptualized in their color palette.

However, in modern communities of artists and designers, in whose activities color hues play an important role, these hues may be singled out as independent prototypes, thereby enriching the set of basic colors. In this case their names may acquire the status of basic terms. For example, designers may use the descriptor "pistachio" ('a pale yellow-green color') directly, without associating it with the color of pistachio nuts; then the adjective *pistachio* would have become a basic color term for the international community of designers.

3.3.5. Lexical indicators of time. Two-stage acquisition of color adjectives by children is also typical of other groups of words that designate various

---

[18] This thought was first formulated by W. Gladstone in 1858. He expressed it while explaining why "the organ of colour and its impressions were but partially developed among the Greeks of the heroic age" (Gladstone 1858, 3: 487–488, 496), cf.: "The perception of color, Gladstone says, seems natural to us only because mankind as a whole has undergone a progressive 'education of the eye' over the last millennia [...] But why, one may well ask, should this progressive refinement of color vision not have started much earlier than the Homeric period? [...] Gladstone's answer is a masterstroke of ingenuity, but one that seems almost as bizarre as the state of affairs it purports to account for. His theory was that color—in abstraction from the object that is colored—may start mattering to people only once they become exposed to artificial paints and dyes. The appreciation of color as a property independent of a particular material may thus have developed only hand in hand with the capacity to manipulate colors artificially. And that capacity, he notes, barely existed in Homer's day: the art of dyeing was only in its infancy, cultivation of flowers was not practiced, and almost all the brightly colored objects that we take for granted were entirely absent" (Deutscher 2010: 38–39).

(alternative) meanings of particular features (common properties). It has been noted above that children confuse indicators of time such as *yesterday / tomorrow*: *My **savtra** xodili v les* 'We went to the wood **tomorrow**' (Nastia, 28 months); *Ya k babushke **vchra** poedu* 'I'm going to my grandma's **yesterday**' (Voeikova 2011: 115–116, 173). Such errors have a similar explanation; the child already distinguishes the feature 'non-present time' from the feature 'present time', but the meanings of the former, 'past-yesterday' and 'future-tomorrow', remain undifferentiated. However, differentiation will happen quickly as it is motivated by the child's daily experience—the daily cycle in which these notions are strictly separate from 'today', and the lexicon (the child keeps hearing the words *yesterday* and *tomorrow* used by others).[19] But in the mental world of the Pirahãs analogous concepts are absent; their life is not divided into daily cycles:

> Pirahãs take naps (fifteen minutes to two hours at the extremes) during the day and night. There is loud talking in the village all night long. [...] Because different fish can be caught at different times of the day and night, Pirahã men can be found out fishing at any time. This means that there is less differentiation between day and night, aside from visibility. A Pirahã man is as likely to be found fishing at 3 a.m. as at 3 p.m. or 6 a.m. [...] If someone catches fish at 3 a.m., then that is when it will be eaten. Everyone will get up to eat as soon as it is brought in (Everett 2008: 77, 79).

This is why there are practically no direct correlates of such lexical indicators of time in Pirahã as *yesterday, today, morning, evening, week*, and so forth, typical for European languages. What Pirahã does have are descriptive time markers that correspond, in their descriptive character, to the descriptive nature of their designations for colors. Here are some of them: *pi'í* 'now', *hoa* 'day' (lit. 'fire'), *ahoái* 'night' (lit. 'be at fire'), *hisó* 'during the day' (lit. 'in sun'), *hisóogiái* 'noon' (lit. 'in sun big be'), *piiáiso* 'low water' (lit. 'water skinny temporal'), *piibigaíso* 'high water' (lit. 'water thick temporal'), *hibigíbagá'áiso* 'sunset / sunrise' (lit. 'he touch comes be temporal'), *'ahoakohoaihio* 'early morning, before sunrise' (lit. 'at fire inside eat

---

[19] A similar phenomenon may be found in the case of many other names for alternating objects and events. For example, when they begin to use personal pronouns children at first confuse them, using *I* instead of *you* and vice versa. Interestingly, this also happens in sign language acquisition; children often use a gesture to point at the interlocutor when referring to themselves, and vice versa (Petitto 1987).

3.3. Systematization of mental representations... 183

go') (Everett 2005: 631). Essentially, all of these are absolute characteristics of time periods immediately recognized by their observable features.

There are both absolute and relative time markers in English, Russian, and other European languages. For example, the words *morning* and *evening* denote relative periods of time (within a sequence of periods, 'night', 'morning', 'day', 'evening') and do not have directly observable visual markers (late in the morning or early in the evening it may be as light as at midday). And the indicators *now, sunrise, sunset, midday* designate visually identifiable periods of time. Compare also the following pairs: *low tide—piiáiso* 'low water'; *midday—hisóogiái* 'in sun big be'.

Thus, there are only absolute temporal markers in Pirahã, while European languages have both absolute and relative temporal markers.

3.3.6. Counting and count words. Commenting on the absence of numerals in Pirahã, Everett writes:

> At first I thought that the Pirahãs had the numbers one, two, and "many," a common enough system around the world. But I realized that what I and previous workers thought were numbers were only relative quantities. [...] And I also noticed that they could use what I thought meant "two" for two small fish or one relatively larger fish, contradicting my understanding that it meant "two" and supporting my new idea of the "numbers" as references to relative volume—two small fish and one medium-size fish are roughly equal in volume, but both would be less than, and thus trigger a different "number," than a large fish. Eventually numerous published experiments were conducted by me and a series of psychologists that demonstrated conclusively that the Pirahãs have no numbers at all and no counting in any form (Everett 2008: 116–117).

Everett's observations allow us to suppose that the Pirahãs have formed only precursory notions of the category "number": *hói* 'a small number', *hoí* 'a large number', *xogió* 'all or almost all' (Everett 2005: 623). However, further differentiation of these notions into concrete sets—exact meanings of the feature Number expressed by count words—appears to have never happened. This fact seems entirely natural in light of the fact that the Pirahãs do not use counting in their daily life at all, cf.: "As I observed more carefully, I saw that they never used their fingers or any other body parts or external objects to count or tally with" (Everett 2008: 116–117).

A genetically conditioned predisposition to count undoubtedly exists in human infants (see, for example, Ivanov 2008: 3), but an external factor—the absence of counting practices—slows its development. It should be noted that it is the absence of such practices (and not of count words) that provides the main evidence for the Pirahãs lacking conceptualizations for exact numbers (quantities). It has been shown experimentally (Frank et al. 2008) that count words do not change our mental representations of number but serve as a tool for dealing with large sets. For example, the Warlpiri (Australian aborigines) use counting despite the fact that the numeral system in their language is impoverished (Everett 2008: 220). This seemingly paradoxical situation can be easily explained. It arises through gestural counting, using fingers (and toes or other body parts). Cf.:

> In the child's developing communication and in the reconstructed languages of many language families, finger gestures serve as symbols for corresponding numbers; this may be considered a universal feature of natural languages in which, as a rule, the numeral 5 used to mean 'one hand', 10 'both hands', etc. […] [N]europsychologists come to the conclusion that language and mathematics are independent of each other, and to the proposition, in the spirit of Plato, that the notion of number appears before the word that stands for it (Varley et al. 2005; Brannon 2005; Dehaene 2007). […] It may be hypothesized that the earlier notion of number was first embodied in gesture, and only later in word (Ivanov 2008: 5, 7).

The need for counting practices is supported by an analysis of count words used by the Mundurukús, a community of hunters-gatherers who also live in Amazonia. As noted by Pica et al. (2004), in contrast to the Pirahãs they have some count words: from "one" to "five." However, the Mundurukús use their words for 'three', 'four', and 'five' to refer not only to the exact numbers but also to amounts close to these numbers; they choose these words intuitively, that is, without making an exact count (Ibid.: 499–500). Nonetheless, some Mundurukús can count exactly (slowly and non-verbally, using fingers or toes); yet, like Pirahãs, they seldom count as they have no practical need for exact counting (Ibid.: 503). For a more detailed analysis of the relationship between counting and count words see Kibrik (2018).

It should be emphasized that number acquisition in children is a two-stage process. First, the feature Number is singled out in their mental representations, followed by its meanings—concrete quantities. Evidence for this two-stage process comes from children's acquisition of count words, a process quite similar to the acquisition of color words described above. Initially, in children's utterances, "numerals appear before the noun, but, as a whole,

3.3. Systematization of mental representations...

the structure only resembles functionally similar utterances of adults because the real number of objects does not correspond to the number named by the numeral" (Voeikova 2011: 115). Only later does the child learn to name numbers correctly.

3.3.7. Absence of the passive voice. According to Everett, the Pirahã culture is based on the **immediacy of perception** principle. According to this principle, the only knowledge that is certain is that which comes from immediate perception or personal experience, or from stories told by eye-witnesses. Practically all the Pirahãs' interests and attention are focused on what happens 'in the here and now'. Cf.:

> [...] Pirahãs don't store food, they don't plan more than one day at a time, they don't talk about the distant future or the distant past-they seem to focus on now, on their immediate experience. [...] The Pirahãs simply make the immediate their focus of concentration [...] They have no craving for truth as a transcendental reality. Indeed, the concept has no place in their values. Truth to the Pirahãs is catching a fish, rowing a canoe, laughing with your children, loving your brother, dying of malaria (Everett 2008: 131–132, 273).

As the above quote demonstrates, Everett believes that this principle predetermines not only the everyday and cultural aspects of the Pirahãs' life (poverty of rituals and folklore, absence of artistic fiction, etc.), but also the unique features of their language—in particular, recursion (cf. Everett 2008: 132–133; Futrell et al. 2016).

Adopting this view as a whole, I will provide a corroborating example. I am going to show that absence of the passive voice in Pirahã relates to the immediacy of perception principle. In order to substantiate this thesis I will rely on a cognitive approach to explaining the meanings of voice (for more details, see Koshelev 2016). The approach consists in explaining visually observed situations with the help of cognitive components not unlike those singled out by Talmy (1985: 57, 61) and used to describe a situation of motor activity—'Figure' (the moving Agent or object), 'Path' (trajectory), and so forth.

The analysis below is based on data from Russian and is given as an illustration; its goal is to show that the meaning of the passive voice is highly abstract. Unlike the meaning of the active voice, which directly reflects an observed event (the Agent, the main participant in the event, is expressed by a nominal subject, etc.), the meaning of the passive voice reflects a specific interpretation of this event (the nominal subject expresses the passive participant in the event, while the Agent is expressed by a noun in the instrumental case). With this in view, it is natural to infer that the Pirahãs might not have any need for such an oblique interpretation of a perceived action. And thus, there is no demand for the passive meaning.

The basis of what follows is a general concept of action. By 'action' I designate observed uniform changes undergone by an object. The action (these changes) may be caused by the object itself (its internal energy)—in which case it is an **independent** action—or by the action of another object, in which case it is a **dependent** action. The voice value of a verb indicates the type of action (dependent or independent) that involves the doer—the referent of the subject. The active voice expresses an **independent** action of the doer, and the passive a **dependent** action of the doer.

Consider (6), where the driver is involved in an **independent** action (the verb *moet* 'is washing' is in the active voice), and (7), where the car (the subject of the verb) is involved in a **dependent** action (the verb *moetsja* 'is being washed' is in the passive voice):

(6) *Šofěr* **moet** *mašinu* 'The driver is washing the car'.

(7) *Mašina* **moetsja** *šofěrom* 'The car is being washed by the driver'.

To clarify our definitions, let us take a closer look at the situation described in (6). The transitive verb *moet* 'is washing' designates not a single transitive action but a tripartite structure—two actions that are in a causal relationship to each other. The first action involves the driver: he dips a rag in a bucket of water, moves the wet rag over the surface of the car body, and so forth. This is an independent action because it is achieved by the driver's energy (activity). The second action involves the car: its surface becomes cleaner. This is a dependent action caused by the first action. Thus, the sentence *Šofěr* **moet** *mašinu* 'The driver is washing the car' describes the following situation:

(8) situation "driver—car" =

> 'the driver is involved in an **independent** action (he dips a rag in a bucket of water, moves the wet rag over the surface of the car body, and so forth)'
>
> THEREFORE
>
> 'the car is involved in a **dependent** action (the car becomes cleaner)'.

3.3. Systematization of mental representations...

Now consider the sentence in (7). Strange as it may seem, it describes the same situation, (8), where the driver is still an active subject whose independent action causes the dependent action that involves the car. This inference is based on our knowledge of the described situation. And yet the meaning of (7) is notably different from the meaning of (6). As may be clearly seen, the difference lies in the different interpretations of the situation, (8), reflected in these sentences. In (6) the Agent, driver (referent of the subject), is the main situation participant and his main action is what he does to the Patient (car) (though while washing the car he might be smoking, talking to a friend, etc.). This interpretation is completely in agreement with the immediacy of perception principle as it is the outwardly more active and salient situation participant that is chosen as the main object of description and his main action is the visually more salient action taking place in the situation. The (physical) contact between the driver and the car also plays an important role; it manifests the causal relationship between the driver's action and the action that involves the car.

> **Note.** In a series of experiments conducted by Leslie (1982; 1984), infants at 3 months of age watched a collision of balls. If the red ball moved up to the green ball and stopped while the green ball immediately came into motion ('direct impact'), infants did not show any surprise (they ceased to pay attention to the event rather quickly). However, if the red ball stopped just a little short of the green ball and the latter nevertheless started to move ('impact without collision'), infants showed surprise. They were also surprised to see the red ball come up to the green ball and stop while the latter started to move, not at once, but with a delay ('deferred impact'). These and many other similar experiments show that very early on children interpret an impact between two active objects as evidence for a causal relationship between the objects' actions (for details, see Subbotskii 2007: 177–178).

Therefore, the sentence *Šofër* **moet** *mašinu* 'The driver is washing the car' directly describes an observed situation using its visual features. In the sentence *Mašina* **moetsja** *šofërom* 'The car is being washed by the driver' the emphasis is different. The car (former Patient), an inactive object that does not draw attention, is designated as the main participant in the situation and the main action is the dependent changes undergone by the car, the surface of the car becoming cleaner. Besides, the active participant in the situation, the driver (former Agent), is expressed by a noun in the instrumental case, that is, he is viewed as a tool that directly causes these changes but does not possess any activity of its own, cf.: *Mašina* **moetsja** *triapkoj* 'The car is being washed with a rag'. Therefore, it is permissible not to mention the tool at all: *Mašina moetsja* 'The car is being washed'. This interpretation seems to contradict the immediately perceived features of the situation participants. What could the possible motivation be in this case? Apparently, it is inclusion of the situation, (4), into a broader context that profiles other features of the situation not related to initial perception. First of all, it is the speaker's interest in the passive object and changes to it caused by an external action, regardless of whose action it was. Such an interpretation fits those situations in which the action may not be directly observed, cf.: *Vaša mašina moetsja* 'Your car is being washed' (it is at the carwash); or the action continues over a long period of time and it is not clear what is happening with the object at a given moment, cf.: *Dom stroitsja* 'A house is being built' (the immediate action is not always obvious even if the house is being directly observed).

Such interpretations are well outside of the immediacy of perception principle that prevails in the world of the Pirahãs.

The immediacy of perception principle acts similarly, but with a more robust effect, in the case of children. Vygotsky (1998) described an experiment conducted by a colleague:

> Two-year-olds repeat without any difficulty sentences such as: "The chicken is walking," "Koko is walking," or "The dog is running." But the child cannot say "Tanya is walking," when Tanya is sitting on a chair before him. This sentence gets the reaction, "Tanya is sitting" (p. 262).

As will be shown in subsection 3.4.1, the Pirahãs' perception of the world is not confined to this principle. But for them to go beyond it, it is necessary for corresponding situations to begin to appear in their everyday lives. And as long as this is not the case it may be assumed that the Pirahãs simply have no need for the use of passive constructions (in subsection 3.2.2 I discussed the conditions for the appearance of such situations and their description in the form of passive constructions).

3.3.8. On the universality of human concepts. The considerations given above allow us to contend that such concepts as color (GREEN, RED, etc.), size (BIG, SMALL, etc.), number (ONE, TWO, THREE, etc.), and others cannot be viewed as **universal** human concepts. With this in mind, let us consider the discussion on the universality of color concepts. As has already been mentioned, Berlin and Kay (1969) claimed that the English basic color terms *black, white, red, yellow, green, blue, brown, purple, pink, orange*

3.3. Systematization of mental representations... 189

and *grey* designate basic categories for which the central prototypes remain the same across different ethnic groups, and although in many languages there are fewer words for basic categories people are able to form all such categories. Wierzbicka (2005; 2008) holds a different view. Starting with the fact that some languages—for example Warlpiri, the language of the Australian aborigines—have neither the word *color* nor basic terms for focal colors, she assumes that color categories do not belong to human universals. Wierzbicka acknowledges that all humans live in the world of many colors, but not all humans conceptualize colors. According to Wierzbicka, for the speakers of languages that lack the word *color*, the question, What color is this? may not be asked and, obviously, does not arise. Therefore, they cannot think about color, either.

For Wierzbicka, the question whether the concept COLOR is universal is a question of principle. Answering this question in the negative, she excludes this concept from her list of universal semantic primes. Contesting Wierbizcka's logic, Kay (2015) notes that some languages lack the words *size*, *big* and *small*, *number*, *quantity*, *one*, *two*, and others, yet, despite this fact, Wierzbicka includes the concepts BIG and SMALL, ONE and TWO into universal semantic primes.

While this discussion cannot be addressed here in detail, note that the explanations given above resolve this conflict. From them it follows that color categories may be viewed as universal only potentially, in the sense that salience of the feature COLOR seems to be genetically conditioned. As for the extent to which the values of this feature develop, it is determined exclusively by external influences—the influences of practical everyday social activities. The same is also true in regard to the feature SIZE (see subsection 3.3.2).

> **Note.** From the preceding arguments it follows that the concept of a 'lexical / grammatical universal' is relative. It applies not to all languages but to a subset of languages that are in the same stage of development—in other words, to the 'Language—Society' pairs for which the societies have the same type of organization (homogeneous or heterogeneous). This should be considered in application to the one-hundred-word Swadesh list that includes, as basic words, the adjectives *green*, *yellow*, *red*, *big*, *small*, and the numerals *one*, *two*.

A similar approach should be taken to the argument between Everett and generativists about the universality of recursion (Everett 2008; 2009; Nevins et al. 2009a; 2009b; Futrell et al. 2016). Though I will not enter into this discussion here, I will simply express solidarity with the proposition that there is a considerable difference between languages with a writing system and those without that should be taken into account when discussing recursion (cf. Burlak 2018; Kibrik 2018).

3.3.9. Concluding remarks. The analysis given above shows the magnitude of the influence exerted by the progress of a ethnogroups (its civilizational component, according to Sapir) on the development of the content component of language—its lexical and grammatical elements. In this way we are able to understand the mechanisms by means of which, as Sapir wrote, the rapid development of Western European culture over the past 2,000 years was accompanied by "a corresponding accelerated rate of change in language" (Sapir 2008: 148).

Regarding Everett's claim that culture directly affects language structure (see subsection 3.1.1), it does not seem to be substantiated by hard evidence. Moreover, it is doubtful whether such a claim is justified at all. Indeed, as has been shown above, the crucial factor in the development of language in a developing society is the constantly arising new professional languages. However, each of these languages inevitably uses the syntax of the base (common) language when defining its new terms and metaphorical and idiomatic expressions. Of course, special constructions may appear in a new language that have not been used before, such as the construction *then, and only then* in mathematics and logic. But they must all be syntactically correct to ensure their unambiguous interpretation.[20] With this in view, it would be natural to assume that the culture of a society in an advanced stage of progress (that is to say, its civilizational progress) is unable to modify the syntax of its language—for example, to change its basic word order (SVO, SOV, etc.), as discussed by Pinker (see subsection 3.1.1).

> **Note.** Everett might be correct in saying that the Pirahã culture affected the structure of their language. The Pirahãs appear to be close to the initial level of civilizational progress, at which, according to Sapir's report 1911, such an influence is possible (see section 3.1.2). Let us consider, for the sake of argument, how such an influence could be produced with regard to basic word order in a sentence. A given word order may be interpreted as indicating the degree of information conveyed by the parts of speech in a sentence.

---

[20] As a matter of fact, this proposition implies that all professional languages are developed sublanguages of the ordinary language of a community.

For example, SVO indicates that the subject is most informative, after which comes the verb and then the direct object. But what it essentially means is that in the ethno-specific representation of the described situation the Agent is the most informative, the Action comes second, and the Patient is third. It reasonable to assume that such ethno-specificity (the informativity hierarchy among situation participants) forms the basis of the representation of the world of a community and may vary with different communities. And since there are grounds to believe that ethno-specific representations of situations are primary with regard to language (cf. Koshelev 2017: 16–21), sentential word order will also differ corresponding to such representations.[21] If this hypothesis is found to be substantiated by typological data, it may be possible to show that in the initial stages of a community's progress its culture may have an effect on its language, just as Sapir indicated in his 1911 report, see also subsections 2.5.5 and 2.6.2.

3.4. On the relative nature of 'exotic' linguistic properties

In this section, I would like to discuss two types of human perception of the world and express a unified point of view regarding the notion of 'exotic (unique) linguistic property', namely, to show its relative nature. The material for our specific discussion will be drawn from Everett's concepts and the Pirahã language.

3.4.1. Two principles of perception. As seen in subsection 3.3.7, Everett believes that the Pirahãs' life is dominated by the 'immediacy of perception principle' (IPP); this principle impedes the formation of general and abstract ideas devoid of concrete perceptual constituents. In particular, this accounts for the use of analogy in descriptions of prototypical colors (using the phrases 'like blood' to describe red, 'not ripe' for green, etc.); such descriptions apply to well-known objects of distinctive color. Everett contrasts

---

[21] This hypothesis is in sync with Paul's (1970: § 86) position, which held word order to be second (after simple juxtaposition of words) in importance among the linguistic means for expressing coherent human ideas, function words and word inflections being the sixth and seventh, correspondingly. He emphasized that, from the listed means of expression of coherence, the latter two might have formed gradually, in the course of long historical development, while the first two might have been at the speaker's disposal from the very beginning.

such descriptions to basic color terms such as *red, green*, etc. characteristic of European languages.

A similar situation is observed, according to Everett, with lexical indicators of time. He points out that Pirahã has no relative temporal markers—*yesterday, today, tomorrow, morning, evening, week, month*, and so forth. At the same time, Pirahã does have temporal markers that correspond, in their descriptive character, to Pirahã analog designations of colors: *hisóogiái* 'noon' (lit. 'in sun big be'), *hibigíbagá'áiso* 'sunset / sunrise' (lit. 'he touch comes be temporal'), *'ahoakohoaihio* 'early morning, before sunrise' (lit. 'at fire inside eat go') (Everett 2005: 631). Essentially, all of these are absolute characteristics of time periods immediately recognizable by their observed features.

Following this line of reasoning, one could inadvertently come to the conclusion that Pirahã follows only the immediacy of perception principle while speakers of European languages, by contrast, adhere to an alternative principle of mediated perception. It is not difficult to show that such a conclusion would not be true to facts. Indeed, as has been shown above, the immediacy of perception principle reflects the syncretic (undifferentiated) nature of the mental representations humans have of the world, and the mediated perception principle their systematicity. For example, the basic color spectrum domain is reflected in a Pirahã's mind as syncretic mental representations; therefore, reference to parts of this spectrum (separate colors) is not possible without the support of an identifying marker as the manifestation of a prototypical color: 'it is like blood'—"red," 'it is not ripe'—"green", etc. For the speaker of a European language, this syncretic spectrum is already differentiated into separate colors—radial categories (Lakoff 1987: chap. 6) with a central member—prototypical color—and other members, colors of the spectrum close to the prototype. For example, the radial category RED includes its central member, the prototypically red ('bloodlike') color, and less central members—brick color, wine purple, etc. I call such a representation of the color spectrum systematic because it is a set of separate but interconnected colors (they all constitute the meanings of COLOR as an object feature). Parts of this spectrum may be designated directly, without the use of the color markers / identifiers *red, green*, etc.

At the same time, as was noted above, ordinary speakers of European languages also have syncretic color representations. These have analog designations for well-known markers of particular colors: *amber, amethyst, bronze, carrot, chestnut,* and so forth. Therefore, speakers of European languages also have syncretic representations of some parts of the color spectrum, which

3.4. On the relative nature of 'exotic' linguistic properties

is a sign of immediate perception. Similarly, there are words in European languages that either designate relative periods of time that have no direct visual markers, such as *evening, morning, tomorrow*, etc., or are analog markers, such as *midday, sunrise, sunset*, etc. that directly describe visually identifiable time periods. The former reflect systemic, and the latter syncretic representations of the time spectrum.

> **Note.** I analyze mental representations of phenomenal events with a perceptual (visual) constituent. For example, the words *morning, day, evening* and *night* designate phenomenal events while the words *week, Monday, Tuesday* and the like do not. The latter are names of purely contemplative and conventional concepts. Therefore, as noted by Pinker and Jackendoff (2005: 206), such concepts may not be acquired without the mediation of language.

The preceding facts give grounds for supposing that speakers of European languages utilize both perception principles: immediate perception (syncretism) and mediated perception (systematicity).[22] I will now show that this conclusion holds true for the Pirahãs as well.

I have already discussed the Pirahãs' syncretic representations (in the color domain and the temporal domain). But there are domains in the Pirahã world whose representations are characterized by a quite detailed systematicity, while for speakers of European languages these domains are reflected in much less systematic representations. For example, the jungle plays a crucial role in the Pirahãs' everyday life. They know a great variety of trees and herbs, their medicinal and other properties, as well as ways of handling and using them. It would seem that the Pirahãs' mental representations in this domain are much more differentiated and systemic than those of the members of industrial societies. Therefore, there is a large class of concrete lexical items in Pirahã used to designate these plants, their properties, and ways of handling them. And this, I argue, stems from the Pirahãs' systemic principle, which governs their perception of the jungle. No less important are fishing, boating, and everything that has to do with the river. This is why their perception of the world is characterized by more minute details than the perception of the world by ordinary speakers of European languages. I will give two episodes from Everett's book that tell us about the Pirahãs' ability

---

[22] Cf.: "[C]ounter to Everett's claim, the 'immediacy of perception principle' is not a unique feature of Pirahã and is manifested in European languages as well, such as Russian and English" (Kravchenko 2019: 158).

to notice important details in the world around them that totally escaped Everett's visual attention.

In the first episode, Everett recalls how he and his daughter Shannon went out in a boat with some men to hunt an anaconda.

> Kóhoi and Poióí both paddled silently to a spot just beneath some overhanging trees on the right bank of the river. Kóhoi turned to me and Shannon and asked, "Do you see its hole there just under the water?" "No," we replied. I didn't see a thing. "Watch!" he said. At this, Kóhoi took his bow, like all Pirahã bows about two yards in length, and probed under the water for a few seconds. "That will make it mad." He giggled. "See it?" he asked. "No," I responded. Neither Shannon nor I could see a thing other than murky water, since it was still the rainy season. "See the dirt!" Kóhoi exclaimed. "It's moving now." I did see a small swirl of mud in the water. Before I could remark, Kóhoi had stood in the boat and drawn his bow. Thwang! Thwang! Two arrows were fired into the water within a second of each other. Almost immediately a ten-foot-long anaconda burst through the surface of the river, thrashing, with long Pirahã arrows through its head and body (Everett 2008: 113).

In the second episode, Everett recounts walking on a narrow jungle path with a teenage Pirahã, Kaioá.

> Suddenly he... said softly, "Look at the caiman up ahead!" I directed the beam of my flashlight up the path. I did not see a thing. "Turn off that lightninglike thing in your hand," Kaioá suggested, "and look in the dark." I followed his instructions. Now I really saw absolutely nothing. "What are you talking about?" I asked, beginning to feel that he was having me on. "There's nothing up ahead." "No! Look!" Kaioá giggled. My inability to see beyond my nose is a source of constant merriment among the Pirahãs. "See those two bloodlike eyes up there?" I strained my own eyes and then, sure enough, I could just make out two red dots about a hundred feet up ahead. Kaioá said that these were the eyes of a small caiman (Ibid.: 247).

In summary, I hypothesize that all childhood representations are initially syncretic. Later, in the course of the child's cognitive and social development, and as the child engages in concrete activities, certain representations become systemic while others remain syncretic.

I will consider numbers in the same way. Everett observes that, unlike European languages with their count words designating exact numbers, Pirahã has only names for approximate numbers: *hói* 'a small number', *hoí* 'a large

3.4. On the relative nature of 'exotic' linguistic properties 195

number', *xogió* 'all or nearly all', etc. However, European languages also have words for inexact numbers. For example, as noted by Burlak (2018), the word *para* 'lit. a couple' in Russian means 'a certain small number'. Thus, as a response to a request for a couple of matches one might receive three or even five matches. There is in addition a special count word *neskol'ko* 'a few' to designate a rough number between two to three and eight to ten. Similar observations can be made with regard to the passive voice absent in Pirahã (see subsection 3.3.7).

The relative nature of contrasts between the properties of Pirahã and European languages comes to the fore when we analyze Everett's famous claim that there is no recursion in Pirahã (Everett 2005: 622). On the one hand, there are in fact domains in European languages where recursion is hardly used at all. As observed by Burlak (2018: 23), "if we turn, not to writing, but to oral, spoken discourse, especially the everyday conversation register," we will find an almost complete reduction of embedded constructions (subordinate clauses, possessive constructions, and the like) (cf. also Dronov 2016: 323). On the other hand, some research (Nevins et al. 2009a; Salles 2015; Kibrik 2018; Nikulin 2018) has shown that certain utterances in Pirahã may actually be interpreted as recursive. The situation is similar in the case of phatic communication, which, according to Everett (2008), is not a feature of Pirahã: "There are no words for *thanks, I'm sorry* and so on" (p. 11). As Kibrik (2018) remarks, "this conclusion might be based on such cases being rather less frequent in the Pirahãs' communicative practices; however, there are many examples in the book which show that the phenomenon itself does exist" (p. 30).

In conclusion, I would like to state that. Both perception principles have been analyzed in the domain of **ordinary** activities and **ordinary** concepts of a society. I aimed to show that an ordinary member of any society, either homogeneous or heterogeneous, has representations of both types: syncretic and systemic. Therefore, typologically, the structure of ordinary concepts characteristic of a society does not depend on the level of its progress. At the same time it may be hypothesized that in societies at different levels of progress the ratio between these types of representations may differ noticeably. Thus, in a homogeneous society the ordinary activities in which its members are engaged are, on the average, much less sophisticated (more integral) than in a heterogeneous (industrial) society—consider, for example, such spheres in the latter as elaborate hygienic procedures, intricate rules for cooking and consuming food, various manipulations with exact numbers (counting), etc.

Therefore, a speaker of a European language will have many more systemic representations than, say, a Pirahã. This means that the progress of a society (expansion of its domain of professional activities) enhances the development of its representations of the world (cf. (3) in subsection 3.2.6), making it more systemic and, therefore, accessible to a deeper level of understanding. This hypothesis agrees with Gurdjieff's proposition that deeper understanding is conditioned by the codependent progress of human knowledge and human existence (cf. section 3.2.8).

3.4.2. 'Exotic linguistic property' as a relative feature. Within traditional linguistics there has long persisted the tendency to generalize theories pertaining to European languages, and primarily for English, across the world's languages (linguistic Eurocentrism). When certain languages or language properties did not fit into these theories, they would often be labeled as exotic. This tendency began to swing in the opposite direction after Dahl's (1990) paper under the symptomatic title, "Standard average European as an exotic language," and this reverse process continued to gather momentum due to publications that followed (Evans, Levinson 2009; Henrich et al. 2010; Majid, Levinson 2010; Dahl 2015; cf. also Kibrik 2018: 33–34). The preceding analysis provides a basis for the claim that the concept of an 'exotic (unique) linguistic property' appears to be a **relative** notion regardless of the accepted point of reference—a group of languages that have been viewed as manifesting the most general typological features. An 'exotic linguistic feature' is conditioned not by some intrinsic factor, such as the development of language as an independent human subsystem, but by the level of social progress indirectly reflected in language.

References

Aksënov, M. S. *Transtsedental'no-kinetičeskaja teorija vremeni* [Transcendental-Kinetic Theory of Time]. Moscow: Jazyki slavjanskix kul'tur, 2011.

Aktivnyj slovar' sovremennogo russkogo jazyka [An Active Dictionary of Modern Russian], edited by Iu. D. Apresian. Pervyj vypusk. Vol. 1, 2. Moscow, 2014.

Andrick, G. R. and H. Tager-Flusberg. "The acquisition of colour terms." *Journal of Child Language* 13 (1986): 119–37.

Apresian, Iu. D. *Leksičeskaja semantika: sinonimičeskie sredstva jazyka* [Lexical Semantics. The synonymical means of language]. Moscow, 1974. 2nd ed., *Izbrannye trudy*. Vol. 1, *Leksičeskaja semantika: sinonimicheskie sredstva jazyka*. Moscow, 1995.

Aristotle. *The categories. On interpretation. Prior analytics.* L.: William Heinemann ltd; Harvard University Press, 1962.

Arnauld, A. and P. Nicole. *Logic Art Thinking*, edited by J. V. Buroker. Cambridge, MA: Cambridge University Press, 1996.

Saint Augustine. *The Confessions of Saint Augustine*, translated by E. B. Pusey. 2002. URL: https://www.gutenberg.org/files/3296/3296-h/3296-h.htm

Austin, J. L. *Philosophical Papers.* Oxford: Clarendon Press, 1961.

Baddelley, A. *Your Memory: A users guide.* Prion Books, 1996.

— —. "Is working memory still working?" *American Psychologist* 56, iss. 11 (2001): 851–64.

Baillargeon, R. "Infants' physical world." *Current Directions in Psychological Science* 13 (2004): 89–94.

Barsalou L. W. "Perceptual symbol systems." *Behavioral and Brain Sciences* 22 (1999): 577–660.

Berlin, B. "The concept of rank in ethnobiological classification: Some evidence from Aguaruna folk botany." *American Ethnologist* 3 (1976): 381–39.

— — and P. Kay. *Basic Color Terms: Their Universality and Evolution.* Berkeley: University of California Press, 1969.

Bernshtein, N. A. *Biomexanika i fiziologija dviženij* [Biomechanics and Physiology of Movements]. Moscow: Medgiz, 1947.

— —. *Očerki po fiziologii dvizhenij i fiziologii aktivnosti* [Essays on the Physiology of Movements and the Physiology of Activity]. Moscow: Medicina, 1966.

Berwick, R. C. and N. Chomsky. *Why Only Us: Language and Evolution.* Cambridge, MA: MIT Press, 2016.

Bickerton, D. *Language and Species.* Chicago: University of Chicago Press, 1990.

———. "Language evolution: A brief guide for linguists." *Lingua* 117 (2007): 510–26.

———. *Adam's Tongue: How Humans Made Language, How Language Made Humans.* N. Y.: Hill and Wang, 2009.

———. "On two incompatible theories of language evolution." In *The Evolution of Human Language: Biolinguistic Perspectives*, edited by R. K. Larson, V. M. Déprez, and H. Yamakido, 199–210. Cambridge: Cambridge University Press, 2010.

———. *More Than Nature Needs.* Cambridge, MA: Harvard University Press, 2014.

Blackwell, A. A. "Acquiring the English adjective lexicon: Relationships with input properties and adjectival semantic typology." *Journal of Child Language* 32, iss. 3 (2005): 535–62.

Bloom, L. *One Word at a Time: The Use of Single-Word Utterances Before Syntax.* The Hague: Mouton, 1973.

Bloom, P. "Generativity within language and other cognitive domains." *Cognition* 51 (1994): 177–89.

Boduen de Kurtene, I. A. *Izbrannyje trudy po obŝemu jazykoznaniju* [Selected Works on General Linguistics]. Vol. I–II. Moscow: Academy of Sciences of the USSR, 1963.

Bolhuis, J., Tattersall, I., Chomsky, N., and R. Berwick. "How could language have evolved?" *PLoS Biology* 12 (2014): 1–6.

Boroditsky, L. "Metaphoric structuring: Understanding time through spatial metaphors." *Cognition* 75, iss. 1 (2000): 1–28.

———. "How does our language shape the way we think?" In *What's Next? Dispatches on the Future of Science*, edited by M. Brockman, 116–29. N. Y.: Vintage, 2009.

Bower, T. G. R. *Development in Infancy.* San Francisco, CA: W. H. Freeman, 1974.

Brannon, E. M. "The independence of language and mathematical reasoning." *Proceedings of the National Academy of Sciences of the USA* 102, iss. 9 (2005): 735–40.

Brown, R. "How shall a thing be called?" *Psychological Review* 65 (1958): 14–21.

———. *Social Psychology.* N. Y.: Free Press, 1965.

Burlak, S. A. "Jazyk piraxan i razgovornaja reč'" [Pirahã and Colloquial Speech]." *Rossijskij žurnal kognitivnoj nauki* 5, iss. 1 (2018): 22–6.

Butterworth, G. and M. Harris. *Principles of Developmental Psychology.* L.: Psychology Press, 1994.

References

Casasola, M. and L. B. Cohen. "Infant categorization of containment, support, and tight-fit spatial relationships." *Developmental Science* 5 (2002): 247–64.

— —, Cohen, L. B., and E. Chiarello. "Six-month-old infants' categorization of containment spatial relations." *Child Development* 74 (2003): 679–93.

Choi, S., McDonough, L., Bowerman M., and J. M. Mandler. "Early sensitivity to language-specific spatial categories in English and Korean." *Cognitive Development* 14 (1999): 241–68.

— — and M. Bowerman. "Learning to express motion events in English and Korean: The influence of language-specific lexicalization patterns." *Cognition* 41 (1991): 83–121.

— — and A. Gopnik. "Early acquisition of verbs in Korean: A cross-linguistic study." *Journal of Child Language* 22 (1995): 497–529.

Chomsky, N. "Language in a psychological setting." *Sophia Linguistica* 22 (1987): 1–73.

— —. *Language and Problems of Knowledge: The Managua Lectures.* Cambridge, MA: MIT Press, 1988.

— —. "Linguistics and cognitive science: Problems and mysteries." In *The Chomskyan Turn*, edited by A. Kasher, 26–53. Cambridge, MA: Blackwell, 1991.

— —. *New Horizons in the Study of Language and Mind.* N. Y.: Cambridge University Press, 2000.

— —. "Some simple evo-devo theses: How true might they be for language?" In *The Evolution of Human Language: Biolinguistic Perspectives*, edited by R. K. Larson, V. M. Déprez, and H. Yamakido, 45–62. Cambridge: Cambridge Univerisity Press, 2010.

Chunharas, C., Rademaker, R. L., Sprague, T. C., Brady, T. F., and J. T. Serences. "Separating memoranda in depth increases visual working memory performance." *Journal of Vision* 19, iss. 4 (2019): 1–16.

Chuprikova, N. I. *Umstvennoe rezvitie. Princip differenciacii* [Mental development. The principle of differentiation]. St. Petersburg: Piter, 2007.

Clark, E. V. *First language acquisition.* 2nd ed. N. Y.: Cambridge University Press, 2009.

Condillac, É. B. de. *Essay on the Origin of Human Knowledge*, translated and edited by H. Aarsleff. Cambridge: Cambridge University Press, 2001.

Corballis, M. C. "Language evolution: A changing perspective." *Trends in Cognitive Sciences* 21, iss. 4 (2017): 229–36.

— —. "Minimalism and evolution." *Frontiers in Communication* (2019). Doi: https://doi.org/10.3389/fcomm.2019.00046.

Dahl, Ö. "How WEIRD are WALS languages?" Paper presented at the conference: Diversity linguistics: Retrospect and prospect, Max Planck Institute for Evolutionary Anthropology, Leipzig, Germany, May 1–3, 2015.

Dehaene, S. "A few steps toward a science of mental life." *Mind, Brain and Education* 1, iss. 1 (2007): 28–47.

Deutscher, G. *Through the Language Glass: Why the world looks different in other language.* N. Y.: Metropolitan, 2010.

Dowty, D. "Thematic proto-roles and argument selection." *Language* 67, iss. 3 (1991): 547–619.

Dronov, P. S. "Tak li už nesovmestimy točki zrenija D. Everetta i generativistov? [How incompatible are D. Everett's and the generativist points of views?]" In Everett, D. *Don't Sleep, There Are Snakes: Life and Language in the Amazonian Jungle*, translated from English by I. V. Mokin, P. S. Dronov, and E. N. Panov, 309–24. Moscow: Izdatel'skij dom Jazyki slavjanskix kul'tur, 2016.

Ebeling, K. S. and S. A. Gelman. "Flexibility in semantic representations: Children's ability to switch among different interpretations of 'big' and 'little'." *Papers and Reports on Child Language Development* 29 (1990): 38–46.

Eliseeva, M. B. *Stanovlenie individual'noj jazykovoj sistemy rebënka: rannie ètapy* [Formation of the Child's Individual Language System: Early stages]. Moscow: Jazyki slavjanskoj kul'tury, 2015.

Evans, N. and S. C. Levinson. "The myth of language universals: Language diversity and its importance for cognitive science." *Behavioral and Brain Sciences* 32, no 5 (2009): 429–92.

Evans, V. *The Language Myth: Why Language is Not an Instinct.* Cambridge: Cambridge University Press, 2014.

Everaert, M., Huybregts, M., Berwick, R., Chomsky, N., Tattersall, I., Moro, A., and J. Bolhuis. "What is language and how could it have evolved?" *Trends in Cognitive Sciences* 21 (2017): 569–71.

Everett, D. "Cultural constraints on grammar and cognition in Pirahã: Another look at the design features of human language." *Current Anthropology* 46 (2005): 621–46.

——. *Don't Sleep, There are Snakes: Life and language in the Amazonian jungle.* N. Y.: Pantheon Books, 2008.

——. "Pirahã culture and grammar: a response to some criticism." *Language* 85, iss. 2 (2009): 405–42.

——. *How Language Began: The story of humanity's greatest invention.* N. Y.: W. W. Norton, 2017.

Ferry, A., Hespos, S., and S. Waxman. "Categorization in 3- and 4-month-old infants: An advantage of words over tones." *Child Development* 81, iss. 2 (2010): 472–79.

Finlayson, N. J., Zhang, X., and J. D. Golomb. "Differential patterns of 2D location versus depth decoding along the visual hierarchy." *NeuroImage* 147 (2017): 507–16.

Fodor, J. "The present status of the innateness controversy." In *RePresentations: Philosophical essays on the Foundations of Cognitive Science*, edited by J. Fodor, 257–316. Cambridge, MA: MIT Press, 1981.

Frank, M., Everett, D., Fedorenko, E., and E. Gibson. "Number as a cognitive technology: Evidence from Pirahã language and cognition." *Cognition* 108 (2008): 819–24.

Fulkerson, A. L. and S. R. Waxman. "Words (but not Tones) facilitate object categorization: Evidence from 6- and 12-month-olds." *Cognition* 105, iss. 1 (2007): 218–28.

Futrell, R., Stearns, L., Everett, D. L., Piantadosi, S. T., and E. Gibson. "A corpus investigation of syntactic embedding in Pirahã." *PLOS One* 3 (2016).

Gallese, V. and G. Lakoff. "The brain's concepts: The role of the sensory-motor system in conceptual knowledge." *Cognitive Neuropsychology* 22, no 3/4 (2005): 455–79.

Gasser, M. and L. Smith. "Learning nouns and adjectives: A connectionist account." *Language and Cognitive Processes* 13, no 2/3 (1998): 269–306.

Gelernter, D. "Recursive structure." Accessed December 3, 2016. https://www.edge.org/response-detail/10574

Gentner, D. and L. Boroditsky. "Individuation, relativity and early word learning." In *Language Acquisition and Conceptual Development*, edited by M. Bowerman and S. Levinson, 215–56. N. Y.: Cambridge University Press, 2001.

—— and M. Bowerman. "Why some spatial semantic categories are harder to learn than others: The typological prevalence hypothesis." In *Crosslinguistic Approaches to the Psychology of Language: Research in the tradition of Dan Isaac Slobin*, edited by J. Guo et al., 465–80. N. Y., NY: Erlbaum, 2009.

Givón, T. *On Understanding Grammar.* N. Y.: Academic Press, 1979.

——. "On the co-evolution of language, mind, and brain." *Evolution of Communication* 2 (1998): 45–116.

Gladstone, W. E. *Studies on Homer and the Homeric Age.* 3 vols. Oxford: Oxford University Press, 1858.

Gleitman, L. and A. Papafragou. "New perspectives on language and thought." In *The Oxford Handbook of Thinking and Reasoning*, edited by K. J. Holyoak and R. G. Morrison, 543–68. Oxford: Oxford University Press, 2012.

Göksun, T., Hirsh-Pasek, K., and R. M. Golinkoff. "Figure and ground: Conceptual primitives for processing events." Paper presented at the conference: Foundations for learning relational terms: What is in an event? Symposium at the 11th International Congress for the Study of Child Language. Edinburgh, 2008.

——, Hirsh-Pasek, K., and R. M. Golinkoff. "Processing figures and grounds in dynamic and static events." In *Proceedings of the 33rd Annual Boston University*

Conference on Language Development, edited by J. Chandlee, M. Franchini, S. Lord, and G. Rheiner, 199–210. Somerville, MA: Cascadilla Press, 2009.

— —, Hirsh-Pasek, K., and R. M. Golinkoff. "Trading spaces: Carving up events for learning language." *Perspectives on Psychological Science* 5, iss. 1 (2017): 33–42.

Goldstein, K. and M. Scheerer. "Abstract and concrete behavior an experimental study with special tests." *Psychological Monographs* 53, iss. 2 (1941): i–151.

Golinkoff, R., Chung, H. L., Hirsh-Pasek, K., Liu, J., Bertenthal, B. I., Brand, R., Maguire, M. J., and E. Hennon. "Young children can extend motion verbs to point-light displays." *Developmental Psychology* 38, iss. 4 (2002): 604–14.

— — and K. Hirsh-Pasek. "How toddlers begin to learn verbs." *Trends in Cognitive Science* 12 (2008): 397–403.

Goodale, M. A., Milner, A. D., Jakobson, L. S., and D. P. Carey. "A neurological dissociation between perceiving objects and grasping them." *Nature* 349 (1991): 154–56.

Grashchenkov, P. V. *Grammatika prilagatel'nogo. Tipologija ad"ektivnosti i atributivnosti* [The Grammar of Adjectives. Typology of Adjectivity and Attributivity]. Moscow: Izdatel'skij Dom JaSK, 2018.

Greenfield, P. "Language, tool and brain: The ontogeny and phylogeny of hierarchically organized sequential behavior." *Behavioral and Brain Sciences* 14 (1991): 531–95.

Griffiths, P. D. and M. Atkinson. "A 'door' to verbs." In *The development of Communication*, edited by N. Waterson and C. Snow, 311–19. L.: Wiley, 1978.

Gvozděv, A. N. *Formirovanie u rebënka grammatičeskogo stroja russkogo jazyka* [Formation of the Russian grammar structure in a child]. Part 2. Moscow: APN RSFSR, 1949.

Hanson, C. and W. Hirst. "On the representation of events: A study of orientation, recall, and recognition." *Journal of Experimental Psychology: General* 118 (1989): 136–47.

Hauser, M. D. *Wild Minds: What animal really think.* N. Y.: Henry Holt, 2000.

— —, Chomsky, N., and W. T. Fitch. "The faculty of language: What is it, who has it, and how did it evolve?" *Science* 298 (2002): 1569–79.

Henrich, J., Heine, S. J., and A. Norenzayan. "The weirdest people in the world?" *Behavioral and Brain Sciences* 33, iss. 2–3 (2010): 61–83.

Hespos, S. J. and R. Baillargeon. "Young infants' actions reveal their developing knowledge of support variables: Converging evidence for violation-of-expectation findings." *Cognition* 107 (2008): 304–16.

— — and T. Piccin. "To generalize or not to generalize: Spatial categories are influenced by physical attributes and language." *Developmental Science* 12 (2009): 88–95.

— — and E. S. Spelke. "Conceptual precursors to language." *Nature* 430 (2004): 453–6.

Hinton, C. H. *The Fourth Dimension*. Leeds: Celephaïs Press, 2004. http://www.astrumargenteum.org/wp-content/uploads/2015/06/Hinton-The-Fourth-Dimension.pdf

Humboldt, W. von. "Über die Verschiedenheit des menschlichen Sprachbaues und ihren Einfluss auf die geistige Entwickelung des Menschengeschlechts." In *Wilhelm von Humboldt's gesammelte Werke*. Bd 6, 1–425. Berlin: G. Reimer, 1848.

— —. "Über das vergleichende Sprachstudium in Beziehung auf die verschiedenen Epochen der Sprachentwicklung." In *Wilhelm von Humboldts Werke*, edited by A. Leitzmann. Bd 4: 1820–1822, 1–34. Berlin: Walter de Gruyter, 1905.

Isenina, E. I. *Doslovnyj period razvitija reči u detej* [The Pre-lexical Period of Speech Development in Children]. Saratov, 1986.

Ivanov, Viach. Vs. "Ob èvolucii pererabotki i peredači informacii v soobŝestvax ljudej i životnyx [On the evolution of information processing and transfer in human and animal communities]." *Voprosy jazykoznanija* 4 (2008): 3–14.

Jackendoff, R. *Semantics and Cognition*. Cambridge, MA: MIT Press, 1983.

— —. *Semantic Structures*. Cambridge, MA: MIT Press, 1990.

— —. "How language helps us think." *Pragmatics and Cognition* 4 (1996): 1–34.

— —. *Language, Consciousness, Culture: Essays on Mental Structure*. Cambridge, MA: MIT Press, 2007.

— —. "Your theory of language evolution depends on your theory of language." In *The Evolution of Human Language: Biolinguistic Perspectives*, edited by R. K. Larson, V. M. Déprez, and H. Yamakido. Cambridge: Cambridge University Press, 2010.

Jerison, H. *Evolution of the Brain and Intelligence*. N. Y.: Academic Press, 1973.

Kasevich, V. B. *Vvedenie v jazykoznanie* [Introduction to Linguistics]. Moscow: Academia, 2011.

Kay, P. "Universality of color categorization." In *Handbook of Color Psychology*, edited by Andrew J. Elliot, M. D. Fairchild, and A. Franklin, 245–58. Cambridge, UK: Cambridge University Press, 2015.

Kibrik, A. A. "Tiranija čužogo uma [The tyranny of others' minds]." *Rossijskij žurnal kognitivnoj nauki* 5, iss. 1 (2018): 27–35.

Kisch, S. "'Deaf discourse': The social construction of deafness in a Bedouin community." *Medical Anthropology* 27 (2008): 283–312.

——. "Demarcating generations of signers in the dynamic sociolinguistic landscape of an shared sign-language: The case of the Al-Sayyid Bedouin." In *Endangered Sign Languages in Village Communities: Anthropological and Linguistic Insights*, edited by U. Zeshan and C. de Vos, 87–125. Berlin: Mouton de Gruyter & Ishara Press, 2012.

Kol'tsova, M. M. *Obobščenie kak funkcija mozga* [Generalization as a Brain Function]. Leningrad: Nauka, 1967.

——. *Dvigatel'naja aktivnost' i razvitie funkcij mozga rebënka (Rol' dvigat. analizatora v formirovanii vysš. nervnoj dejatel'nosti rebënka)* [Motor Activity and Development of Brain Functions in Children (The role of motor analyzer in shaping the child's higher nervous activity)]. Moscow: Pedagogika, 1973.

——. *Razvitie signal'nyx sistem dejstvitel'nosti u detej* [Development of Reality Signal Systems in Children]. Leningrad, 1980.

Koshelev, A. D. "O sxeme leksičeskogo značenija predmetnogo suščestvitel'nogo i eë funkcionirovanii v akte kommunikacii [On the lexical meaning schema of a concrete noun and its functioning in the act of communication]." In *Verenica liter: Sb. st. k 60-letiju V. M. Živova*, 516–70. Moscow: Jazyki slavjanskix kul'tur, 2006. http://akoshelev.net/?part=11&m-32

——. "V poiskax universal'noj sxemy razvitija [In search of a universal development schema]." In *Integracionno-differencionnaja teorija razvitija*, compiled by N. I. Chuprikova and A. D. Koshelev, 217–34. Moscow: Jazyki slavjanskix kul'tur, 2011. https://independent.academia.edu/AlexeyKoshelev

——. *Kognitivnyj analiz obščečelovečeskix konceptov* [Cognitive Analysis of Universal Human Concepts]. Moscow: Rukopisnye pamjatniki Drevnej Rusi, 2015. https://independent.academia.edu/AlexeyKoshelev

——. "O strukturnom i genetičeskom sxodstve leksičeskix i grammatičeskix značenij (kognitivnyj analiz glagol'noj perexodnosti i zaloga) [On structural and genetic similarities of lexical and grammatical meanings (a cognitive analysis of verb transitivity and voice)]." *Izvestija RAN. Serija literatury i jazyka* 75, iss. 3 (2016) 19–39.

——. *Očerki èvoljucionno-sintetičeskoj teorii jazyka* [Essays on the Evolutionary-Synthetic Theory of Language]. Moscow: Izdatel'skij dom Jazyki slavjanskix kul'tur, 2017. https://independent.academia.edu/AlexeyKoshelev

——. "O vlijanii kul'tury sociuma na ego jazyk (na primere amazonskogo plemeni piraxa) [On the influence of culture on language (the case of the Amazonian tribe Pirahã)]." *Rossijskij žurnal kognitivnoj nauki* 5, iss. 1 (2018a): 44–62. URL: http://cogjournal.org/5/1/index.html

— —. "Ob otnositel'nosti 'ekzotičeskix' svojstv jazyka indejcev piraxa i ix principov vosprijatija mira [On the relativity of "exotic" features of Piraha and the principles underlying their worldview]." *Rossijskij žurnal kognitivnoj nauki* 5, iss. 1 (2018b): 7–9. http://cogjournal.org/5/1/index.html.

— —. *Essays on the Evolutionary-Synthetic Theory of Language.* Moscow; Boston: LRC Publishing House; Academic Studies Press, 2019.

Kosslyn, S. M. *Image and Brain: The resolution of the imagery debate.* Cambridge, MA: MIT Press, 1994.

— —. "Scanning visual images: Some structural implications." *Perception & Psychophysics* 14 (1973): 90–4.

— —. "Mental images and the brain." *Cognitive Neuropsychology* 22, iss. 3–4 (2005): 333–47.

Kravchenko, A. V. "Naskol'ko ėkzotičen 'princip neposredstvennosti vosprijatija' v jazyke piraxa? [How exotic is the 'immediacy of experience principle' in Pirahã?]" *Sibirskij filologičeskij žurnal* 1 (2019): 148–60.

Lakoff, G. *Women, Fire, and Dangerous Things: What Categories Reveal about the Mind.* Chicago: University of Chicago Press, 1987.

Lakusta, L., Wagner, L., O'Hearn, K., and B. Landau. "Conceptual foundations of spatial language: Evidence for a goal bias in infants." *Language Learning and Development* 3 (2007): 179–97.

— — and S. Carey. "Infants' categorization of sources and goals in motion events." Paper presented at the conference: Conceptual primitives for processing events and learning relational terms. Symposium at the XVIth International Conference on Infant Studies. Vancouver, Canada, 2008.

— —, Spinelli, D., and R. Garcia. "The relationship between pre-verbal event representations and semantic structures: The case of goal and source paths." *Cognition* 7, no. 164 (2017): 174–87.

Landau, B., Smith, L. B., and S. S. Jones. "The importance of shape in early lexical learning." *Cognitive Development* 3, no 3 (1988): 299–321.

Langacker, R. W. *Foundation of Cognitive Grammar.* Vol. 1, *Theoretical Prerequisites.* Stanford: Stanford University Press, 1987.

Lepskaia, N. I. *Jazyk rebënka. Ontogenez rečevoj kommunikacii* [The Child's Language. Ontogeny of speech communication], compiled by T. V. Bazzhina. Moscow: RGGU, 2013.

Leslie, A. M. "The perception of causality in infants." *Perception* 11 (1982): 173–86.

— —. "Spatiotemporal continuity and the perception of causality in infants." *Perception* 13 (1984): 287–305.

Longman Dictionary of Contemporary English. Italy, 2009.

Maguire, M. J., Hirsh-Pasek, K., Golinkoff, R. M., and S. M. Pruden. "The way you do that thing you do: Attention to path and manner in action words." Paper presented at the conference: How event cognition turns into event language. Symposium presented at biennial meeting of the Society for Research in Child Development. Tampa, FL, 2003 (April).

Majid, A. and S. C. Levinson. "WEIRD languages have misled us, too." *Behavioral and Brain Sciences* 33, iss. 2–3 (2010): 103.

Mandler, J. M. "How to build a baby: II. Conceptual primitives." *Psychological Review* 99 (1992): 587–604.

— —. *The Foundations of Mind: Origins of conceptual thought.* N. Y.: Oxford University Press, 2004.

— —. "Actions Organize the Infant's World". In *Action Meets Word: How children learn verbs*, edited by K. Hirsh-Pasek and R. M. Golinkoff, 111–33. N. Y.: Oxford University Press, 2006.

Markson, L., Diesendruck, G., and P. Bloom. "The shape of thought." *Developmental Science* 11, no 2 (2008): 204–8.

Marr, N. Ia. *Izbrannye raboty* [Selected Works]. Vol. I. Leningrad: USSR Academy of Sciences Publishing, 1933.

— —. *Izbrannye raboty* [Selected Works]. Vol. III. Leningrad: USSR Academy of Sciences Publishing, 1936.

Mel'čuk, I. A. *Language: From Meaning to Text.* Moscow: LRC Publishing House & Boston: Academic Studies Press, 2016.

Mervis, C. "Early lexical development: The contributions of mother and child." In *Origins of Cognitive Skills*, edited by C. Sophian, 339–70. Hillsdale, N. J.: Lawrence Eribaum Associates, 1984.

— —. "Child-basic object categories and early lexical development." In *Concepts and Conceptual Development: Ecological and Intellectual Factors in Categorization*, edited by U. Neisser, 201–33. N. Y.: Cambridge University Press, 1987.

Moore, G. E. *Principia Ethica.* Cambridge: Cambridge University Press, 1903.

Morgan, L. H. *Ancient Society, or Researches in the Lines of Human Progress from Savagery through Barbarism to Civilization.* Culcutta: BHARTI LIBRARY, Booksellers & Publishers, 1944.

Müller, F. M. *Lectures on the Science of Language.* Vol. 2. Longmans, Green, and Company, 1885.

Munnich, E., Landau, B., and B. Dosher. "Spatial language and spatial representation: A cross-linguistic comparison." *Cognition* 81 (2001): 171–208.

Nelson, K. "Some evidence for the cognitive primacy of categorisation and its functional basis." *Merrill-Palmer Quarterly* 19 (1973): 21–39.

Nevins, A., Pesetsky, D., and C. Rodrigues. "Pirahã exceptionality: A reassessment." *Language* 85, iss. 2 (2009a): 355–404.
— —, Pesetsky, D., and C. Rodrigues. "Evidence and argumentation: A reply to Everett." *Language* 85, iss. 3 (2009b): 671–81.
Nietzsche, F. *Thus Spake Zarathustra*, translated by Th. Common. Edinburgh, 1906.
Nikulin, A. V. "Princip neposredstvennosti vosprijatija i jazykovye fakty [The immediacy of perception principle and linguistic data]." *Rossijskij žurnal kognitivnoj nauki* 5, iss. 1 (2018): 81–93.
Norbury, H. M., Waxman, S. R., and H. Song. "Tight and loose are not created equal: An asymmetry underlying the representation of fit in English- and Korean-speakers." *Cognition* 109 (2008): 316–25.
Ouspensky, P. D. *A New Model of the Universe: Principles of the Psychological Method in Its Application to Problems of Science, Religion and Art*, translated from the Russian by R. R. Merton, under the supervision of the author. N. Y.; L.: Knopf; Routledge, 1931.
— —. *In Search of the Miraculous: Fragments of an unknown teaching*. San Diego: Harcourt. 2001.
Padden, C., Meir, I., Sandler, W., and M. Aronoff. "Against all expectations: Encoding subjects and objets in a new language." In *Hypothesis A / Hypothesis B: Linguistic Explorations in Honor of David M. Perlmutter*, edited by D. Gerdts, J. Moore, and M. Polinsky, 383–400. Cambridge, MA: MIT Press, 2010.
Paducheva, E. V. *Dinamičeskie modeli v semantike i leksike* [Dynamic Models in Semantics and Lexis]. Moscow: Jazyki slavjanskoj kul'tury, 2004.
Paivio, A. *Imagery* and *Verbal Processes*. N. Y.: Holt, Rinehart & Winston, 1971.
— —. *Mental Representations*. N. Y.: Oxford University Press.1973.
— —. "Dual coding theory and education." Draft paper for The Conference on Pathways to Literacy Achievement for High Poverty Children. The University of Michigan School of Education, September 29—October 1, 2006.
Partee, B. "Compositionality." In *Varieties of Formal Semantics*, edited by F. Landman, F. Veltman, 281–312. Dordrecht, 1984.
Paul, H. *Prinzipien der Sprachgeschichte*. Studienausgabe der 8. Aufl. Tübingen: Max Niemeyer Verlag, 1970.
Pereira, A. F. and L. B. Smith. "Developmental changes in visual object recognition between 18 and 24 months of age." *Developmental Science* 12 (2009): 67–80.
Perelmutter, I. A. "Aristotle." In *Istorija lingvističeskix učenij. Drevnij mir* [A History of Linguistic Teachings. The Ancient World], edited by S. D. Kacnel'son and A. V. Desnickaja, 156–79. Leningrad: Nauka, 1980.

Petitto, L. A. "On the autonomy of language and gesture: Evidence from the acquisition of personal pronouns in American Sign Language." *Cognition* 27, iss. 1 (1987): 1–52.

Pica, P., Lemer, C., Izard V., and S. Dehaene. "Exact and approximate arithmetic in an Amazonian indigene group." *Science* 306 (2004): 499–503.

Pinker, S. *The Language Instinct: The New Science of Language and Mind.* L.: The Penguin Press, 1994.

— —. *How the Mind Works.* N. Y.: W. W. Norton & Company, 1997.

— —. *The Stuff of Thought: Language as a Window Into Human Nature.* N. Y.: Viking, 2007.

— —. *Language, Cognition, and Human Nature: Selected Articles.* Oxford: Oxford University Press, 2013

— — and R. Jackendoff. "The faculty of language: What's special about it?" *Cognition* 97 (2005): 201–36.

Potebnia, A. A. *Polnoe sobranie trudov. Mysl' i jazyk* [Complete Works. Thought and Language]. Moscow: Labirint, 1999.

Pruden, S. M., Hirsh-Pasek, K., Maguire, M. J., and M. A. Meyer. "Foundations of verb learning: Infants form categories of path and manner in motion events." In *Proceedings of the 28th annual Boston University Conference on Language Development*, edited by A. Brugos, L. Micciulla, and C. E. Smith, 461–72. Somerville, MA: Cascadilla Press, 2004.

— —, Hirsh-Pasek, K., and R. M. Golinkoff. "Current events: How infants parse the world and events for language." In *Understanding Events: How Humans See, Represent, and Act on Events*, edited by T. F. Shipley T. F. and J. M. Zacks, 160–92. N. Y.: Oxford University Press, 2008.

— —, Göksun, T., Roseberry, S., Hirsh-Pasek, K., and R. M. Golinkoff. "Find your manners: How do infants detect the invariant manner of motion in dynamic events?" *Child Development* 83 (2012): 977–91.

— —, Roseberry, S., Göksun, T., Hirsh-Pasek, K., and Golinkoff R. M. "Infant categorization of path relations during dynamic events." *Child Development* 84 (2013): 331–45.

Pulverman, R., Brandone, A., and S. J. Salkind. "One-year-old English speakers increase their attention to manner of motion in a potential verb learning situation." Paper presented at the 29th Annual Boston University Conference on Language Development. Boston, MA, 2004.

— —, Chen, J., Chan, C., Tardif, T., and X. Meng. "Cross-cultural comparisons of attention to manner and path: Insights from Chinese infants." Poster presented at the meeting of the Society for Research on Child Development. Boston, MA, 2007 (March).

Pulverman, R., Golinkoff, R. M., Hirsh-Pasek, K., and J. Sootsman-Buresh. "Infants discriminate paths and manners in nonlinguistic dynamic events." *Cognition* 108 (2008): 825–30.
Pustejovsky, J. "The generative lexicon." *Computational Linguistics* 17, iss. 4 (1991): 409–41.
———. "Type theory and lexical decomposition." In *Advances in Generative Lexicon Theory*, edited by J. Pustejovsky, P. Bouillon, H. Isahara, K. Kanzaki, and C. Lee, 9–38. Dordrecht: Springer, 2013.
Pylyshyn, Z. W. "What the mind's eye tells the mind's brain: A critique of mental imagery." *Psychological Bulletin* 80 (1973): 1–24.
———. "Mental imagery: In search of a theory." *Behavioral and Brain Sciences* 25 (2003): 157–237.
Rakison, D. H. "When a rose is just a rose: The illusion of taxonomies in infant categorization." *Infancy* 1, no 1 (2000): 77–90.
—— and G. Butterworth. "Infants' use of parts in early categorization." *Developmental Psychology* 34, iss. 6 (1998): 1310–25.
—— and L. B. Cohen. "Infants' use of functional parts in basic-like categorization." *Developmental Science* 2 (1999): 423–32.
Ramscar, M. and U. Hahn. "What family resemblances are not: The continuing relevance of Wittgenstein to the study of concepts and categories." In *Proceedings of the 20th Annual Conference of the Cognitive Science Society*, edited by M. A. Gernsbacher and S. J. Derry, 865–70. Mahwah, NJ: Lawrence Erlbaum, 1998.
Richardson, J. T. E. *Mental Imagery and Human Memory*. N. Y.: St. Martin's Press, 1980.
Richardson, A. *Mental Imagery*. N. Y.: Springer, 1969.
Rosch, E. (Eleanor Heider). "Natural Categories." *Cognitive Psychology* 4 (1973): 328–50.
———. "Cognitive Reference Points." *Cognitive Psychology* 7 (1975a): 532–47.
———. "Cognitive Representations of Semantic Categories." *Journal of Experimental Psychology: General* 104 (1975b): 192–233.
———. "Principles of Categorization." In *Cognition and Categorization*, edited by E. Rosch and B. B. Lloyd, 27–48. Hillsdale, NJ: Erlbaum. *1978*.
———, Mervis, C. B., Gray, W. D., Johnson, D. M., and P. Boyes-Braem. "Basic objects in natural categories." *Cognitive Psychology* 8, no 3 (1976): 382–439.
Rozengardt-Pupko, G. L. *Reč' i razvitie vosprijatija v rannem vozraste* [Speech and Development of Perception in Young Children]. Moscow: Učpedgiz, 1948.
———. *Formirovanie reči u detej rannego vozrasta* [Formation of Speech in Young Children]. Moscow: Učpedgiz, 1963.

Ryle, G. "Ordinary language." In *Philosophy and Ordinary Language*, edited by C. E. Caton, 128–53. Urbana, 1960.

Salles, R. "Understanding recursion and looking for self-embedding in Pirahã. The case of possessive constructions." A Master's Thesis, PUC-Rio, Rio de Janeiro, 2015.

Sandler, W. "Vive la différence: Sign language and spoken language in language evolution." *Language and Cognition* 5 (2013): 189–203.

— —, Meir, I., Dachkovsky, S., Padden, C., and M. Aronoff. "The emergence of complexity in prosody and syntax." *Lingua* 121, iss. 13 (2011): 2014–33.

Santos, L. R., Sulkowski, G. M., Spaepen, G. V., and M. D. Hauser. "Object individuation using property / kind information in rhesus macaques (Macaca mulatta)." *Cognition* 83 (2002): 241–64.

Sapir, E. *Language. An Introduction to the Study of Speech*. Oxford: Oxford University Press, 1921.

— —. *The Collected Works of Edward Sapir*. Vol. 3, *Culture*, edited by R. Darnel, Regna, J. T. Irvine, and R. Handler. Berlin, N. Y.: Mouton de Gruyter, 1999.

— —. *The Collected Works of Edward Sapir*. Vol. 1, *General Linguistics*, edited by P. Swiggers. Berlin: Mouton de Gruyter, 2008.

Sechenov, I. M. *Izbrannye proizvedenija* [Selected Works]. Vol. 1, *Fiziologija i psixologija* [Physiology and Psychology], edited and foreword by Kh. S. Koshtoiants. Moscow: Akad. nauk SSSR, 1952.

Seston, R., Golinkoff, R. M., Ma, W., and K. Hirsh-Pasek. "Vacuuming with my mouth? Children's ability to comprehend novel extensions of familiar verbs." *Cognitive Development* 24, iss. 2 (2009): 113–24.

Shepard, R. N. and J. Metzler. "Mental rotation of three-dimensional objects." *Science* 171 (1971): 701–3.

Slobin, D. I. *Psycholinguistics*. Glenview: Scott, Foresman & Company, 1979

— —. "From 'thought and language' to 'thinking to speaking'." *Rethinking Linguistic Relativity*, edited by J. J. Gumperz and S. C. Levinson, 70–96. Cambridge, United Kingdom: Cambridge University Press, 1996.

— —. "From ontogenesis to phylogenesis: What can child language tell us about language evolution?" *Biology and Knowledge Revisited: From neurogenesis to psychogenesis*, edited by J. Langer, S. T. Parker, and C. Milbrath, 255–85. Mahwah, N. J.: Lawrence Erlbaum. 2004.

Solov'ëv, V. S. *Sočinenija* [Works], in 2 vols. Vol. 2. Moscow: Mysl', 1988.

Song, L., Golinkoff, R. M., Seston, R., Ma, W., Shallcross, W., and K. Hirsh-Pasek. "Action stations: Verb learning rests on constructing categories of action." Poster presented at 31st Boston Language Conference. Boston, MA, 2006.

Spencer, H. *The Principles of Biology*. Vol. 1. L; N. Y., 1864.
Squire, L. R. "Mechanisms of Memory." *Science* 232 (1986): 1612–19.
Stout, D. "Skill and cognition in stone tool production: An ethnographic case study from Irian Jaya." *Current Anthropology* 45, iss. 3 (2002): 693–722.
— —. "The social and cultural context of stone-knapping skill acquisition." In *Stone Knapping: The necessary conditions for a uniquely hominin behavior*, edited by V. Roux and B. Bril, 331–40. Cambridge: McDonald Institute for Archaeological Research, 2005.
Subbotskii, E. V. *Strojaščeesja soznanie* [Consciousness Constructed]. Moscow, 2007.
Talmy, L. "Semantics and syntax of motion." In *Syntax and Semantics 4*, edited by J. P. Kimball, 181–238. N. Y.: Academic Press, 1975.
— —. "Lexicalization patterns: Semantic structure in lexical forms." In *Language Typology and Syntactic Description*. Vol. III, *Grammatical Categories and the Lexicon*, edited by T. Shopen, 57–149. N. Y.: Cambridge University Press, 1985.
Tardif, T. "Nouns are not always learned before verbs: Evidence from Mandarin speakers' early vocabularies." *Developmental Psychology* 32 (1996): 492–504.
Testelets, Ia. G. *Vvedenie v obščij sintaksis* [Introduction to General Syntax]. Moscow, 2001.
Tomasello, M. *Origins of Human Communication*. Cambridge: MIT Press, 2008.
Tseitlin, S. N. "Usvoenie rebënkom prilagatel'nyx [Acquisition of adjectives by children]." In: *Detskaja reč': norma i patologija* [Child Speech: The Norm and Pathology], 4–15. Samara: Samara State University Press, 1996.
— —. *Jazyk i rebënok: Lingvistika detskoj reči* [Language and Child: The Linguistics of Child Speech]. Moscow: Vlados, 2000.
— —. *Očerki po slovoobrazovaniju i formoobrazovaniju v detskoj reči* [Essays on Word Formation and Form Building in Child Speech]. Moscow: Znak, 2009.
Tsien, J. Z. "Neural coding of episodic memory." In *Handbook of Episodic Memory*, edited by E. Dere, A. Easton, L. Nadel, and J. P. Huston, 399–416. Amsterdam etc.: Elsevier, 2008.
— — et al. "On initial brain activity mapping of episodic and semantic memory code in the hippocampus." *Neurobiology of Learning and Memory* 105 (2013): 200–10.
Tulving, E. "What is episodic memory?" *Current Directions of Psychological Science* 2 (1993): 67–70.
Ushakov, D. N., ed. *Tolkovyj slovar' russkogo jazyka* [An Explanatory Dictionary of Russian]. 4 vols. Moscow, 1934–40.

Varley, R. A., Klessinger, N. J. C., Romanowski, C. A. J., and M. Siegal. "Agrammatic but numerate." In *Proceedings of the National Academy of Sciences of USA* 102, iss. 9 (2005): 3519–24.

Vendler, Z. "The grammar of goodness." In Vendler, Z. *Linguistics in Philosophy*, 172–95. Ithaca, NY: Cornell University Press, 1967a.

———. "Facts and events." In Vendler, Z. *Linguistics in Philosophy*, 122–64. Ithaca, NY: Cornell University Press, 1967b.

Voeikova, M. D. *Rannie ètapy usvoenija det'mi imennoj morfologii russkogo jazyka* [Early Stages in Acquisition of Nominal Morphology of the Russian Language by Children]. Moscow: Znak, 2011.

———. *Stanovlenie imeni: rannie ètapy usvoenija det'mi imennoj morfologii russkogo jazyka* [The Formation of Name: Early stages in children's acquisition of the Russian nominal morphology]. Moscow: Jazyki slavjanskoj kul'tury, 2015.

———, Kazakovskaia, V. V., and D. N. Satiukova. "Semantika prilagatel'nyx v reči vzroslyx i detej [Semantics of adjectives in adult and child speech]." In *Jazyk i mysl': sovremennaja kognitivnaja lingvistika*, edited by A. A. Kibrik, A. D. Koshelev, A. V. Kravchenko, Iu. V. Mazurova, and O. V. Fëdorova, 488–540. Moscow: Jazyki slavjanskoj kul'tury, 2015.

Vygotsky, L. S. *Thought and Language*, newly revised, translated, and edited by A. Kozulin. Cambridge, MA: MIT Press, 1986.

———. *The Collected Works*. Vol. 5, *Child Psychology*, edited by R. W. Rieber, translated by M. J. Hall. N. Y.: Plenum, 1998.

Wagner, L. and L. Lakusta. "Using Language to Navigate the Infant Mind." *Perspectives on Psychological Science* 4, iss. 2 (2009): 177–84.

Waxman, S. R. "All in good time: How do infants discover distinct types of words and map them to distinct kinds of meaning?" In *Infant Pathways to Language: Methods, Models, and Research Directions*, edited by J. Colombo, P. McCardle, and L. Freund, 99–118. Mahwah, NJ: Lawrence Erlbaum Associates, 2008.

——— and I. Braun. "Consistent (but not variable) names as invitations to form object categories: New evidence from 12-month-old infants." *Cognition* 95 (2005): B59–B68.

Weinreich, U. "Explorations in semantic theory." In *Current trends in linguistics*. Vol. 3, *Theoretical Foundations*, edited by A. Sebeok, 395–477. The Hague, 1966.

Werner, H. *Comparative Psychology of Mental Development* (with a new prologue by Margery B. Franklin). Clinton Corners, NY: Percheron Press, 2004.

Whorf, B. L. "The Relation of Habitual Thought and Behavior to Language." In *Language, Thought, and Reality: Selected Writings of Benjamin Lee Whorf*, edited by J. B. Carroll, 134–59. Cambridge, MA: MIT Press, 1956.

Wierzbicka, A. *Semantics: Primes and Universals.* Oxford: Oxford University Press, 1996.

———. "There Are No 'Color Universals' but There Are Universals of Visual Semantics." *Anthropological Linguistics* 47, iss. 2 (2005): 217–44.

———. "Why there are no 'colour universals' in language and thought." *Journal of the Royal Anthropological Institute* 14 (2008): 407–25.

Wiese, H. *Numbers, Language, and the Human Mind.* Cambridge, UK: Cambridge University Press. 2003.

Wilcox, T. "Object individuation: Infants' use of shape, size, pattern, and color." *Cognition* 72, iss. 3 (1999): 125–66.

Wittgenstein, L. *Philosophical Investigations*, translated by G. E. M. Anscombe. N. Y.: The Macmillan Company, 1953.

Xu, F. "The role of language in acquiring object kind concepts in infancy." *Cognition* 85 (2002): 223–50.

———. "Sortal concepts, object individuation, and language." *Trends in Cognitive Sciences* 11 (2007): 400–6.

——— and S. Carey. "Infants' metaphysics: The case of numerical identity." *Cognitive Psychology* 30 (1996): 111–53.

———, Carey, S., and N. Quint. "The emergence of kind-based object individuation in infancy." *Cognitive Psychology* 49 (2004): 155–190.

Zacks, J. M. and B. Tversky. "Event structure in perception and conception." *Psychological Bulletin* 127 (2001): 3–21.

Zadeh, L. "Fuzzy Sets." *Information and Control* 8 (1965): 338–53.

Zholkovskii, A. K., Leont'eva, N. N., and Iu. N. Martem'ianov. "O principial'nom ispol'zovanii smysla pri mašinnom perevode [On an Essential Use of Meaning in Machine Translation]." In: *Mašinnyj perevod.* Vol. 2, 17–46. Moskva: Institut točnoj mexaniki i vyčislitel'noj texniki AN SSSR, 1961.

Zubkova, L. G. *Èvoljucija predstavlenij o jazyke* [Evolution of Ideas about Language]. Moscow: Jazyki slavjanskoj kul'tury, 2015.

———. *Teorija jazyka v eë razvitii: ot naturocentrizma k logocentrizmu čerez sintezk lingvocentrizmu i k novomu sintezu* [Linguistic Theory and its Development]. Moscow: Izdatel'skij dom JaSK, 2016.

Name index

Aksënov M. S. 170, 197
Andrick G. R. 176, 197
Antakova-Fomina L. V. 137
Apresian Iu. D. 10, 52, 61, 62, 65, 197
Arcimboldo G. 94
Aristotle 6, 64, 66, 124, 125, 130, 168, 197
Arnauld A. 33, 66, 197
Aronoff M. 207, 210
Atkinson M. 88, 202
Augustine 118, 197
Austin J. L. 47, 197

Baddelley A. 68, 72, 197
Baillargeon R. 78, 197, 202
Barsalou L. W. 9, 31, 197
Baudouin de Courtenay J. 147, 149, 162, 172, 198
Berlin B. 20, 115, 179, 188, 197
Bernshtein N. A. 145, 197
Bertenthal B. I. 202
Berwick R. C. 40, 43, 66, 120, 121, 123, 126–130, 135, 143, 198, 200
Bickerton D. 66, 111, 120, 122, 123, 198
Blackwell A. A. 176, 198
Bloom L. 69, 198
Bloom P. 133, 198, 206
Bogdanov A. 12
Bogusławski A. 65
Bolhuis J. 129, 198, 200

Boroditsky L. 131, 133, 134, 138, 198, 201
Bower T. G. R. 42, 70, 170, 173, 174, 198
Bowerman M. 77, 138, 199, 201
Boyes-Braem P. 209
Brady T. F. 199
Brand R. 202
Brandone A. 208
Brannon E. M. 184, 198
Braun I. 139, 212
Brown R. 20, 115, 198
Burlak S. A. 190, 195, 198
Butterworth G. 101, 118, 198, 209

Carey D. P. 202
Carey S. 77, 96, 176, 205, 213
Casasola M. 77, 78, 107, 199
Chan C. 208
Chen J. 208
Choi S. 77, 199
Chomsky N. 5, 6, 40, 42, 43, 64–66, 111, 116, 117, 120–130, 133, 135, 142, 143, 172, 198–200, 202
Chung H. L. 202
Chunharas C. 72, 199
Chuprikova N. I. 12, 173, 199
Clark E. V. 68, 88, 96, 199
Cohen L. B. 77, 101, 107, 199, 209
Condillac É. B. de. 38, 136, 199
Corballis M. C. 133, 199

Name index

Dachkovsky S. 210
Dahl Ö. 196, 199
Dehaene S. 184, 200, 208
Descartes R. 64
Deutscher G. 181, 200
Diesendruck G. 206
Dosher B. 206
Dowty D. 77, 200
Dronov P. S. 163, 164, 165, 195, 200

Ebeling K. S. 176, 200
Eliseeva M. B. 88, 200
Evans N. 196, 200
Evans V. 66, 200
Everaert M. 120, 200
Everett D. L. 6, 65, 146, 147, 152, 153, 178, 180, 182–185, 189–195, 200, 201, 207

Fedorenko E. 201
Ferry A. 140, 200
Finlayson N. J. 170, 200
Fitch W. T. 202
Fodor J. 65, 201
Frank M. 184, 201
Frege G. 5, 42
Fulkerson A. L. 139, 178, 201
Futrell R. 147, 185, 189, 201

Gallese V. 20, 201
Garcia R. 205
Gasser M. 176, 201
Gelernter D. 39, 201
Gelman S. A. 176, 200
Gentner D. 138, 201
Gibson E. 201
Givón T. 72, 109, 111, 120, 122, 135, 201
Gladstone W. E. 181, 201

Gleitman L. 134, 201
Göksun T. 77, 78, 90, 96, 138, 201, 202, 208
Goldstein K. 178, 202
Golinkoff R. M. 3, 52, 77, 138, 201, 202, 206, 208, 209, 210
Golomb J. D. 200
Goodale M. A. 178, 202
Gopnik A. 77, 199
Grashchenkov P. V. 46, 202
Gray W. D. 209
Greenfield P. 119, 129, 202
Griffiths P. D. 88, 202
Gurdjieff G. I. 167, 171, 196
Gvozdëv A. N. 88, 202

Hahn U. 47, 209
Hanson C. 75, 202
Harris M. 118, 198
Hauser M. D. 121, 123, 124, 139, 178, 202, 210
Hegel G. 12
Heine S. J. 202
Hennon E. 202
Henrich J. 196, 202
Hespos S. J. 78, 138, 200, 202, 203
Hinton C. H. 170, 203
Hirsh-Pasek K. 77, 201, 202, 206, 208, 209, 210
Hirst W. 75, 202
Humboldt W. von. 120, 122, 133, 136, 203
Huybregts M. 200

Ibn Sina (Avicenna) 168
Isenina E. I. 91, 95, 118, 203
Ivanov Viach. Vs. 183, 184, 203
Izard V. 208

Jackendoff R. 77, 120–122, 124, 132–134, 138, 193, 203, 208
Jakobson L. S. 202
Jerison H. 131, 132, 203
Johnson D. M. 209
Jones S. S. 205

Kasevich V. B. 100, 203
Kay P. 115, 179, 188, 189, 197, 203
Kazakovskaia V. V. 212
Kibrik A. A. 154, 184, 190, 195, 196, 203
Kisch S. 165, 204
Klessinger N. J. C. 212
Koffka K. 12
Kol'tsova M. M. 69, 90, 91, 95, 137, 138, 204
Komensky J. 12
Koshelev A. D. 5, 7, 12, 14, 15, 22, 23, 28, 33, 40, 44–46, 51, 53, 54, 56, 58, 62, 70, 75, 80, 98, 107, 113, 119, 123, 132, 144, 146, 147, 155, 159, 163, 173, 174, 176, 178, 185, 191, 204, 205
Kosslyn S. M. 9, 68, 205
Kozlov M. 7
Kravchenko A. V. 7, 69, 91, 95, 138, 172, 193, 205

Lakoff G. 20, 22, 47, 66, 108, 115, 179, 192, 201, 205
Lakusta L. 77, 78, 90, 96, 205, 212
Landau B. 174, 205, 206
Langacker R. W. 60–62, 205
Leibniz G. W. 64
Lemer C. 208
Leonardo da Vinci 168
Leont'eva N. N. 65, 213
Lepskaia N. I. 45, 68, 69, 107, 205
Leslie A. M. 187, 205

Levinson S. C. 196, 200, 206
Lewin K. 12, 72
Liu J. 202
Lomonosov M. 168

Ma W. 210
Maguire M. J. 77, 202, 206, 208
Majid A. 196, 206
Mandler J. M. 77, 138, 199, 206
Markson L. 174, 206
Marr D. 3, 32
Marr N. Ia. 156, 206
Martem'ianov Iu. N. 65, 213
McDonough L. 199
Meir I. 207, 210
Mel'čuk I. A. 65, 119, 134, 141, 206
Meng X. 208
Mervis C. B. 20, 115, 206, 209
Metzler J. 9, 68, 210
Meyer M. A. 208
Milner A. D. 202
Moore G. E. 175, 206
Morgan L. H. 150–152, 206
Moro A. 200
Mozart W. A. 170
Müller F. M. 122, 206
Munnich E. 138, 206

Nelson K. 20, 206
Nevins A. 147, 189, 195, 207
Nicole P. 33, 66, 197
Nietzsche F. 172, 207
Nikulin A. V. 195, 207
Norbury H. M. 138, 207
Norenzayan A. 202

O'Hearn K. 205
Ouspensky P. D. 167, 170–172, 207

Name index

Padden C. 163, 165, 207, 210
Paducheva E. V. 126, 207
Paivio A. 9, 10, 207
Papafragou A. 134, 202
Partee B. 126, 207
Pascal B. 64
Paul H. 191, 207
Pechenkova E. 7
Peirce Ch. 42
Pereira A. F. 175, 207
Perelmutter I. A. 125, 207
Pesetsky D. 207
Petitto L. A. 182, 183, 208
Piantadosi S. T. 201
Pica P. 184, 208
Piccin T. 78, 203
Pinker S. 4, 32, 33, 47, 48, 65, 66, 108, 121, 122, 124, 131–134, 137, 139, 140, 142, 147, 155, 190, 193, 208
Plato 184
Potebnia A. A. 133, 134, 136, 208
Pozner V. 172
Pruden S. M. 75, 77, 78, 90, 96, 138, 206, 208
Pulverman R. 77, 78, 208, 209
Pustejovsky J. 66, 174, 209
Pylyshin Z. W. 9, 209

Quine W. 42
Quint N. 213

Rademaker R. L. 199
Rakison D. H. 20, 101, 209
Ramscar M. 47, 209
Richardson A. 209
Richardson J. T. E. 9, 68, 209
Rodrigues C. 207

Romanowski C. A. J. 212
Rosch (Heider) E. 20, 47, 115, 179, 209
Roseberry S. 208
Rozengardt-Pupko G. L. 176, 209
Ryle G. 157, 210

Salkind S. J. 208
Salles R. 195, 210
Samarina T. 7
Sandler W. 163, 207, 210
Santos L. R. 139, 210
Sapir E. 121, 122, 136, 147–149, 190, 191, 210
Satiukova D. N. 212
Scheerer M. 178, 202
Sechenov I. M. 12, 42, 173, 175, 210
Serences J. T. 199
Seston R. 78, 210
Shallcross W. 210
Shepard R. N. 9, 68, 210
Siegal M. 212
Slobin D. I. 45, 77, 111, 122, 210
Smith J. 7
Smith L. B. 175, 176, 201, 205, 207
Solov'ëv V. 12, 173, 210
Song H. 207
Song L. 96, 107, 210
Sootsman-Buresh J. 209
Spaepen G. V. 210
Spelke E. S. 78, 138, 203
Spencer H. 12, 173, 211
Spinelli D. 205
Sprague T. C. 199
Squire L. R. 157, 211
Stearns L. 201
Stout D. 160, 211
Subbotskii E. V. 187, 211
Sulkowski G. M. 210

Tager-Flusberg H. 176, 197
Talmy L. 77–79, 185, 211
Tardif T. 77, 208, 211
Tarski A. 42
Tattersall I. 198, 200
Testelets Ia. G. 100, 119, 211
Tomasello M. 118, 177, 211
Troje N. 87
Tseitlin S. N. 45, 107, 122, 126, 176, 178, 211
Tsien J. Z. 70, 211
Tulving E. 72, 211
Tversky B. 75, 213

Ushakov D. N. 50, 211

Varley R. A. 184, 212
Vendler Z. 68, 175, 212
Voeikova M. D. 45, 107, 176, 177, 182, 185, 212
Vygotsky L. S. 72, 91, 110, 129, 188, 212

Wagner L. 77, 78, 90, 205, 212
Waxman S. R. 95, 107, 139, 140, 176–178, 200, 201, 207, 212
Weinreich U. 126, 212
Werner H. 12, 173, 212
Whorf B. L. 179, 212
Wierzbicka A. 47, 64, 65, 108, 141, 181, 189, 213
Wiese H. 132, 213
Wilcox T. 140, 213
Wittgenstein L. 1, 2, 47, 54, 115, 209, 213

Xu F. 77, 79, 139, 176, 213

Yakovleva E. 7

Zacks J. M. 75, 213
Zadeh L. 115, 213
Zhang X. 200
Zhigalkin S. 7, 120, 136, 170
Zholkovskii A. K. 65, 213
Zubkova L. G. 7, 125, 135, 213

Subject index

biconcept 99–100, 103, 113, 116, 127–128
    non-predicative 94, 100
    predicative (elementary proposition) 99, 100, 103

category
    adjectival 140
    classical 48, 49, 51, 54, 56, 60–61, 73, 111, 114, 118
    non-classical 1, 54
    color 153, 189
    dual 48, 73
    "Games" 1–2, 54
    "Person is walking" 2
    "Person is running" 2

cell of the conceptual matrix
    <ARMCHAIR> 142
    <BANANA> 112, 113
    <RUN> 113
    <TREE> 112

cell of the propositional matrix
    <PERSON IS RUNNING> 112, 114

cell's point of entry 112–115, 117, 142

classification of the visible world 111–116
    conceptual 111–113, 116
    propositional 113–116

cognitive unit
    pre-conceptual 6, 64, 67
    perceptual 9–12
    functional 6, 9–12, 21
    primary 64, 67–68, 110, 115

elementary 9, 12, 23, 74, 90, 95, 102, 108, 110–111, 135, 143–144
non-verbal 10, 20, 50, 75
independent 23, 93, 111

concept
    adjectival 44–46, 116, 123, 173–174
    adverbial 116, 123
    age 56–59, 170–171
    basic 10, 13, 17, 20–34, 36–39, 46–53, 55–56, 58–59, 61, 73, 79, 86–88, 91–93, 96–97, 102, 104–106, 109, 111–112, 114–115, 117–119, 121, 127, 130–133, 135, 141–144, 156–158, 173–174
        ARMCHAIR 48, 50–51, 142
        BANANA 6, 11, 22–23, 26, 30, 35, 37–39, 44–45, 59–60, 61, 62, 63, 112, 113, 116, 117, 175
        CHAIR 6, 13, 24, 41, 49
        EAT-BANANA 22
        GLASS 6, 24
        LAKE 6, 25
        MAN-RUNNING 53
        MAN-WALKING 53
        MOTHER 108
        PATH 11
        RUN 6
        TREE 6, 25–26, 28, 55
    developed (adjectivally)
        BANANA 37, 38
        GLASS 36
    developed (partitively)
        BANANA 30
        CHAIR 13, 30, 41
        GLASS 30
        LAKE 29
        TREE 29
    developed (adjectivally and partitively)
        BANANA 39
    integral 170–171
        BANANA 171
        TREE 171

motor 6, 9, 21–22, 35–36, 44–45, 49, 64, 67, 68, 79, 91, 93, 95–98, 100, 108–109, 112–113, 115–116, 120, 123, 127–128, 133, 135, 145
    EAT-BANANA 22
    KILL (X KILLS Y) 88, 89
    MAN-RUNNING 53
    MAN-WALKING 53
object 6, 9, 21–22, 26, 35–36, 38–39, 44–46, 64–65, 68, 79, 91, 95–98, 108, 113, 115–116, 120, 123, 127–128, 133, 135, 139–140, 145
    ARMCHAIR 50
    BANANA 11, 22, 23
    CHAIR 13, 24, 49
    GLASS 24
    LAKE 25
    MOTHER 108
    PATH 11
    TREE 25, 55
specific 13, 86–93, 102, 104–106, 109, 112, 117, 130–131, 143–144, 174
    BOY 105, 106
    PATH 106
    ROAD 105, 106
    WOMAN 105
whole 13–17, 108, 174–175

conceptual matrix 111–112, 114–115, 117–118, 142

definition of the term 'situation' 75–77

development
    schema 13–15, 17–18, 35, 57, 67, 77, 81, 95
    theory 12–19, 29, 168, 173

dichotomy
    phenomenon *vs.* function 35
    phenomenon *vs.* noumenon 35
    semantic (linguistic) and pragmatic (encyclopedic) components 60–61
    visual (exogenous) *vs.* functional (endogenous) units 6, 9, 12, 20–21

dual structure "Prototype ← Function" 22, 27, 48, 75, 82–83, 92, 97–98

ethnogroup (ethnic group)
    heterogeneous 150–151, 162–163, 166–167
    homogeneous 150–151, 157, 165–166

evolution
    human 111, 121, 123, 127–129, 135, 167
    of human thought 43, 117, 120
    of language 43, 66, 111, 117, 120–123, 127
        Bedouin Sign Language (ABSL) 163–164
    of pre-human animals 111, 172

exotic linguistic property / feature 146, 150, 191–196

flower schema 18–19, 31–32

full lexical meaning 37–39

independent
    action 21, 76, 186–187
    concept 34, 94, 106
    function 23, 33, 75, 93–94
    goal 21
    notion 33–34, 61, 93–94
    object 32–33
    part 13–14, 34, 94, 112
    property 178, 181
    prototype 21, 23, 179, 181
    representation 35, 68, 139
    situation 94
    status 12, 87, 95, 125, 162, 178

Homo
    perfectus 6, 167–172
    sapiens sapiens 6, 129, 136, 168–172
    syntheticus 168
    early 121, 123, 135, 136
    first 111, 122, 123, 129

knowledge
    ordinary 157–158, 162, 166
    professional 158–159, 162, 168
    pseudo-professional 162–163, 166

Subject index

language of thought (LOT) 5–6, 20, 44–46, 64, 116–117, 127, 142

leaps and gradualness in the child's cognitive development 143–144

life cycle 56–63, 112, 170
    BANANA 59–60, 63
    TREE 57–59, 63

matrix
    conceptual 111–112, 114–115, 117–118, 142
    linguistic 117–120
    propositional 113–117, 120

meaning
    lexical (see also Lexical index)
        full 37–39
        armchair 50
        banana 26, 30, 38, 60
        chair 26, 30, 38, 49
        glass 26, 30
        lake 26, 29
        run (*the man is running*) 52, 53
        tree 26, 29, 59
        walk (*the man is walking*) 52, 53
    grammatical 6, 107, 118, 124, 146, 149, 161
    of genitive construction YX-Gen ('Y of X') 4, 27–28, 46–47
    pseudo-professional 161

mental representation
    syncretic representation 149, 173–174, 177, 192–195
    systemic representation 42, 77, 193–196

model
    of activity development
        for human individuals 6, 146, 150–158
        for ethnic groups 6, 146, 150–158
    of a fruit tree 44, 62–63, 95
    of thought and language 6, 128
    of the world 132, 176–177

neurobiological memory code 23, 43, 70–71, 142

ordinary
> activity 150, 153–154, 157, 162, 163, 166, 168, 180, 195
> knowledge 157–158, 162, 166
> language 150, 157–158, 161–163, 166, 190

ostensive definition 117–119

participant (of a situation)
> main 35, 45, 67, 74, 79, 81, 85–86, 91, 108, 114, 185, 187
> supplementary 35, 67, 79, 81, 108, 114

pathway (schema) of knowledge of an object 35, 36, 39–40

perception principle
> immediacy of perception principle (syncretic perception) 146, 150, 153–154, 178, 185–187, 191–193, 195
> mediated perception principle (systemic perception) 146, 150, 192–193, 195

professional
> activity 132, 150–154, 157–158, 160, 162–163, 165, 168–169, 196
> knowledge 158–159, 162, 168
> language 149, 150, 157, 158, 160, 162, 168, 169, 190

protoconcept
> basic
>> GOAL-EXISTS 81, 85–88, 101–104
>> PERSON-IS RUNNING 80–86, 88–89, 93, 96–97, 102–107, 143–144
>> SURFACE-LIES/EXISTS 80–81, 85, 87–89, 96, 101–104
>
> specific
>> BOY-IS RUNNING 86, 88–90, 143
>> MAN-IS RUNNING 86, 88, 99, 143
>> PATH-LIES 87–89
>> ROAD-LIES 87–90
>> WOMAN-IS RUNNING 86, 88–89, 143–144

protolanguage 122–124, 127, 129–130, 135–136
> asyntactic 122
> syntactic 123

protosituation 83–86, 88, 99, 103, 107, 110, 117, 122, 129, 139–140
> basic 89, 91
> specific 88–90

Subject index 225

psychophysical states 23, 41–43, 50, 69

reference relation 5, 42

relationship
   adjectival 12, 44, 46
   binary 6, 12, 15–16, 29, 117, 119, 175
   case 45, 116, 119
   causal 186–187
      cause-and-effect 148
      cause to become not alive 108–109
      causation of killing 108
      conceptual (between concepts) 66–67
   generic (genus ▷ species) 73, 174
      COLOR ▷ RED 175
      IS RUNNING ▷ RUNNING-JOGGING 105, 144
      IS RUNNING ▷ RUNNING-MINCING 105, 144
      PERSON ▷ BOY 105, 144
      PERSON ▷ WOMAN 105, 144
      PERSON-IS RUNNING ▷ BOY-IS RUNNING 88, 89
      SIZE ▷ MEDIUM 176
   hierarchical 6, 18, 64, 67
   object 45, 96, 119
   predicative 12, 45, 98–100, 103, 119
   role 6, 15–16, 18–19, 29, 31, 35–36, 41, 43–45, 57–59, 64, 67, 77, 79, 81–85, 89, 91, 96, 98, 102, 106–107, 110, 114, 119–122, 128–129, 131, 140–141, 145
   spatial 21–22, 78, 96, 131
   syntactic (of syntactic dependence) 45, 110, 119, 121, 124, 133
      Containment 78
      Earlier ⇒ Later 57, 59
      Object ⇒ Property 44–45, 116
      Part ⇐ Object (partitive) 18, 45–47, 116, 119
      Whole ⇒ Part (Component) 18, 84, 102
      Support 78

representation (mental)
   actions (of actions) 6, 35, 38, 96
   analytical 154

basic 44
ethno-specific 133–134, 136, 156, 179, 191
events (of events) 193
folk 134
functional 128, 132
hierarchical 9, 177
holistic 9, 18, 34, 42, 168
independent 35, 61, 139
linguistic 46
medical 158–159
of object 6, 13–14, 20, 29, 31, 34–35, 38–39, 42, 96, 173–175, 177
pre-conceptual 6, 66, 140
situation (of situation) 6, 35, 44, 64, 67–68, 70, 73, 77–78, 90, 95, 103, 109, 117, 120, 141, 191
spatial 39, 103, 107, 170
syncretic 149, 173–174, 177, 192–193, 195
    child's (children's, childhood) 6, 13–14, 23, 29, 35, 38, 44, 64, 67, 68, 77–78, 86, 88, 90, 109, 115, 117, 134, 140, 144, 174, 184, 194
    color 192
    of time spectrum 193
systemic 77, 194–196
visual 68, 103
world (of world) 6, 9, 12, 64, 67–68, 115, 122, 128, 131–134, 143–144, 149, 154–158, 162, 167–169, 172, 191, 192, 196

situation
    basic 73–79, 84, 86, 89, 91, 93, 95, 115, 144
        PERSON IS RUNNING 71, 73–74, 84, 89, 103, 105–106
    conceptual 102–104, 106, 114
    holistic 35, 67, 69,
    specific 73–74, 84, 86, 89–90, 106
        BOY IS RUNNING ON THE PATH/ROAD 73–74
    syncretic (whole) 6, 40, 64, 67–68, 75, 77, 84–86, 91–92, 103, 108–111, 114–115, 117, 120, 141

stage
    differentiation 12–16, 29, 98
        complete 15, 110
        partial 14–15

Subject index

integration 12–14, 16, 29, 58, 100
   complete 16, 17, 67, 83
   partial 16, 17, 35, 67, 83, 113

structure
   age 55
   argument 117
   conceptual 6, 41, 44, 64, 70, 142, 195
   developed 44, 175
   dual 27, 48, 67, 75, 82–83, 92, 98
   hierarchical 9, 26, 30, 62, 66–67, 120, 122, 127–128, 173–174
   role 35, 37, 40, 120
   partitive 18, 31, 62
   tree-like 29, 68, 116

system
   adjectival 35–37
   dual 17, 35–36, 83, 96, 98–99, 135
   hierarchical 20, 29–30, 57–59, 174–175
   of situation participants 37, 44, 70, 85, 109
   partitive (system of parts) 13–15, 17–19, 20, 29–32, 34–35, 37–38, 40–41, 46, 175
   role 18, 32, 35–37, 67, 144

tree of decomposition of elementary units 144

world
   inner (internal, functional) 42, 111, 116
   visual (perceptual, external, phenomenal, sensory, perceived, visible, physical, material, surrounding) 42, 67–68, 93, 99, 111, 113–116, 124, 131–132, 141, 143–144, 154, 165

Lexical index

Basic lexical meanings in their development in ontogenesis and anthropogenesis.

Primary lexical meanings of a child (up to 2 years)
    armchair 50
    banana 11, 26
    chair 26, 49
    glass 26
    path 11
    lake 26
    tree 26, 55
    run (*the man is running*) 53
    walk (*the man is walking*) 53

Developed lexical meanings of a child (after 2,5 years)
    banana 30, 38–39
    chair 30
    glass 30
    lake 29
    tree 29

Lexical meanings of an adult (*Homo sapiens sapiens*) native speaker
    banana 60
    tree 59

Hypothetical lexical meanings of an adult (*Homo perfectus*) native speaker
    banana 171
    tree 171

www.ingramcontent.com/pod-product-compliance
Lightning Source LLC
Chambersburg PA
CBHW052018290426
44112CB00014B/2290